Persons and Personality

Persons and Personality

A Contemporary Inquiry

Edited by
ARTHUR PEACOCKE AND
GRANT GILLETT

Ian Ramsey Centre Publication No. 1

Basil Blackwell

First published 1987

Basil Blackwell Ltd
108 Cowley Road, Oxford, OX4 1JF, UK

Basil Blackwell Inc.
432 Park Avenue South, Suite 1503
New York, NY 10016, USA

British Library Cataloguing in Publication Data

Persons and personality : a contemporary
  enquiry.
  1. Personality
  I. Peacocke, A.R.   II. Gillett, Grant
  155.2   BF698

  ISBN 0-631-15102-8

Library of Congress Cataloging in Publication Data
Persons and personality.

  Based on papers from seminars on "Conceptions of
the person and their ethical implications", held by
the Ian Ramsey Centre, from the middle of 1985 to
March of 1986.
  Includes bibliographies and index.
  1. Self (Philosophy)——Congresses. 2. Personality——
Congresses. I. Peacocke, A. R. (Arthur Robert)
II. Gillett, Grant, 1950–   III. Ian Ramsey Centre
(St. Cross College)
BD450.P4622 1987 126   87-10974
ISBN 0-631-15102-8

6/6/90

Typeset in CG Times 10/12½pt by
System 4 Associates, Gerrards Cross, Buckinghamshire
Printed in Great Britain by T. J. Press Ltd, Padstow

Contents

Preface

The Ian Ramsey Centre, which was established at St Cross College, Oxford, at the beginning of 1985, has, as its principal aim, the interdisciplinary study of both ethical problems arising from scientific and medical research and practice and the underlying philosophical and theological issues. Early on, it became clear that beneath controversies concerning a whole range of ethical issues, especially those in the field of medicine or what has come to be known more widely as 'bioethics', reside profoundly different conceptions of the human person and of the relation of the person to the human body, to nature, and to society. This would not have surprised Ian Ramsey, after whom the Centre is named; for, both as Nolloth Professor at Oxford and later as Bishop of Durham, he was particularly active and effective in thinking through with the appropriate experts many aspects of our understanding of the human person in the light of new knowledge.[1]

From the middle of 1985 to March of 1986, the Centre held a number of open seminars on 'Conceptions of the Person and their Ethical Implications', presented by representatives of different disciplines; a number of these presentations are included, albeit with some modification, in this volume. This series of seminars, fascinating though it was, made me realize that a more intensive study was required, one that would bring together in one place spokesmen for the distinct clusters of conceptions of the person that I was able to identify with the invaluable research assistance of Dr Grant Gillett, a neurosurgeon also qualified in psychology and philosophy of mind and now the co-editor of this volume.

We were fortunate in being able to assemble at a 24-hour workshop entitled 'Persons and Values', during the weekend of 6–7 December 1985, six speakers representing both various combinations of naturalism, reductionism, existentialism, dualism, and theism and various scientific and philosophical disciplines. Their papers constitute the core of the present volume, together with abbreviated versions of the discussions which they provoked among some twenty other participants invited because of their known contributions to or interest in this area of inquiry.

This volume is offered as a contribution by a group of original thinkers to that elucidation of our conception of the person which alone can form an adequate basis for the even more difficult inquiry into the relationship between the notion of a 'person' and that of 'values'. Confusion about this relationship is endemic in contemporary discussions of the ethical problems generated by scientific and medical research and practice. Its clarification constitutes unfinished business for all of us.

The production of such a volume inevitably involves efforts of many different kinds. As Director of the Centre, I am particularly grateful for the encouragement given me in this enterprise by Professor Basil Mitchell, FBA, Chairman of its Management Committee. The whole exercise has rested heavily on the skills of Mrs Elizabeth Foster-Hall, Secretary to the Centre, and on the transcribing expertise of Miss Humaira Ahmed; both editors would like to express their gratitude to them for all the hard work involved. The preparation for the press of such a wide range of manuscripts has demanded the highest possible editing skills, and we were again fortunate in the availability of Dr Jean van Altena for her percipient and professional work on our behalf. We are grateful both to her and to Julia Mosse and Stephan Chambers of Basil Blackwell Limited for their encouragement and cooperation in this first major publication of the Centre.

Finally, I acknowledge gratefully, on behalf of the Management Committee of the Centre, the financial support afforded by grants from the All Saints Educational Trust, the Culham Educational Foundation, the Hockerill Educational Foundation, St Luke's College Foundation, the Rhodes Trust, the Sarum St Michael Educational Charity, an anonymous trust and the contributions of a number of anonymous private donors, without all of which the work of the Centre in general, and this exercise in particular, would not have been possible.

Arthur Peacocke
Ian Ramsey Centre
St Cross College
Oxford

Acknowledgements

Chapter 2, 'Purposeless People', copyright © Peter Atkins 1987. Chapter 3, 'The Structure of the Soul', copyright © Richard Swinburne 1987, is based on material contained in *The Evolution of the Soul* (Clarendon Press, Oxford, 1986). The author and publisher are grateful for permission to reproduce this essay here. Chapter 4, 'The Person as Object of Science, as Subject of Experience, and as Locus of Value', copyright © David Wiggins 1987. Chapter 5, 'Reasoning about Persons', copyright © Grant Gillett 1987; 'A Response', copyright © Derek Parfit 1987. Chapter 6, 'Persons and Selves', copyright © Rom Harré 1987. Chapter 7, 'The "Person" in Law', copyright © Richard Tur 1987. Chapter 8, 'Is Medicine a Branch of Ethics?', copyright © William Fulford 1987. Chapter 9, 'Jung's Concept of Personality' copyright © Anthony Storr 1987. Chapter 10, 'Personality and Poetry', copyright © Anthony Nuttall 1987. Chapter 11, 'A Theology of Personal Being', copyright © John Macquarrie 1987. Chapter 12, 'Christian Theism and the Concept of a Person', copyright © Adrian Thatcher 1987. Chapter 13, 'The Unity of the Human Person according to the Greek Fathers', copyright © Kallistos Ware 1987.

1

Introduction

GRANT GILLETT AND ARTHUR PEACOCKE

For centuries, one might venture to assert, the idea of the 'person' has been a central concern of the humanities, especially theology, and has been an abiding topic of inquiry in ethics; yet a very wide range of conceptions of the human person and of what constitutes personality continue to be held. These underlying conceptions, or preconceptions actually, since they are often implicit rather than explicit, underlie many contemporary controversies regarding the ethical implications of scientific and medical research and practice.

The diversity of conceptions is itself generated by the diversity of disciplines and perspectives involved, disciplines and perspectives which take account of a multiplicity of features of the perceived data concerning the 'person'; but inevitably they converge in the questions they raise: Is a person a body with an essential inner, or 'spiritual', self which confers a special status on all our discussion of these areas? Or is a person merely a biological entity around which we have woven a tracery of elaborate metaphor? Does the human mind represent a dimension which is different from that explored by physical science? Can human beings come to a true knowledge of themselves? Can we arrive at a rational conception of human worth? How can human organisms be said to know a transcendent God?

It is within this complex of connected questions that the significance of persons will be examined here. Because persons are not only entities in the world, but are also conscious of it, think about it, and seek to understand it, such questions constantly confront them. We wonder about the origin and meaning of the world and of human life within it, and attempt to understand the mysteries which surround us. In this activity we are dependent on our minds, which tend both to a critical contemplation of what they encounter and to a deeply personal involvement in it.

So it is not surprising that much of the discussion in this book centres on the human mind. But not exclusively; for, if there is one thing on which the contributors might be said to agree, it is that 'mind', conceived of as pure ratiocination, is by itself an inadequate designation for the concept of 'person'. But this leaves open what an adequate designation might be. Hence our authors represent a variety of philosophies – naturalism, reductionism, existentialism, dualism, theism, and others less easily labelled.

This volume opens with two contributions that represent a polarity that is not merely contemporary, but that has deep roots both in the Enlightenment and further back in Greek philosophy. It is the polarity between a materialist, reductionist understanding of human beings, on the one hand, and a theistic dualism which affirms that the 'soul' is the essential component of human personhood, on the other. These two extremes are represented here by Dr Peter Atkins and Professor Richard Swinburne, respectively, whose papers have been given first place to act, as it were, as markers, by reference to which the ensuing chapters and discussions may be situated.

Peter Atkins, in his chapter entitled 'Purposeless Persons', sets out to explain how persons are no more than random products of a few simple causal processes. He asserts that we must openly face the possibility that 'we might be creatures of chance, nothing more than fragments of highly organized matter', with nothing special about us except the complexity of our responses. He urges that the vocabularies of the humanities and religion are nothing but an unnecessary 'sugar-coating' on a stark, scientifically describable reality. In his view, all phenomena in the world are not only subject to scientific explanation, but are potentially completely understandable in scientific terms.

Atkins sees the free-wheeling of all systems in the direction of increasing universal chaos, in accordance with the second law of thermodynamics, as the source of all change in the universe – including the construction of cathedrals, symphonies – and indeed of all human actions. People have emerged from this 'efflorescence of chaos' and represent a passing phase in the descent of the universe into total disorder. Consciousness and thought are merely manifestations of brains assembled out of simple elements through the reactions of organisms to their environment. So consciousness falls within the 'kingdom of science'.

The ethical implication of this view that consciousness must be 'admitted to the kingdom of scientific explanation', as Atkins puts it, is that there is no ethical attitude which is in any way privileged, and that views which are extant are the outcome of survival pressures. Since, for him, no ethical view is more principled than any other, the chief criterion is survival, which, he contends, may or may not involve my brain having respect for and interacting with the brains of others who also take pleasure in being in the world. He concludes that science specifies, as it were, a 'sea-level' for discussions of the concept of person, and that any accretions to its account of the world as a purposeless unwinding into chaos and oblivion are gratuitous. Science itself affords an enthralling vision of deep-rooted simplicity erupting in the complexity of the perceived world. The belief that science is all-competent, which is based on the observation that 'science has never encountered a barrier that it has not surmounted or that it cannot reasonably be expected to surmout eventually' is for him a deeply enriching one.

Richard Swinburne, in his contribution entitled 'The Structure of the Soul', takes the Cartesian position, arguing that man is a dual creature comprising body and soul as two distinct components. He regards the soul as that inner, conscious entity which both constitutes us as the thinking, morally significant beings that we are, and allows for the possibility of life after death. Because mental predicates are in principle distinct from physical events, they cannot be grounded in the attribution of certain physical properties, even those of the brain. He argues that, because I can conceive of myself as a continuing conscious being without a body, the conscious mental entity that is me cannot in any way just consist in, or be reduced to, some facts about my physical existence. Armed with this dualist basis on which to construct a philosophical anthropology and psychology, Swinburne goes on to suggest that the inter-action between the soul and the body/world must be effective in both directions. For there must be a certain autonomy in the mental realm whereby belief is sensitive not merely to causal influences, but also to rational considerations and can thereby be justified. It is, he says, indubitable that the conscious intentions, desires, and projects of rational beings act upon the world. Given the logical distinction between the soul and the body, we thus arrive at a view of the mental attributes of a human being as categorical states of a mental entity which is in interaction with the physical world. This entity, or 'soul', has a structure such that conscious beliefs and desires and unconscious mental propensities interact to explain or determine the behaviour of the thinking being. Swinburne leaves us with the picture of a structured soul in intimate contact with a (structured) brain such that, in principle, it could be taken from its particular embodiment and given another embodiment, should some omnipotent being wish to effect such a transfer.

At this early point in the book, it will already have become clear to the reader that there are potentially serious linguistic confusions concerning the use of the word 'person'. More sophisticated philosophical analysis is therefore crucial, and for this we turn to Mr David Wiggins and Dr Grant Gillett. In 'The Person as Object of Science, as Subject of Experience, and as Locus of Value', Wiggins addresses the philosophical problems of our concept of a person. He identifies three elements which need to be brought into a single focus: the notions of the person as biological entity, subject of consciousness, and bearer of ethical attributes.

He insists on the need to distinguish the *sense* of the term 'person' from its *reference*. In other words, we need to know not only what the term stands for, but also how it is being used, or the way of thinking implied by it. He notes that many words can be defined by some description or other, but that others are not susceptible to this kind of specification, so that one must appeal to what the entities being denoted are, what they are like. He suggests that 'person' is a term like this, that what it stands for and the way of thinking implied by it can only be grasped adequately by encounter with persons – indeed, with human beings. We need the idea of 'human being' to give some matter and substance to our idea of 'person'.

To strengthen this claim, Wiggins turns to P. F. Strawson's notion that 'person' is a primitive concept in our practices of mental and physical ascriptions to human beings. He regards Strawson's 'P-predicates' (that is, predicates *not* ascribable to material objects, such as actions, intentions, thoughts, feelings, perceptions, memories, sensations and so on) as predicates which stand for properties that are not reducible to predicates proper to the physical sciences, but which are also matter-involving. If we remove a certain technical difficulty from Strawson's definition of these things, then perhaps every P-property is also an M-property (one ascribable to material objects). Wiggins illustrates this by reference to perception and memory. Turning to Locke's conception of what it is to be a person, he proposes that a person is one of a kind whose typical members perceive, feel, think, take up attitudes to themselves, and so on. The 'and so on' indicates that the indefinite set of further properties which we bring to our concept of a person has to be filled out in the light of our experience with human beings. In this experience, human beings are not only conscious, but also make sense of one another. In so far as we do this – and there is no alternative but for us to try to do this – we are engaged with others. Other persons and their thoughts and feelings cannot help but be significant to us. In so far as we understand others, we see them not only as organisms of a certain type, but also as thinking subjects and as objects of reciprocity – indeed, to put the culmination of a Humean argument in more Kantian terms, as members of the kingdom of ends.

Philosophical analysis is further pursued by Dr Grant Gillett, who in his title, 'Reasoning about Persons', alludes to Derek Parfit's recent book *Reasons and Persons*.[1] Gillett emphasizes that the concept of a person must be regarded as the keystone of our conception of mind, and stresses its importance in understanding our experience of the world. He suggests that the claim that persons are mere collections of conscious mental states is illfounded. Examining recent formulations of personal identity which have sought to reduce the concept of a person, he finds no evidence for such claims in the neuro-psychological data to which their proponents often appeal. He then argues more generally that, although one can imaginatively extend one's conception of a person in certain rather bizarre circumstances, the general features of the concept and its conditions of proper use must be linked to a substantial view of human beings as the conscious, rational, public beings whom we identify in everyday experience. The argument is that, when a concept is strained by employing it under conditions substantially different from the norm, many subtle and complex assumptions may be violated; we thereby deprive what we say of the meaning we take it to have.

Gillett then argues that the very nature of concept use, and hence of discursive thought, implies that there is a single, re-identifiable psychophysical subject who participates in interpersonal activities and practices, and, in the process, attains a grasp and then a mastery of the concepts he or she uses. Finally, he introduces the idea that a person not only serves as a substrate for a set of experiences, but exercises an active narrative role in reflecting and comment-ing on these experiences and weaving them together into an informal autobiography. Thus the phenomena of human experience require an appeal to a unitary subject of experience which transcends the contents of that experience. Throughout, he sees the human person in living relationships with others, and so claims that 'person' is essentially an ethical concept.

Dr Gillett's presentation is followed by a response from Mr Derek Parfit. He challenges Gillett's interpretation of brain bisection cases, and then goes on to discuss teletransportation and the production of a psychophysical replica of a given person. He documents the tension between our intuitive, identity-based view of persons and a reductionist view which trades exclusively in links of mental continuity and connectedness. He argues for a view of personal identity based on the existence of such links, and spells out the transformation in our ethical theory to which it would give rise.

Now it is widely accepted among developmental psychologists that the sense of being a 'person' is intimately linked with our interaction with other persons, especially during early childhood. Moreover, social anthropological studies have revealed how the conceptions that people have of themselves as persons vary historically and geographically, as is well expounded in a recent volume[2] that explores the implications and subsequent studies inspired by a seminal lecture of Marcel Mauss in 1938. In the present volume, this approach is represented principally by the next two chapters, one by a philosopher of science in general and of psychology in particular, Mr Rom Harré, and one by a student of jurisprudence, Mr Richard Tur.

In 'Persons and Selves', Rom Harré suggests that each of us forms a concept of self informed by the concept of person operative in the dealings we have with others. The concept that each of us has will be a joint product of common human tendencies and capacities and our particular cultural context. It provides each of us with an organizing principle or concept to bring to bear on our experience, and thereby also provides us with first-person knowledge. We learn as individuals the judgements and practices of reflective commentary that are applied to and by individuals within a social setting. By thus acquiring the knack of referring to ourselves and making the sort of judgements about ourselves that others might make, we each become conscious of self as an active being and are able to stand back from ourselves in thought. Hence, self-reflective judgements avail themselves of the kinds of predicates that we use in talking of others and are influenced by the beliefs current in our community of reference. Self-consciousness is the learned ability to speak, and thereby to think, of oneself in ways that spring from our encounters with other thinking beings. Harré claims that the self is not some inner entity, but an intersubjective mode of being. The way in which this should encourage us to think about persons is sufficiently revolutionary, he thinks, to overturn many of the traditional notions clustering around their purported significance.

Law has always been an instrument whereby the relations between what we call 'persons' have been regulated. Hence it is not surprising that it has always had to operate, implicitly or explicitly, with some kind of working definition of the entities between which relations are being legally regulated. Richard Tur discusses 'The "Person" in Law' by turning first to Roman law. He explains how the idea of legally specified life conferred a certain status, or mode of public being, on a person. In Roman law, one had a *status libertatis*, a *status civitatis*, and a *status familiae*. Legal penalties were assessed in terms of what legal status was lost as the result of a misdemeanour. The relation between the person as construed legally and a natural human life was not a one-to-one matter. This evinced the idea of a *persona*, a mask or role, through which one acts and which partially defines the significance of one's actions and one's being as an agent.

He notes that, in the eyes of the law, a 'person' is a party to implicit and explicit agreements, obligations, and commitments, rather than an actual or potential rational conscious being. In English law, the concept of person can be quite bewildering, for it is not co-extensional with the idea of agency, and, even more than in Roman law, is a matter of degree. He illustrates this with reference to who had the vote at the turn of the century and to contemporary debates regarding abortion and contraception. Throughout, Tur emphasizes that legal personality is a matter of a rather subtle conglomerate of capacities, rights, obligations, and liabilities. He concludes that legal personality is derivative from all sorts of beliefs, common wisdom, and social custom. He thereby returns the determination of the concept of what it is to be a person to the realm of extralegal reasoning, reserving as the proper concern of the law only a diverse and shifting set of practices through which our more general beliefs are enacted and in which the idea of the person at law is constituted.

At this point, we look at concepts of the person operating in another profession, medicine. In a chapter entitled 'Is Medicine a Branch of Ethics?', Dr William Fulford shows how ethical theory can be employed to restore what he calls the patient-as-a-person to a properly central place in the concerns of everyday medical practice. He reminds us that the patient-as-a-person has, over recent years, increasingly been displaced by the patient-as-a-machine. This has been a natural consequence of the development of science in medicine. Yet with this development have come ever more pressing ethical difficulties. And this trend, Fulford argues, will continue until we come to recognize fully that, however important the contribution of science to clinical work, medicine is at heart not a scientific, but an ethical, discipline.

This challenging conclusion he derives from a consideration of the concepts by which medicine is defined, the concepts of 'illness' and 'disease'. The importance of science in medicine is such that these concepts, although apparently evaluative concepts, have generally been regarded, at least in medical usage, as factual concepts – this is so, for example, in the recent extensive literature on the concept of 'mental illness'. However, acknowledgement that they are really evaluative concepts in no way impedes the progress of science to medicine, while, on the other hand, it allows us to explore and explain the way in which they are used by drawing on everything that has been written about the logic of value-terms in general, notably in the literature on the 'is-ought' debate. Nor is this a result of merely theoretical significance. For it has a number of important practical consequences; and it is by way of these that the patient-as-a-person is restored to pride of place in medicine. The full realization of these consequences, as Fulford emphasizes in his conclusion, is a philosophical task still to be completed. But so important is this task, that we may anticipate, as a direct response to it, the appearance of a new medicine–philosophy hybrid, a hybrid which will eventually prove as powerful in dealing with the patient-as-a-person as the already well-established medicine–science hybrid has proved in dealing with the patient-as-a-machine.

Dr Anthony Storr then examines the conception of personality advocated by one of the most influential thinkers of this century, Carl Jung, who was trained in medicine and then in psychiatry at the time when the latter was taking on its modern form. He became fascinated by the unity that subjects impose on their conscious lives, a unity that can become dramatically fragmented in the presence of psychiatric disorders. His work exposed the often covert or partly submerged complexities of personality. Jung claimed that 'the psyche is a self-regulating system that maintains its equilibrium just as the body does', and that there is a compensatory relation between the conscious and the unconscious. According to him, what really matters is a person's relationship with the unconscious; and, at the beginning of his autobiography, he describes his own life as 'a story of the self-realization of the unconscious'.

Jung's greatest interest was in individuals who pursue their own paths, heedless of convention, for he saw the highest achievements as always individual. Indeed, he defines personality as 'the supreme realization of the innate idiosyncrasy of a living being'. This process of realization, or 'individuation' as Jung, following Schopenhauer, calls it, is a religious one, in that it involves a denial of the claims of the ego and an acknowledgement of a guiding, integrating factor not of one's own making.

Jung does not deny the importance of interpersonal relationships; but, unlike social psychologists, he does not give them pride of place. In this, Storr sees him as providing a necessary corrective to the overly social theory of personality prevalent today.

In his chapter entitled 'Personality and Poetry', Mr Anthony Nuttall is also concerned with the human psyche, preferring the Platonic term *psuché*, which includes mind, intelligence, and character, to the term 'soul', with its religious overtones. Like Plato, he believes that there are many real and important things in the world, such as justice and other abstract universals, which are not simply physical facts, and that the psyche is one such fact, albeit with the difference that it may not be timeless, or immortal. None the less, to be human is to participate in the non-material as well as the material, which is why attempts to give an account of the world solely in physical terms – such as those of the behaviourists – are unconvincing, and why Plato's argument regarding the psyche 'continues to nag, to pluck at the sleeve of the mind', as Nuttall puts it.

A similarly unsatisfactory situation has arisen in recent years in the field of literary criticism. First, there was the New Critic, elevating the poem as the sole determinant of meaning, regardless of the intention of the author. Then came the structuralist, claiming that the meaning of a poem resided in the wider literary context; and, following that, the deconstructionist, questioning the very possibility of meaning. Nuttall says: 'It is as if the analytic intelligence, for considerable stretches of human history, operates as a sort of death-ray, withering all that lies in its path.'

In both pursuits – that of the psyche and that of the meaning of a poem – the object of inquiry has seemed to recede – indeed, to be dissolved. What seems to have gone wrong in both cases is that there has been an artificial separation of different orders of being and discourse, with a 'subsequent wanton privileging of one order over all the rest', and a concomitant loss of the sense of the whole, whether person or poem.

At this point, we move on to theological news of the person, and more specifically, Christian views. In a chapter entitled 'A Theology of Personal Being', Professor John Macquarrie considers three aspects of what it is to be a human person. He argues first that persons are always 'beings-on-the-way', beings in the process of change; and thus that human nature is constituted by an activity in which persons grow and, in so doing, create themselves. They thereby become both what they are and what they will be. Since we both choose and create, we have radical responsibility for what we actually make of ourselves. Macquarrie links this idea with that of transcendence, which expresses the 'going beyond' that occurs when we transform both what we are and the world in which we live.

Second, he stresses the world-involving nature of human life; for we are 'beings-in-the-world', entities that are essentially embodied. Man is an embodied spirit as the Bible teaches, and within this totality reside the distinction, limitations, and the possibilities of human existence. Finally, Macquarrie like many of our contributors, stresses that we are 'being-with-others'. The dialogue between persons, in which the 'I' and the 'thou' mutually constitute each other, leads us to realize that any purportedly Christian view that focuses solely on the individual human being is a distortion of the biblical perspective, which emphasizes our social, interpersonal being. Macquarrie concludes by provoking us to reflect on the ethical implications of his approach, on those ethical dilemmas which we face in a shared world, as beings with responsibility for ourselves, the world, and each other.

We turn next to 'Christian Theism and the Concept of a Person', in which Dr Adrian Thatcher examines a number of different uses of the concept *person*, specifically with regard to how these might be applied to the personal God in whom Christians believe. In particular, he is concerned to show that neither the Christian conception of God nor the Christian understanding of the human person requires a Cartesian dualism in order to be credible. He sees human beings as persons not by virtue of any inner essence or mental substance, but in part, at least, because of their essential involvement in the world. Indeed, Thatcher wants to say that the bodily nature of human life is precisely what gives death its importance and makes it a matter of faith that some substantial, eternal being is conferred on us by God; for it is not a natural feature of our constitution. He maintains that there are no theological reasons for favouring some kind of philosophical dualism, and that the doctrines of Creation, Incarnation, Resurrection, and Ascension all support a non-dualist view.

He goes on to discuss the new concept of matter, describing it as 'a gift of the physical sciences to theology'. This new concept of 'matter' is open, emergent, and fathomless as to its ultimate nature; moreover, the term 'matter' now becomes inclusive of both 'form' – since it is self-organizing – and 'mind' – since mental activities emerge at an advanced stage in the hierarchical organization of matter. He regards this dynamic view of matter issuing in life, thought, and creativity as entirely consistent with Christian theology. It gives rise to views of the person which place a positive value on those features of our experience that are intimately embedded in our bodily nature. God remains a mystery, but has given us a medium, as it were, through which this mystery is, at least in part, disclosed: the person of Jesus the Christ. It is on the positive ground afforded by this last claim, Thatcher urges, that we see God clothed in personhood in all its aspects. Thus God both communicates himself to us as God, and provides for us a pattern of what it is to be fully human.

Thatcher speaks of the 'mystery' of God and of the claim that a particular person in history is the means by which this mystery is disclosed. But there is a reciprocity involved in such a disclosure, for there is a mystery about persons, as Dr Kallistos Ware emphasizes at the beginning of the final chapter, entitled 'The Unity of the Human Person according to the Greek Fathers'. He quotes David Jenkins as saying that 'The mystery of the fact of being a person' cannot be 'reduced to the facts of the appropriate sciences'; and he himself goes on to assert that 'The reality of our personhood is far more than any explanation that we choose to give it. It is an intrinsic feature of personalness to be open, always to point beyond', which echoes Macquarrie's theme of persons as beings-on-the-way. More particularly, he finds this to be a recurrent feature of the understanding of the human person among the Greek Fathers of the Christian Church in the first few centuries after Christ. For them, the basis for the mysterious, indefinable character of the person is that the human being is made in God's image and likeness (Gen. 1: 26–7). As Ware puts it, 'The human person is a created icon of the uncreated God; since God is incomprehensible, so also is the human person.' Beneath the apparent Platonism of much of the thought of the Fathers, we find evidence of a more integrated, holistic conception.

Our human personhood is also a microcosm, an image, or icon, of the world, because, existing as it does on both the spiritual and material levels, it can reflect and embrace these two different aspects of the created universe. Indeed, it is our human vocation to reconcile and harmonize the differing levels of reality in which we participate, and so to draw them all in to unity. This is a theme of Jewish Hasidic writers, as well as of the Greek Fathers, though in the latter this mediatorial function is specifically assigned to Christ, who is taken as the model of what it means to be human.

However, the Greek Fathers also saw the human role as extending to the task of unifying the created and the uncreated, of mediating between extremes, and so uniting them to God. In this human persons transcend the limits of their created nature and are 'taken up into the eternal life of God', thereby being rendered godlike. this is possible because the human person is not only the universe in miniature, but also God in miniature, *microtheos*. Indeed, the true greatness of human personhood consists in our being made in the image of the Creator.

One cannot help wondering at this point whether the polarities represented by the first two contributors have not in some way been transcended already in the very biblical thinking of these early Christian writers. It is not for us, as editors, to pronounce on this, but rather to encourage the reader to follow a trail in search of appropriate and sufficiently rich conceptions of the person and of personality, mindful that this may lead to a growing sense of mystery regarding the nature of what is sought.

2

Purposeless People

PETER ATKINS

When confronted with the analysis of any concept, however complex, the only intellectually honest approach is to explore the extent to which an absolutely minimal explanation can account for the reliable evidence. There is no justification for departing from this procedure when the complex concept in question is that of the person, however deeply emotive it may be, and however much we may long for a reassuring outcome. Only if a minimal approach is explicitly demonstrated to be inadequate may there be some justification for indulging in the soft furnishings of additional hypotheses. We should begin our exploration, therefore, by asking whether the concept of person, which I take to be the concept of our individual existence, persistence, and role in this universe, can be explained without the sugar-coating of invented attributes of persons, additions that have been proposed by the under-informed or the wiley perhaps, and have been adhered to generally by the religious.

We should ask whether the concept of personal existence can survive stripped-down explanations and their ramifications. Is there any support for the existence of something beyond the absolutely sparse? Is there life beyond bones? Are the fat and tallow of religious, philosophical, and psychological forms of justification necessary and not merely desirable? And if fat and tallow are found to be unnecessary, is there any justification for an ethical view amid the bones of people's purposelessness?

I will argue that it is intellectually dishonest at this stage of human development to resort to the artifice of supposing man's existence to be justified by recourse to something beyond this world. I will argue that the time is ripe for the faithful to relinquish their prejudices and to examine with an open mind the possibility that the world is a happy accident, that we might be creatures of chance, nothing more than fragments of highly organized matter, and that there may be nothing intrinsically special about us apart from the complexity of our responses. I will also argue that the long-term future of everything is oblivion and annihilation.

I challenge anyone who seeks, hopes, and believes in a seductively richer option and a rosier destiny to accompany me to the bedrock of existence and to build their beliefs on it only in so far as their shelter is shown to be essential. I will argue that *all* softenings of my absolutely barren view of the concept of person and of the foundations of this wonderful, extraordinary, delightful world are sentimental wishful thinking.

THE OMNICOMPETENCE OF SCIENCE

The spring of my apparently barren but, as I hope to show, deeply enriching world-view, is my belief that science is all-competent.

I base this belief on the observation that science has never encountered a barrier that it has not surmounted or that it cannot reasonably be expected to surmount eventually. I admit that this is only a belief, but I will argue that it is supportable, and that it is simpler than the alternatives and should therefore be given priority over more elaborate views. In alluding to domains not yet fully conquered, I have in mind the at least arguable – and certainly not yet explicitly denied – view that, in due course, science will be equipped to deal with aesthetic and religious experience, and will be able to account for our perception of ourselves as distinct, responding entities. It will do so, I believe, by showing that the characteristically human capacities which we lump together for convenience of discourse as 'human spirit' or 'soul' are no more than states of the brain, and likewise that extension of the idea of a soul to expectation of eternal persistence is already quite plainly explicable in terms of a deep-seated desire to avoid, and the inability to come to terms with, the prospect of one's own annihilation.

I do not see any evidence to support the claim that there are aspects of the universe closed to science. Given the success of science in encroaching on the territory traditionally regarded as that of religion, I can accept that many people *hope* that its domain of competence will prove bounded, with things of the spirit on one side of the fence, things of the flesh on the other. But *until it is proved otherwise*, there is no reason to suppose that science is incompetent when it brings its razor to bear on belief. Until the day that science is explicitly shown to be incompetent, we should acknowledge that its not-yet-stopped razor is slicing through the fabric of the heavens and leading us towards an extraordinary deep understanding of the composition, organization, and origin of the world.

As science's razor continues to slice, so it is revealed that much that was once inexplicable stems from the workings of laws that are simplicity itself. What grounds are there for assuming that the razor will become blunt or will run against the uncuttable? Pessimism? Fear? Outrage? Surely such emotional cringing is poor reason for not permitting this supreme device of the human intellect, our science, to run its course.

If we are to approach our topic with an open mind, we should prepare ourselves to see sliced from the concept of person many of some people's most cherished beliefs. It would be premature to say that science, which at present is undeniably in full flood, cannot deal with the great questions. Give science time: it is in the midst of its achieving; do not yet merely deny its omni-competence, and do not resort to traditional explanations unnecessarily. In assessing whether a purely scientific world-view is likely to be complete, do not assume that because religious views have been around longer, they are more likely to be right. In wondering whether a sparse scientific view of the person could suffice, I think it only fair to play the game of reversing history, of envisaging a religious upstart battling against a high ground held for millennia by science. Could anyone seriously take religion's mysteries to be more compelling than science's public achievements? I picture a dog suddenly woken into our intellectual level and presented with the offerings of religion and science. What dog, unfettered by our cultural heritage and free from the iron grip of religion's social, economic, private, and artistic propaganda, would opt for religion's 'explanations'? Surely, any honest dog would accept that science was so well along the road to full explanation, that it should side with science and discard religion, at least until – if ever – science failed to deliver.

THE JOURNEY INTO SIMPLICITY

My attitude is that the omnicompetence of science and, in particular, the simplicity revealed by its insights should be accepted as a working hypothesis until, if ever, it is proved inadequate. This is relevant to our discussion in a multitude of different ways. Among them is the lesson taught by science about the power of the unconstrained and undirected to lead to rich consequences, consequences that are so rich that they can readily be mistaken for purposeful, directed events.

I think it worth exploring this last statement more deeply, for many non-scientists see science as an increasingly complex edifice, with each new discovery, each new theoretical concept, adding one more pimple to an already over-carbuncled and bunioned body. Such a view could not be further from the truth. Each new discovery of fundamental science – and we are not at this stage concerned with its applications – reveals one more facet of an underlying *simplicity*, a simplicity, that allows more to be explained by fewer concepts and precepts.

Not all scientists, never mind non-scientists, recognize or acknowledge this simplicity. Some see only the enormous effort and complex equipment needed to make even the seemingly most trivial advance in understanding and confuse the complexity entailed in gathering information with the underlying simplicity revealed by the information so gathered. Some, seeing how new ideas over-throw old familiar ones, as when quantum theory replaced classical mechanics, do not see beyond the loss of the familiar to the sharp insight that comes from discarding approximations and shifting viewpoint. Some, seeing the mathematics required both to express an idea and to relate it to an observa-tion, confuse the complexity with which simple concepts band together to masquerade as complex phenomena with the simplicity of the concepts themselves.

If there is a deep message that a scientist should convey to non-scientists, it is that simplicity can have consequences of extraordinary complexity, a revelation resulting from science's ability to discern the ways in which these simplicities tangle into testable, observable complexities.[1]

THE MOTIVE POWER OF CHANGE

I must take you to one more level of scientific explanation if you are to appreciate the power of science to attack great problems, and if you are to see what I have in mind when I speak of complexity as the child of simplicity.

The second law of thermodynamics,[2] that child of the steam-engine, has, in the course of the nineteenth and twentieth centuries, grown to become the greatest liberator of the human spirit, and the steam-engines from which it sprang can now be seen to have forged wings for humanity's aspirations. Sadi Carnot – and it is fitting that he was named after a poet – pointed the way to the formulation of this law that acts as signpost in the direction of natural change, a law of such universality that it applies to every kind of change, from the most primitive – such as the cooling of hot metals and the expansion of gases – to the marginally more complex – such as the synthesis of ammonia and the rusting of iron – to the most complex – such as the emergence of new species, the formation of opinions, introspection, hallucination, self-deception, and comprehension.

Carnot's reflections leading to this law, as well as those of his successors Kelvin and Clausius, who formulated it rigorously and explored some of its consequences, were views of matter and its behaviour as seen from the outside.

Theirs were powerful formulations of descriptions which did not, on their own, lead to insight into the spring of the world. It was left to the short-sighted Boltzmann to see further than all his contemporaries and to formulate an explanation of the second law in terms of the behaviour of atoms before their existence was generally accepted. Many of his contemporaries doubted the credibility of Boltzmann's assumptions and feared that his work would dethrone the concept of purpose that they presumed to exist within the world of change, just as Darwin had recently dispossessed its outer manifestations. Suffering from their scorn, Boltzmann, himself committed to the omnicompetence of science, was overcome by instability and unhappiness, and killed himself.

Yet now we know that Boltzmann's interpretation of the second law in terms of atoms was right in broad terms. Today no one seriously doubts the existence of atoms, and no one has reason to suppose that they are driven by a sense of purpose. They are driven by forces, their intrinsic properties – their mass, their charge, and, more deeply, their wave nature – determining their response and their paths through the world, bundled together as an element here and an elephant there. In the late twentieth century, we see that the direction of natural, spontaneous change, the direction taken by events when the universe is left to free-wheel, is that of increasing universal chaos.

Boltzmann's insight into the deep structure of natural change, which accounts for all the events of the world captured by Carnot's, Kelvin's, and Clausius's phenomenological thermodynamics and has now been extended beyond them, is that the universe is sinking, purposelessly, into ever greater chaos. Thus, energy tends to disperse from compact, highly concentrated regions, such as a nucleus, a lump of coal, a sandwich, or the sun. Similarly, the energy of orderly motion tends to become chaotic, as when a bundle of atoms grouped together as a ball hits a wall and the uniform motion of its atoms is rendered chaotic by the collision, and the net motion is randomized into chaotic thermal motion. Likewise, the location of particles becomes chaotic, when they move, collide, and spread, as when a gas expands into a vacuum.

These three kinds of sinking into chaos account for all natural change.[3] That they account for the decay and decomposition of matter may be self-evident. But the richness of these processes, and that of science, is due to the fact that the very same processes also account for the emergence of structures. That is, the second law allows for the abatement of chaos in one region, as long as there is a greater flood elsewhere, so that, overall, the universe becomes more chaotic. This extraordinary, creative, constructive characteristic of the collapse into chaos is a result of the universe being a network of inter-dependences: pull a string here and a lever moves there. Falling water here drives a lathe there. A chemical reaction here is linked to another reaction there. A new substance produced in one reaction is used in another linked reaction, and together they add to the chaos of the world; but whereas one reaction has resulted in decay, as when a sandwich is eaten, the other has given birth to a protein.

The universe is an astonishingly, but not incredibly, rich, interconnected network of events. It moves forward as a result of its gradual sinking into chaos, but its interconnectedness is so rich that a surge of chaos there may effloresce into a cathedral, a symphony, or a deed here. Structures – in the broadest sense, including raising a stone in a field to build a house – moving a molecule in a brain to form an opinion – are local abatements of chaos, driven by a greater surge of chaotic dispersal elsewhere.

CHAOS, PURPOSE, AND THE EMERGENCE OF PEOPLE

Of course, we cannot yet trace a surge of chaos at some point and identify it with a particular deed. Perhaps we never will be able to, for it is undeniable that the brain is an exceptionally complex test-tube. Yet this criticism is irrelevant. It is enough for our present purposes to expose the bedrock of the scientific explanation of events: that the chaotic dispersal of energy and matter is interconnected in an intricate web, as in a diabolical organ where depressing one key may sound a chord of a billion unpredictable notes.

As yet, little has been said of purpose. At this stage science can perform its elucidation without appealing to the shroud of obscurity of man-made artifice. A block of hot metal will cool, not because its purpose is to cool, but because the spontaneous chaotic dispersal of its energy results in it cooling. A shoot emerges from a seed and grows into a plant, not because the seed's purpose is to grow, but because the intricate network of reactions in its cells are gearboxes that propel its growth as the rest of the world sinks a little further into chaos. The lily is a flag hoisted by collapse into purposeless chaos. All the extraordinary, wonderful richness of the world can be expressed as growth from the dunghill of purposeless, interconnected decay.

People, too, have emerged as the same dunghill has effloresced. One molecule capable of reproducing itself in its own image is all it needs to set the world on the progress that has culminated in it being peopled with persons. All that was needed initially was a supply of suitable molecules that could be linked together into one larger molecule with the capacity to act as a template for its own replication. There are several conjectures as to how the appropriate organic molecules might have accumulated in the warm, wet, storm-ridden, and ultra violet-soaked conditions prevailing on this planet three and a half billion years ago, and how they might have been combined into molecules that are the ancestors of today's DNA. Science, although far from sure, is certainly not defeated when it comes to suggesting how chance may have transformed the inanimate into the animate, with the potential for humanity.

One such global grandfather molecule could have entered the world through the blind, purposeless action of the second law, and at its inception become king. The blind activity of the second law, leads to replications of the king, and with more than one king, the world is at war and natural selection rules. I do not intend to trace the steps of evolution,[4] except to say that we can see in broad outline, and here and there in detail, how, given the conditions prevailing on this planet, the grand sinking into chaos led to us.

We have inherited the earth, at least temporarily, because our ancestors were equipped by chaos with mobility and brains that could respond ever more adroitly to the pressures of circumstance. We are, in a word, the children of chaos. At root there is only corruption and the unstemmable tide of chaos. That is the bleakness we should accept, as the starting-point for our analysis of the concept of person, for science can account for our emergence without the imposition of any extraneous view; it does not need to smear on to its clear, sinewy explanations any invented concept, particularly that of purpose. Purpose is unnecessary; all that is required to account for the emergence of people is interconnectedness and time.

Yet, when we look around and see beauty, when we look within and experience consciousness, when we participate in the delights of life, we feel in our hearts that the heart of the universe is richer by far. But do not be seduced: that is sentiment, and not what we should know in our minds. Unless it can be explicitly demonstrated otherwise, we should adopt the view that all attributes of persons have grown in response to the pressures for survival, and that any rationalization of them in terms of *additional* hypotheses, such as that of a creating, rewarding, or admonishing god or a teleological sense of purpose, are unjustified, superfluous superimpositions.

The bare bones of the scientific explanation of the emergence, existence, and temporary persistence of persons are that the universe is sinking into chaos. Faith in things beyond is a psychologically motivated fat and tallowing of these bones: God, an afterlife, the concept of purpose, are merely attempts to ameliorate the prospect of death, to unload the burden of guilt, and to soften the hardships of life. There is not one iota of justification for them beyond assertion, wishful thinking, and hallucination.

THE FUTURE

This bleak view, it seems to me, is only roughened into greater harshness when we pursue it with intellectual honesty into the future.

Although I can see that there is in some sense a justifiable temporally local sense of purpose – as for example, when I attempt to persuade others to my views (for reasons I could state), and more generally to contribute to the cultural heritage of the world; but I know that in the long term such activity is futile. For, after billions of years, even though we may have mastered the galaxies, founded new, young worlds, built our own private utopias next to stars we have learnt to ignite and perhaps refresh, and have individually acquired physical and mental immortality, there will come a time when activity in the universe will cease. Then, at the dead end of the world, when all matter has decayed, when the expansion of the universe has distended space so much that it is a perfect void, we and all our achievements will come to naught. In the end there will be only dead flat space-time, our castles will have gone, as well as our libraries, our achievements, our selves. We, who will no longer be, will then listen in vain in the void for the Last Trumpet.

The sound of the Last Trumpet could, I suppose, be that of the Big Crunch, when the expanding universe, gripped by its own gravitation, ceases its current expansion, falls back on itself like a returning high-thrown ball, and crashes together in a final fury. Such a crunch could be the precursor of another Big Bang, a new First Trumpet, another cycle of expansion and contraction, another episode of groping for understanding in the liberty of newly refreshed space-time. But, aside from the fact that I consider it more likely that this is a one-shot universe, with a window briefly and only once opened for comprehension and aspiration, the Big Crunch would erase the tracks of our progress through this episode, and so, just as surely as in a one-shot universe, our achievements would be as though they had never been.

There is no reason to believe, except wishful thinking, that the long-term future of the human race, if it has one, even if it should evolve into superhumans, will be anything other than annihilation and oblivion. The long-term future, and in that sense purpose, of humanity should be regarded as empty. We came from nothing and will return to nothing, leaving behind neither material nor intellectual castles. All traces of our wars, poems, theories, and aspirations, all traces of our existence, and all traces of the existence of all matter will be erased.

THE SPARSE MODEL OF PERSONS

My scientific world-view of humanity is obviously bleak with regard to its origins, its motivations, and its future. Yet, unless it can be explicitly demonstrated otherwise, it should be the sparse working hypothesis underlying our concept of person. If everything in the world can be accommodated in this bare-bones view, then there is no justification for imposing on our understanding the hypothetical extraneous.

But does this view account for everything? Does the spare eschew the fat? What sense of being a person is not, in principle at least, explicable in these terms?

Being a person includes a sense of identity and a sense of distinctness from one's surroundings, surroundings normally presumed to contain other persons. On the sparse model, such a sense is nothing more than the response of the brain to its sensory input: I do not see that there is anything particularly odd about a brain treating its nerve endings as its boundaries. Consciousness is a manifestation of the brain, and on the sparse model it is no more than a fascinating property that depends on, and is the non-linear summation of, the physical states of nerve cells.

This, of course, is where some would wish to challenge, claiming that consciousness is irreducible; but when it comes down to what it means to give a scientific explanation. Although I am a reductionist, I wish to make it plain that, like most reductionists, I suspect, I am actually an assemblist. That is, I regard it as the task of a reductionist intent on explaining the brain (or any other complex device) to show that from a set of components and normal physical principles, defined as deeply as you wish, a working brain can be assembled. As a reductionist, I claim that it is possible to reproduce consciousness or any other property by synthesis; but I do not claim that it is necessarily possible to comprehend it analytically, or to comprehend any other complex property of any other composite entity, by treating it as an agglomeration of functioning parts. Synthetic, assemblist explanation may seem weak by comparison with truly analytical classical explanation, but I do not see that it is unworthy of the name 'explanation', nor do I accept that being limited to synthetic explanation is tantamount to denying that we have reached a stage of comprehension.

There is no reason why consciousness should not be admitted to the kingdom of scientific explanation. I would stress, however, that I do not claim that consciousness has yet been 'explained'. I am claiming merely that it is open to scientific explanation, and that there is no evidence that the brain's workings require non-physical impositions. I claim that the principal activity of the brain, that of sustaining a sense of consciousness through a lifetime, is open to explanation in terms of its physical structure (as governed by the genes that the body inherits which find expression through the purposeless workings of the second law, essentially building on the purposeless collapse of sandwiches into chaos) and its chemical activity (which is also a manifestation of the second law in precisely the same way).

Once consciousness is admitted to the kingdom of science, then all mental atrributes of the person are open to comprehension. The brain is subtle and capable, it seems, of infinite understanding of itself, its individual origin, its cosmic origin, the origin of the cosmos, and of the cosmos's immediate, intermediate, and long-term featureless future. However, like other complex instruments, the brain can make errors, especially when the opinions it expresses have been pressed on it and are widely supported by others. Thus the brain can hallucinate; it can become perplexed; moreover, armchair brains can avoid unnecessary exercise by adopting easy explanations. Some of these failures lead to poetic expression, others to religious fervour, and some to undisguised madness. But they are an abnegation of the brain's true power of understanding, which is to be found only in scientific, reductionist (that is, assemblist) explanation.

THE ETHICS OF PURPOSELESS DECAY

If persons are the inevitable outcome of the collapse into chaos, acting through essential physical laws and fundamental constants without which this universe could neither have come into being nor persist, and if chance has located a stage for this comedy on earth, or even if persons are the result of chaos pulling the strings of an accidental blend of laws and constants, can there be any fundamental ethical view?

If we accept, at least as a working hypothesis, that the world is barren of purpose, devoid of a long-term future, and free of godlike intrusions and excrescences, then what are the ethical implications? If persons are accidents, merely the outcome of chaos, can there be an ethical view of the person? (I am dismissing as not worthy of consideration, of course, the converse of this argument, that there is an intrinsic ethical commitment, and hence that persons cannot be merely accidents.) In a word, no. There cannot be a fundamentally justifiable ethical view in a world free of purpose, one that explores its own destiny blindly. All ethical views have stemmed from human attitudes, and their justification is to be found in history and psychology, not in anything more fundamental.

The adoption, elaboration, and persistence of the ethical values adopted by societies could be yet another aspect of natural selection. Pragmatically advantageous values can emerge at the level of interpersonal behaviour and be frozen into the structure of society by legislation. Thus, an incipient society without rules or with rules that lead to self-destruction, would be incapable of development and survival. Only societies in which individuals interact constructively can develop and flourish. It is better for the species, the society, or whatever is being selected, if wanton random killing is taboo and if mutual back-scratching is encouraged.

We humans have a non-Darwinian advantage. The ethical views most conducive to the survival of the society can be perpetuated through our advantage of language, for such views need not be inherited genetically or even be appropriate under contemporary conditions, but can be drilled into the brains of succeeding generations and disguised, for the sake of digestion and acceptance, as God-given. I am not saying that ethical views may not be wise: they may constitute a valuable framework for survival by providing protection without too great an inhibition of personal aspiration. What I *am* saying is that ethical views, except in so far as they are seen to be invented, are without foundation.

CONFLICTING ETHICS

Although my world-view does not imply an ethical framework, it may be worth exploring whether some ethical attitudes are compatible with it and others not. One attitude implied by my view is that, since we are all accidents, decaying helter-skelter into chaos, driven by purposelessness and governed by decay, then each of us has an equal right to fulfil our aspirations as long as we do not transgress and thwart the aspirations of others. *Soft universal liberalism*, respect for more or less any aspiration, would seem to be one ethical implication of my nihilism.

Unfortunately, my nihilism can also be turned around and used to support *hard universal tyranny*. For, if we are all accidents, and if there is no great monitor in the sky and no prospect of punishment in an afterlife, then there is no particular reason, apart from our own safety or the safety of our species, why we should maintain that it matters how we behave.

I see no *a priori* distinction between being agreeable and respectful to everyone, on the grounds that we are equal accidents, and killing at will, on the same grounds. I see plenty of *a posteriori* distinction, however, not least my own survival and the retention of my liberty to use my brain and body to seek enjoyment, by respecting the laws that my society has evolved to sustain itself. I see no deeper reason than the love I have of comprehending, the respect my brain has for itself and for the brains of others, and my hope that knowledge and understanding will grow among all people.

My view that *any* ethical view can be argued from first principles is an important one, I think, for those who seek to impose moral attitudes. If I have any positive view at all, it is that humanity is *completely free* to impose its own rules, for better or worse, on itself and its societies. If societies are to survive, they need rules, and at least in their early days, before education has become universal and successful, it may be wise to pretend that the rules that have been invented were originally carved on stones by vigilant deities who, if transgressed, will either punish immediately or scorch for eternity. However, I do not think a continuation of such an approach to be worthy of respect, once the vacuity of its foundations has been exposed. And if the lie has to be retailed to peoples for the structural stability of the society or the species, then at least the retailers should be clear in their own minds that they are liars.

Why, then, do I bother to do anything? Why, given the prospect of personal annihilation and, in the long and cosmic term, universal oblivion, is life still worth living as positively as possible and, within limits, without transgressing the aspirations of others, while helping them, as an educator to realize their hopes? For me, it boils down to pleasure, the pleasure of sensing, participating in, and understanding the world. I revel in the pleasure of sensing a rose, seeing a sunset, perceiving the world. I also revel in the understanding that comes from knowing how an atom contributes to the world, in knowing why a rose is red, in understanding the sunset, in knowing why a stone falls. In particular, I revel in the delight of knowing that all this can come from deep-rooted simplicity erupting into the perceived world disguised as apparently unresolvable complexity. This enthralling vision is something worth sharing.

CONCLUSION

I have tried to argue that science provides a complete (and, by implication, the only) pathway to fundamental knowledge, that in doing so it specifies a sea-level for discussions of the concept of person and that all mountains must be argued for. Science is proving omnicompetent, showing (at this stage of its development, largely in principle) that every aspect of the world can be regarded as the outcome of the purposeless unwinding of the universe; it also strongly suggests that the long-term future is oblivion.

I have argued that any accretions to this picture are gratuitous and based on sentimental wishful thinking, hallucinations, loneliness, misunderstanding, cultural conditioning, psychological defectiveness, personal insufficiency, and so on. I have also argued that those who doubt that my bare-bones picture is complete should nevertheless adopt it until it has been explicitly demonstrated to be deficient, for only then will their cherished preconceptions have been shown, after all, to be possibilities.

I have argued that we are all chance efflorescences emerging amid the purposeless collapse of the universe, and that we should not regard ourselves as some special creation or as the zenith of evolution. This desolate, but, in my opinion, deeply enriching view is the foundation of no system of ethics, for it can be used to argue for perfect respect for people, slugs, and rocks, or for the inconsequentiality of persons and as justification for waging random death. What it teaches is that no system of ethics based on accretions to this bare-bones world-view should be respected, except in so far as they are pragmatic, have given societies and species stability, and have allowed time for the realization to emerge that their foundations are empty. Any ethical code must be seen as being in humanity's gift, and hence as artificial as any game yet invented.

DISCUSSION

MICHAEL RUSE. I want to go back to the beginning, where Atkins said he was going to put forward a reductionist, minimalist position, for basically that is what his philosophy is; if one can speak in terms of one thing, then it is better to do so than to use two, and two is better than three, and so on.

This seems to me to be in itself a value judgement, though not necessarily a *moral* value judgement. It is a value judgement, nevertheless, because I did not hear any kind of Kantian transcendental deduction or anything else to prove that reduction to one is more true than reduction to two, or to two than to three. I share the same presuppositions; but nevertheless, it is a judgement made at the beginning, and I wonder if one might not be justified in seeing this as the thin end of a very wide wedge. The critic might well say: 'You are admitting that your science is itself structured according to certain preferences, limitations, and prior judgements. Therefore it suggests to me that your science is not quite a disinterested, true mapping of ultimate reality. Rather, you have led us to believe that "science", which is going to explain all to us, is itself a great deal more human than you allow. And perhaps, in fact, there are other value judgements which went into the making of your "science".' Speaking as one concerned with biology and its dynamics, I know that a great many value judgements of one sort or another have been imported into science at various times. What I am asking is whether your bleak, but enriching, picture, as you call it, is itself not so much a wonderful inference from the only true way of looking at the world that any reasonable man or woman may subscribe to, but rather a function of a particular philosophy, one you adopted right from the beginning, which would mean that it is no surprise that you come out with your particular conclusions.

ROGER TRIGG. I would like to apply what Ruse said not just to what you, personally, think, but to scientists in general. Consciousness is a manifestation of the brain; it is open to scientific explanation; it is rooted in physical structure. I conclude from that that science as an agreed, accepted body of theory is just a manifestation of a group of brains; that it is rooted in physical structures: it is therefore ultimately accidental. Its purposelessness means that it is something of which I need take no notice whatsoever. I wonder if a nihilism of your kind does not in the end undercut itself in this way, so that we are left with an inability to claim truth even for science itself, the truth of which I take was your underlying assumption. If you are an absolute reductionist, I think you have got to take the argument from reflexivity seriously, and apply it to science, so that human knowledge as such turns out not to be knowledge at all. It is just the accidental product of brains reacting in a haphazard way.

ATKINS. I am inviting you to explore the possibility that 'one is better than two', and am simply asking you to lay down your 'two' and pick up 'one' and see whether it could work just as well. I think one should go through such an exercise. I am exploring the possibility that all accretions are unnecessary. It is ceretainly possible to begin with the view that the world has apples in it and that is that. I am inviting you to a simpler view of the world: that it does not just have apples in it, but that it has something simpler, and that one ought to see if apples will emerge automatically. Looking for a minimal explanation seems to me to be the intellectually honest way of proceeding. If a minimal explanation works, then you have to argue the case for any additions.

MICHAEL LOCKWOOD. You suggested that anyone who submits the matter to the judgement of his intellect in a totally dispassionate way is likely to realize that any kind of enrichment of an austere scientific view of the kind you propose is a product merely of sentiment. In my own case, however, I think the exact reverse is true. I share your atheism; I share your belief that there is no ultimate purpose; and I agree that your cosmological scenario is, on the whole, favoured by the currently available evidence. It seems to me, however, that the view you presented, dispassionately regarded, just will not work as a rational scheme of things. I think that what you are presenting is, in a way, a view that is enormously biased in the direction of evidence drawn from sense perception as opposed to introspection. If one looks, for example, to early thinkers – first to animist religions and subsequently to Aristotle – what seems to be happening is that the paradigm of explanation is being taken from within, from looking within themselves. People find purpose and so on – we ourselves, after all, have purposes – and they then impose what they find on external nature, yielding a teleological view of all natural processes. That was a mistake. I think today, however, we have the opposite bias. We look outwards, through the spectacles of modern physical science, and all we see is the apparently purposeless and insensate operation of causal laws; and we then try to impose that inwards, upon our own inner workings, including the operations of our own minds. I think that is simply to commit the opposite mistake to that of

Aristotle and the animists, and that it results in a world-view that is likewise inadequate.

I am convinced – for entirely intellectual reasons, not sentimental ones – that it is impossible in principle to accommodate the data provided by introspection within a description of the world couched purely in the language of physics. Here I am not talking about anything high-flown, such as religious experience, but things which are much more mundane than that: the sense of blueness, for example; not that blueness which is a property of physical objects or their surfaces, but the character or content of the corresponding state of awareness, sometimes called by philosophers 'phenomenal blue'. Equally puzzling is the 'aboutness' of thoughts, what philosophers call 'intentionality' – the fact that our thoughts are intrinsically meaningful in a way that, for example, printed words and the operations of computers are not; the latter, by contrast, are meaningful only by virtue of their connection to thought. Both these features of mind, and many others, seem to me to defy adequate explanation in terms of physics or physiology, as currently conceived. Consciousness itself is an enormous puzzle, an incredible enigma. Even if we had an understanding of the workings of the brain that was in physico-chemical terms complete, it would still be a total mystery why there was, in Nagel's phrase, a 'what it is like to be me' at all.[5] Surely an adequate world-view must somehow bring together – synthesize, if you like – the kinds of things that we know of ourselves through introspection and what we know of the external world through observation and experiment. I do not look for God. I do not look for ultimate purpose. But it seems to me that, simply on rational grounds, the kind of reductionism you propose is philosophically untenable. It is not a question simply of discovering new facts or introducing new particles, new forces, new laws, or what have you into physical theory. The point is rather that the conceptual resources of the physical science are, at present, simply too meagre to encompass the kind of phenomena that I have instanced.

ATKINS. I said that I was an assemblist, and in that sense not a disconnector of pieces. I maintain that if we put together physical matter into a brainlike arrangement, we would find it conscious.

GUY SCOTT. I spend a lot of my time trying to teach computers to make scientific discoveries, to be scientific or to perform very ordinary acts of perception. The problem in both cases, as I am sure you are aware, is that we have a lot of variables and not enough equations. So it is not entirely obvious on what one is going to base one's solution. The dissolution of structure really has beauty. If you show a computer a movie of, let us say, something simple like planets moving through the sky, and ask it to give you back an account, a model and an interpretation of what it 'sees', you very quickly realize that you have either a trivial or an impossible problem. Why is it that Copernicus is better than Ptolemy? They had exactly the same explanatory power, exactly the same predictive power. To us, one is obviously right, the other obviously wrong; but to a computer, nothing is obvious. What is it that underpins 'obviousness'? This opens up the whole area of aesthetics. It seems to me that science, and thus your sort of view, has a problem with aesthetics, because this challenges where science is coming from, what its roots are. In discussing science's own roots, we have no languages other than those of poetics, faith, taste, or aesthetics – all very human.

WILLIAM FULFORD. Is the view that you, Atkins, are expressing itself a scientific view? If it *is*, what would you offer as something that would, as it were, falsify that view? If it is *not*, does not that in itself suggest a limit to what science can do?

ATKINS. These remarks of Scott and Fulford are related. Science is not a matter of aesthetics. Science works; that is the dimension left out of Scott's remarks. One can actually do calculations and make predictions that can be shared with others. There is no mystery in science. It actually maps out the real world. There is a tangible difference between the affirmations of science in successfully predicting the density of lead and the striving of poets for emotional resonance. My attitudes are a part of science in the sense that I can demonstrate that they work in practice.

FULFORD. But how? By what experiment? What test? What would be something that would lead you to say, 'Now I can see that everything is *not* going to be scientifically explicable'? It seems to me that there is a crack of non-falsifiability built into your view.

ATKINS. Science proceeds by measurement, and it has built all its success on measurement and reproducibility. Those are the criteria that I would expect to apply.

TRIGG. It seems to me that what is built into this kind of theory is a refusal to take seriously anything that cannot be measured, and that therefore it is made true by definition that what is real is what is measurable. If it is beyond what is measurable, it is not real. That is not dissimilar to the line the positivists originally took, a view now widely discredited. Such a view is not acceptable, because it rules out a lot of what everyone considers to be important and, indeed, to be real.

RICHARD DAWKINS. Atkins is assuming that a simple view is more virtuous than a complex view, and that we all accept that. I myself do, but many do not. They, it seems, are prepared to say that even if you have two views of the universe which are both equally capable of explaining the facts, and that one of them is simple and the other complicated, it is not obvious that we have to accept the simpler one. So we have to say why the simple one is preferable. One possible way of doing so would be to argue that the moment we allow ourselves the luxury of accepting a more complex view, given that there are several views that account for the facts, then there is no limit to the number of more complex views that are in a sense equally capable of explaining them. As a Darwinian who occasionally has to debate matters with fundamentalist creationists, I frequently meet arguments of the form, 'God not only created the universe: he also created it so as to make it *look* as though evolution has occurred.' So one can construct a highly elaborate view of the universe which is utterly irrefutable, like Bertrand Russell's 'Holes in our socks'. It is clear that there is an infinite number of such highly elaborate world-views. Even if it has no other virtue, the simplest hypothesis at least has the virtue of uniqueness. It is one way, and almost obviously, the best way, of choosing among the infinite range of hypotheses which there will be as soon as you throw out that razor.

JOHN DURANT. I agree with that, but I think there may be another problem. As I understand it, what Dawkins has said would apply where we know we have rival hypotheses each of which could, in principle, explain a certain phenomenon. But there is disagreement among us about whether, in principle, certain kinds of hypotheses – simple, physicalist hypotheses – *can* explain what needs to be explained. Lockwood's position is that the physicalist position presented by Atkins cannot do the job for which it is intended, simply or otherwise. There may be a similar problem with notions of simplicity when we go further back to the origins of the universe, as well. I wonder whether there is some other way of resolving this problem, apart from resorting to the principle of simplicity.

RICHARD SWINBURNE. I too believe in simplicity, and that is my ground for believing that there is a God. Now the principle which you are advocating is that entities should not be multiplied beyond necessity. The question is, what counts for necessity? That is to say, if your principle of simplicity is only to postulate entities which are entailed by your observations, then you will not get atoms, molecules, or electrons, or anything like that. But you want to postulate atoms, electrons, and molecules in science, and so do I. *You* do so, because by postulating a few kinds of entities interacting in mathematically simple ways, you are led to expect the diversity of phenomena we actually find. That is a good reason for believing that there are such entities. So postulate the simplest account of the universe which will allow you to find and explain the diversity of phenomena around you. But then the issue becomes a little more complex than you have represented it to us. Because it is a question of whether your ontology – your atoms, molecules, and so on – is a simpler ontology than the one which I would produce as a rival, and whether each is equally able to lead you to expect the phenomena which you find. Now I am not disagreeing with your ontology; I am just throwing in an extra entity – God.

Why should I throw the extra one in? Because I think that if you start from there, you will be led to expect what you find in a way that you would not if you started from your rather (I would say) complex ontology. Your ontology postulates at the beginning of things many, many, many different electrons, all with the same properties of interaction and so on. I would want to say that there is a very remarkable and extraordinary coincidence, which you as a scientist are refusing to face up to, because you have decided to start from it. You will say that that is how it is. Electrons are manifold. They just happen to have the same properties at all times and places. If you are being true to your own principles, you will say that here is something that I ought to look for an explanation of, and that if I can find one, by postulating a simpler entity, lying yet further behind, then I ought to accept it. Now you may disagree with my particular system, but I am making this point to suggest that the issues are very much more complex than you represent them. That is to say, whether one system is simpler than another is not in the least obvious. Even if it includes an extra entity, it may be a simpler system, because that extra entity may lead you to expect the other entities from which you have started.

ATKINS. If I had time, I would pursue my rigorous scientific view to its limit. I agree that if I had to stop at the level of electrons, then I would have to admit to failure, and that I would need to introduce your Conductor-God to marshal them into some sort of orchestra. But I do not stop at electrons. I think that it is necessary for modern physics to pursue the structure of the world back to the point where it can see that it has emerged from nothing, without intervention. That is, I wish to regard this world as starting from zero. If it can be demonstrated that this world cannot start from absolutely zero, then you win. But I believe that science will find a way, and I can certainly speculate upon that way.

GRANT GILLETT. It seems to me that accounts may be complete in a variety of ways. For instance, a reductionist-materialist police-officer may well say, 'I know why Mr Jones was murdered. He was murdered because a bullet left the gun propelled by an explosion and lodged itself in his heart.' This is a completely adequate explanation of why Mr Jones died, and therefore of the *fact* that he was murdered. However, a less materialistic police-officer might say, 'Well, we all know that Mr Jones died, and the impact of the bullet is a complete explanation as far as it goes, but what I am more interested in is working out why somebody should want to kill him in the first place.' It does not seem to me that this is the same kind of explanation at all. There is an important and definite issue here: namely, that questions of reasons, thoughts, meaning, significance, beauty, and so forth may just not be commensurable with the kind of limited and, on your own account, austere, view of the nature of reality that your physical scientism propounds.

ATKINS. But you are not saying that a motive represents anything other than a state of a brain, are you?

GILLETT. It might represent the thoughts and feelings of a person and thus involve semantic relations, aesthetic appreciation, moral commitments, religious ideas, etc., all of which have content and an importance that goes beyond the concepts and entities discovered in the brain sciences.

ATKINS. That is just a lack of clarity of vision about what a brain is doing.

SCOTT. If you accept for the moment that the study of artificial intelligence is a scientific undertaking, it is quite interesting to see how it has worked out. In the early days of cybernetics, attempts were made, in some sense, to model the brain directly. One went to the neurophysiologist for the experimental facts, and then returned to construct something to which we might impute motives, feelings, and so forth, and thus constitute a reductionist-assemblist model of a person. Things have changed since then. We have been forced to talk 'scientifically' about the 'mind', about the 'motive', 'belief', and 'desire' of a person. For the whole discourse becomes hopeless if you reduce your terms to those of conditioned reflexes. If you try to make this kind of reduced level an explanation, it does not work, certainly in relation to any theories of the universe and its possible meaning.

RUSE. I think that at one point you implied that ethics is permissible pragmatically, but does not have any ultimate ontological validity or justification. I am now wondering why the same argument does not apply to mathematics and science itself. Suppose I were to say, 'I think that an ultimate ethical value is treating other people as ends rather than as means,' and you were to reply, 'No, that is just a matter of sentiment, and it is nothing ultimate.' You could hold that perhaps in Andromeda they do believe something else. Why should not exactly the same argument apply to your belief in the second law of thermodynamics?

KENNETH WILSON. In order to continue to substantiate the thesis that Atkins is putting forward, will it not be necessary to sustain a society in which other views are equally assumed? Otherwise one would have a society which has come to believe what you yourself have said is a hypothesis which must be held until it has been shown to be false. We need, therefore, a context in which testing of that point of view can continue, and not simply one which accepts it.

ATKINS. It may be the case that no other society exists in which it can be tested, but that does not deny its validity.

WILSON. It does not deny that it is accepted empirically. However, it is very important when offering a thesis as 'scientific' that it should be possible to continue to test it.

ATKINS. It is not necessary, though. It may still be true, yet cannot be tested. For example, one might have a supportable view about the origin of this universe, even though one did not have other universes on which to test it. LOCKWOOD. I asked earlier what was meant by scientific explanation. What I understand by scientific explanation is the application to natural phenomena of rationality and clear thinking with an eye to constructing hypotheses that render them intelligible, in a manner guided by observation and experiment. I am inclined to agree with you that there is no reason to suppose that there are any phenomena which in principle defy any possibility of scientific explanation, understood in that broad sense. But that doesn't force one to accept the kind of reductionist view that you offer. In one sense, reductionism is probably true: presumably there is some fundamental level of explanation from which everything else follows. But there seems to me to be, in your account of things, an unfounded bias in the direction of physics, and an assumption that the language of physics is adequate to describe the reality that we know. As I said earlier, there seem to me to be decisive philosophical objections to that point of view. I regret this in a way, since in certain moods I yearn for the simplicity and austerity of the kind of position you advocate. Having wrestled with the mind–body problem, however, I have become convinced that the only kind of physics that has any hope of accommodating what we know about the workings of the brain 'from the inside', from introspection, must be richer, in a qualitative sense, than what we have at present. Some radical conceptual shift seems to me to be called for.

ATKINS. I am looking for an explanation rooted in physics, which means an explanation rooted in mathematics, and that, I think, is an entirely different level of understanding. You do not believe, surely, that the brain needs more than physical inputs to bring about its operation?

LOCKWOOD. There are two sorts of doubts one might have about the adequacy of the language of physics or physiology to describe the operations of the brain. Some may believe that human beings can do things which would defy any attempt at physical explanation, in the sense that no adequate physico-chemical explanation could ever be given as to why such and such operations occurred. I have no particular doubts on that score; I do not expect the enterprise of explaining the operations of the brain in terms of physics and chemistry to break down in its own terms. Mine is a different sort of doubt, which has to do with the question of whether explaining the operations of the brain at the level of physics – by which I mean the kind of physics we are familiar with – could ever explain the character of one's awareness, for example, the sensory qualities, such as perceived blue. That there should be this 'inner perspective' at all seems totally inexplicable from the standpoint of present-day physics or physiology. And one would not in the least have succeeded in explaining it merely by correlating states of awareness with states of the brain. For the mystery is why there is this conscious dimension to reality at all, just how mind is to be accommodated within a scientific world-view. DAWKINS. I too, like Lockwood, find myself baffled when I try to give an account of what it is like to have a conscious sensation. He was making a distinction, in agreement with Atkins, between saying, on the one hand, that there is nothing going on in the brain that is not a molecular event, and, on the other hand, that we cannot yet give an account of what *is* going on. This seems to me to be a limitation of language. I cannot give an account of what is going on on all sorts of occasions, or of what it is like to feel something I cannot describe. Nevertheless, I agree with both of them that there is nothing going on that is not part of the manifestation of the laws of physics. However, some people feel that there is also something more mysterious going on: the kinds of reasons that we have heard for that view have seemed to me to be very unconcinving. We have heard, for example, from the investigator of artificial intelligence [Scott] that people who have done such research for 25 years have, with today's limited computers, found it difficult to account for the problems that they face when they find that their computers will not do human-like things. Surely the answer must be that we just have not given it long enough. If you think there is something in brains that is not in computers, what do you think we are? Is anybody going to deny that a monster electronic box constructed as a precise mimic of the brain, with mimic-neurons behaving like our neurons, would have motives, purposes, emotions, and the sensation of seeing green in exactly the same way as we do? If somebody *does* deny that, then we have a real argument on our hands.

3

The Structure of the Soul*

RICHARD SWINBURNE

Persons are beings capable of sophisticated thought and action. But the only ones known to all of us on Earth are human beings or men. I wish to argue that man on Earth is body plus soul, two components (combined undoubtedly in an intimate unity). The soul is an immaterial thing; and the conscious life of thought, sensation, and purpose which belongs to a man belongs to him because it belongs to his soul. The functioning of the soul consists in its having a conscious life. The soul is the essential part of me, and it is its continuing in existence which makes for the continuing of me. My soul may not be able to function on its own; but it is the principle of identity which, when linked to a body, either this present one or some new one, makes that body my body, and the reconstituted man, who thinks, feels and acts, me. And it is to the soul, I shall argue, that character also belongs.

MENTAL EVENTS

I begin my defence of my view of human nature by distinguishing between the mental and the physical states and events which characterize man. The physical characteristics of man are those which characterize his body and which he and others are equally well positioned to study. Weighing ten stone, being pale in colour, or having a brain with a certain rhythm are physical properties

* This paper is based on material contained in my book *The Evolution of the Soul* (Clarendon Press, Oxford, 1986) and is published by kind permission of Oxford University Press. It provided the core of my Inaugural Lecture as Nolloth Professor of the Philosophy of the Christian Religion in the University of Oxford, delivered on 18 October 1985.

of a man. But as well as his physical characteristics, man has a range of characteristics to which he has privileged access, for example, his sensations. You can study my brain and my public behaviour and on the basis of that make well-justified claims about my sensations. But whatever evidence of this public kind you can have, I can have also; I can read your reports of my behaviour, and with the aid of a mirror see what you can see through the hole in my skull. Yet I have a further source of information about my sensations which you cannot have – I actually experience them, and whether or not that gives me infallible knowledge of what they are, it certainly gives me better knowledge of them than the outsider can ever have; it gives me privileged access to them. I call states to which their subject has this privileged access his mental states. Mental states are of two kinds. First, there are conscious events, states of which not merely can the agent be aware if he chooses, but of which he will necessarily be aware while they last. His sensations (for example, the pattern of colour in his visual field), his occurrent thoughts ('it is now 5.20 p.m.' striking the lecturer), and his purposes (the intentions in the movements which he is making) are all conscious episodes. But as well as conscious episodes, there are continuing mental states, states which may continue while the subject is unaware of them and they do not impinge on his consciousness; these are, I suggest, of two kinds – desires and beliefs. By an agent's desires I mean the inclinations to action with which he finds himself, whether or not he ever yields to them. Some of these are fairly short-lasting: the desire to post a letter or to open a window, for example. Some short-lasting desires, such as desires for food and rest, recur regularly. Other more general desires last many years. The desire to become Prime Minister or to write a book or to walk across Antarctica, say. Many desires last for periods while the subject is giving them no thought; even while he is asleep. The same goes for beliefs. Some of my beliefs last but a short while – I shall soon forget my belief, recently acquired through perception, that there is a piece of chalk on that shelf. But other beliefs last a lifetime, again over long periods of time while the agent is giving them no thought, and they do not reach his consciousness.

ARGUMENTS FOR THE EXISTENCE OF THE SOUL

The Simple Argument

Now the continued existence and functioning of a person consists in the continuing of his conscious life. Those of us who hope for a life after death, hope that we will continue to think thoughts and do actions; whether it will be through our present bodies that our actions are performed and our thoughts caused is irrelevant to that for which we hope, our future life. But the continued operation of this body will not satisfy my hopes unless it is I who feel the sensations in these limbs or move these lips. Someone else could take it over (either by some of his brain replacing mine, or by some other means), and then its functioning would not satisfy my hopes for survival. It is this fact, that the continued existence and functioning of a person consists in the continuing of his conscious life, which gives rise to a very simple logical argument for the view that man consists of two components – body and soul, an argument so simple that it will not initially convince those who do not initially accept its conclusion; and which in consequence I shall back up with two more detailed considerations.

The simple argument, put forward in essence by Descartes,[1] among many others, is this. If I am to continue to exist, some part of me must continue to exist; if you destroy every part of me, I cannot any longer exist. However, it is logically possible, there is no contradiction in supposing, that I shall continue to have a conscious life and so exist (with a new body or no body at all) even if you destroy my present body. Indeed that could happen, whatever else compatible with my now being conscious might now be the case with me. Hence my now being conscious must consist in some present part of me other than a bodily part being conscious; and to this immaterial part I give the traditional name of 'soul'. It can only be logically possible that I continue to exist when this body is destroyed (and any other changes are made compatible with my remaining currently conscious) if there is now in actuality more to me than this body, my soul, whose existence is involved in my very being conscious. It is not even logically possible that this table continues to exist when you destroy every atom of which it is made. But since it is logically possible that I continue to exist when you destroy every atom of which I am made and any other part of me leaving me still conscious, there must be more to me than those parts – not, it is logically possible that there be, but there must now actually be more.[2]

Arguments from Brain Research

This argument for the existence of the soul as the essential part of a man seems to me of irrefutable cogency; but as it may seem to others too slick, I now argue that my account of man as body plus soul can account simply and naturally for two sets of puzzling empirical phenomena concerned with personal identity to which modern brain research has drawn our attention. First, there is the fact that we may know everything about the state of a human body and brain, and yet not know how many centres of consciousness, that is, persons, there are connected with that brain. The brain consists of two very similar hemispheres, the right hemisphere and the left hemisphere. The right hemisphere is involved in causing the movements of limbs on the left side of the body and in processing sensory input from the left side of the body and the left halves of both eyes. The left hemisphere is involved in causing speech and the movements of limbs of the right side of the body and in processing sensory input from the right side of the body and the right halves of both eyes. If, through disease or as the result of an operation, the main neural link between the two hemispheres, the *corpus callosum*, is severed, the two sides of the body act in certain situations independently of each other. The mouth and left limbs show knowledge of information conveyed to the left side of the body, but not of information conveyed to the right side of the body, and conversely. Neurophysiologists therefore wonder whether the severing of the *corpus callosum* has created two persons locked into one body, where there was only one before. The behavioural evidence is, however, capable of being interpreted in either way.[3] And more and more investigation of the brain, of the extent and speed of neural connections, will not tell you for certain, and may not even indicate probably, whether there is one subject of experience (one subject who sees the signals sent to both eyes) or two (each subject seeing only the signals sent to one half of the eyes). But there is a truth here, whether there is one subject of experience or two, and yet a truth which lies beyond the evidence, which points uncertainly to it. The model of man as body plus soul gives a ready explanation of why there is a truth to which the public evidence does not give total access. For on that model the truth is a truth about souls and the evidence arises from study of bodies, and the two are distinct entities.

The account of man as body plus soul is equally well able to account for the phenomena which, there is good reason to suppose, will occur when surgeons start transplanting brains or, worse, brain hemispheres. Let me remind you of the problem. Note first that what happens to me is obviously separate from what happens to parts of my body other than my brain. I may survive an accident or operation even if I lose my legs or arms, and am given a new heart and lungs. But, we suspect, a person goes where his brain goes. If you take my brain out of this skull and transplant it to another skull (from which the brain has just been removed) and the transplant takes and there results a living conscious person, that person, we are inclined to suspect, is me. We think that because, all the evidence suggests, the brain is the vehicle of memory and character. The resulting person will have my apparent memories (will claim to remember doing the things that I did) and my outlook on the world. And that is evidence, though not, I shall argue, conclusive evidence, that that person is me. I go where my brain goes. But now suppose that only one brain hemisphere is transplanted and the transplant takes and there results a living conscious person. Evidence suggests that that person will also have my apparent memories and my outlook on the world. Not perhaps as many memories or quite as similar an outlook as if the whole brain was transplanted, but enough to make the resulting person much like me, to provide good evidence that that resulting person is me. Men can certainly survive with little more than half a brain; and there is every reason to suppose that if a hemisphere were taken from this body and transplanted, it could survive to produce a living and apparently conscious person. There are certainly formidable technical difficulties involved in splitting the brain-stem, and maybe a new half-brain-stem would need to be added to a hemisphere from some other source before you would have a functioning person. But, formidable though they are, these difficulties give every appearance of being mere technical ones.

Now, suppose my right hemisphere is transplanted into an empty skull, and my left hemisphere into another, and both transplants take so that we have two living and apparently conscious persons, which would be me? There are four initially possible answers – neither, the one with the left hemisphere, the one with the right hemisphere, both. But in a literal sense the fourth answer cannot be right. If both later persons were me, then they would be the same persons as each other. But they would not be; they would be living different lives, having different experiences, performing different actions, unaware of each other's mental life. Some writers, notably Derek Parfit,[4] have said that although both later persons would not, strictly speaking, be me, they would be successor persons of me, partly me, my later 'selves'. Just as a later car may be in part the same as, in part different from, an earlier car, may it not be like that with persons? But it is not very easy to give sense to this notion of partial survival, when we are dealing with conscious agents rather than inanimate things. If I became partly both the later persons, I would presumably in part have both their experiences; yet how on earth can this be, since there would be no one person who has simultaneously the experiences which each of the subsequent persons has at a given time?

It is tempting to say that it is a matter of arbitrary definition which of the four answers is correct (or three answers, if we rule out the fourth as incoherent). But this temptation must be resisted. There is a crucial factual issue here – which can be shown if we consider the situation of someone knowing that his brain is about to be split, knowing that the person to be formed from his left hemisphere is to have a happy life and the person to be formed from his right hemisphere is to lead an unhappy life. Whether my future life will be happy is a clearly factual question, and yet, as I await the transplant and know exactly what will happen to my brain, I am in no position to know the answer. Maybe neither future person will be me – it may be that cutting the brain-stem destroys the locus of consciousness, and though both subsequent persons behave much like me, they are unconscious robots. Maybe it will be the left hemisphere person, or maybe it will be the right hemisphere person who will be me. Both will bear some resemblance to me in their character and memory claims, and even if one is more like me than the other, that one might not be me; any evidence from past transplants could yield no certain conclusion. And even if the fourth answer, that they are both to some extent me (and so either choice brings me roughly the same fate), were (despite its apparent incoherence) correct, neither science nor philosophy can show that to us. Maybe the division has created two new persons (who each thinks, falsely, that he is me); or one new person who thinks falsely like the other person, who thinks truly that he is me; or at least one new unconscious robot out of whose mouth come claims to be me and yet who really has no thoughts or feelings.

What all this shows again is that, however much we humans know about the fate of my brain and the subsequent behaviour of bodies, that does not entail what happens to me. It is easy to understand why this is so if I am body plus soul. However much we know of the fate of the body, we may still be ignorant of the fate of a separate entity connected with it, the soul. Normally I go where my brain goes, but in difficult cases (for example, when my brain is split), it is uncertain where I go – and that is because the essential part of me is not a bodily part (about the fate of which we are well aware), but an immaterial part. The problems about personal identity raised by brain bisection and brain transplantation are easily solved by the supposition that man consists of two parts, body and soul (the soul being the essential part). I believe that my earlier argument for the view was decisive, but I hope that I have reinforced plausibility by considerations of a more modern and scientific character.

So man on Earth is body plus soul. With its present link to a brain and so a body, the soul is obviously dependent for its operations on the functioning of that brain. The brain needs to tick over in a certain way before the soul can have its thoughts and feelings. In deep sleep the soul seems not to operate. Nothing I have said would give any support to the doctrine of the *natural* immortality of the soul, in the sense of its natural eternal functioning. But clearly an omnipotent God has it in his power to make my soul to function again after the dissolution of this earthly body; and he may well choose to do so by giving it a new and nobler body.

THE NATURE OF THE SOUL – THREE THEORIES

The Epiphenomenalist Theory

But if he does so choose, what will that revived soul be like? I come now at last to argue for the central thesis of this paper – that the soul has a structure.

There are three possible theories of the nature of the soul, differing according to the power and structure which they ascribe to it. The first theory is the minimalist theory of the epiphenomenalist. An epiphemomenalist is one who holds that physical events cause conscious events, but conscious events never cause either physical events or other conscious events. Souls make no difference to anything. My brain events produce sensations and thoughts, but these make no difference either to my behaviour or to my subsequent conscious life. Superficially we think that they do – my pain apparently causes me to cry out. Not so, says the epiphenomenalist, appearances are deceptive. The storm follows a fall of the barometer needle, but the fall of the barometer needle does not cause the storm; rather, both have a common cause in the decline of air pressure. It is like that, says the epiphenomenalist, with soul and body. The brain event which causes my pain also causes me to cry out; my pain itself causes nothing. When I form an intention to move my arm, that does not cause my arm to move; rather, the brain event which causes the formation of my intention also causes its execution. And the only conscious aspects to belief and desire, the subject's awareness of them in consciousness, according to the epiphenomenalist makes no difference to anything. The conscious is, according to the epiphenomenalist, like a shadow or a shimmer on a surface which makes no difference to any physical behaviour.

There are many different objections which could be made to epiphenomenalism, but I choose one crucial one. Epiphenomenalism is self-defeating; if it were true, we would never have any justification for believing it to be true. The epiphenomenalist must hold that our judgements (our conscious expressions of belief to ourselves) are caused by brain states and these brain states by other brain states, and these ultimately by physical states outside the body. They will not be formed by chains of cogent thoughts. Now, the belief that my belief B is formed through a causal chain as such in no way impugns my justification for holding B. Thus my belief that my belief B that there is a table in front of me is caused by a series of brain and then bodily and then extra-bodily causes in no way impugns my justification for holding B, since I will believe that among the causes of B is the table being in front of me; and so, that I would not have held B but for B being true. But the belief that there are no conscious items among the causes of B puts B into a certain category, the category of perceptual or semi-perceptual beliefs which are non-reasoned responses to the environment – beliefs which are not held because they are justified by other beliefs. Such beliefs form the foundations on which other reasoned beliefs are built – or so we normally think. But if epiphenomenalism is true, it will not be so; *all* beliefs – be they about cosmology, or quantum physics, logic . . . or epiphenomenalism itself – will be in the same category of intuitive responses to the environment, not grounded in other beliefs. Our belief in that case that epiphenomenalism itself is true will not be something which we hold because of reasons (for we would hold it just because the right brain event occurred, whatever other beliefs we held) or which we can get others to hold by getting them to consider reasons. The epiphenomenalist's arguments, whatever they may be, play no role in the formation of his beliefs or those of anyone else. But although my belief that there is a table in front of me needs no arguments by which to justify it, my beliefs in complicated world-views – including epiphenomenalism itself – surely do, at any rate sometimes when they are the subject of serious dispute. A man who believes a disputed theory on hunch alone in the face of counter-argument lacks the justification for his beliefs possessed by the man who forms it in response to evidence which he has carefully considered. But if such high-level beliefs cannot, as the epiphenomenalist holds, be held on the basis of perceived grounds, they cannot be held with that justification. Epiphenomenalism is self-defeating. Only if our large-scale beliefs arise from reflection upon other beliefs will they be justified, and according to epiphenomenalism that is never the case. The very practice of psychology itself as a science which produces justified, argued, reasoned beliefs about human nature necessitates a certain view of its subject matter.

The Moderate Theory

So I come to the second theory of the soul, let us call it the moderate theory. On this theory, the soul has sensations and thoughts, and these make a difference to how the subject behaves, it forms intentions, and these intentions affect behaviour. There is a two-way interaction. But on the moderate theory the only mental states which take part in such interaction are conscious states. We saw earlier that there are two kinds of mental state – conscious events and continuing mental states (beliefs and desires) which latter continue while the subject is giving them no attention. But there are two accounts of what the continued existence of beliefs and desires while the agent is giving them no attention amounts to – the dispositional account and the categorical account. On the dispositional account the only real, actual, categorical state which continues while the agent is thinking about other things is a brain state. At appropriate times that brain state causes conscious desire or belief – awareness of an inclination to act (how much the agent wants to become Prime Minister or to have a rest) or of a conscious belief (the agent makes a judgement that Aquinas lived in the Middle Ages or that John was at home on Monday); and also at appropriate times the brain state causes inclination to action (causes the agent to desire to have a rest, in the absence of any belief that it would be bad to rest) or causes the agent to execute his intentions in a certain way (causes him to say, when he seeks to give this information about where John was on Monday, that John was at home). The subject's privileged access to his beliefs and desires is simply accesss to their conscious aspects, which exist only while the agent is paying attention to them. Why the same beliefs and desires persist for some time is because the same brain state persists for some time.

On the categorical account beliefs and desires are no mere dispositions to thought and action. They are attitudes to the world (beliefs about it and inclinations to do something in it) which persist at the subconscious level of the soul, differing only from beliefs and desires of which the agent is aware simply in that the agent is giving them no present attention. They remain attitudes embedded in his soul.

The moderate theory of the soul adopts the dispositional account of belief and desire. A subject's beliefs and desires affect his behaviour; but, according to the moderate theory, this is only a case of soul affecting body if the beliefs and desires have reached the surface of the subject's consciousness. The theory is therefore committed to the view that the mechanism by which belief and desire affect behaviour is crucially different according to whether the subject is at the time aware of his beliefs and desires, or not. If I take a certain path as a result of saying to myself 'That's the way home', then the soul has affected the body; but if I just take the path because I believe that the path leads home and never comment consciously to myself on the fact, then brain processes alone have operated. Belief has affected behaviour, but what belief amounts to when the subject is giving it no thought just is a brain state with a disposition to cause behaviour of a certain sort. The trouble is, though, that there is such continuity between the beliefs and desires of which we are conscious and those of which we are not conscious that it is very odd to suppose that, as we become less conscious of our beliefs and desires, a radically different mechanism suddenly begins to operate.

This general point of the continuity of conscious belief and desire with non-conscious belief and desire will lead shortly to two more detailed arguments against both the dispositional account of desire and belief and of the moderate theory of the soul which includes it, and in favour both of the categorical account of belief and desires (that they continue to exist as subconscious states while the subject is giving them no attention) and of my third theory of the soul, which I shall call the mental structure theory. The mental structure theory adopts the categorical account of belief and desire and holds that beliefs and desires causally affect public behaviour and the conscious life and also the formation of other beliefs and desires, even when the subject is giving them no conscious attention. The soul is a structure of subconscious beliefs and desires, of which the subject becomes conscious from time to time, and against the background of which he has his sensations, forms his thoughts, and executes his purposes.

The Mental Structure Theory

Before coming to two detailed arguments in favour of this account of mental structure, I draw your attention to reasons why we should think of belief and desire (whatever their nature) as forming a structure.

Quine taught us many years ago that our beliefs do not exist in isolation from each other.[5] In his analogy, beliefs form a net which impinges on experience only at the edges. The beliefs at the edge are beliefs about particular facts of present experience – that I am now seeing a table, that the clock reads 5.40 p.m., that there are five people in the front row – and of past experience, that I was in Blackwell's yesterday, that I was in Canada a few months ago, and so on. Next comes a ring of beliefs about the history and geography of the physical world, and of the agent's more immediate environment (that Aberdeen is to the North of Edinburgh, that the Second World War ended in 1945). Then there come more fundamental particular beliefs – that I live on the Earth, that it is spherical, and millions of years old. Then come general beliefs about how the world works – that bodies on Earth fall to the ground, that dry twigs and paper ignite easily but water does not. And finally, close to the middle of the net, there are an agent's most general metaphysical beliefs – that there are other people who have feelings and thoughts, that memory is generally reliable, and that there is a public world.

The point of the net analogy is that an agent's beliefs cannot be obviously inconsistent with his other beliefs, and must be rendered to some extent probable by those other beliefs. In consequence, if you give up one belief, you have to change, introduce, or abandon others; and the more central a belief is, the greater the difference to other beliefs a change in it will make. If I am to come to believe that the world began in 4004 BC, I have to give up thousands of beliefs about prehistory, about the respectability of geology and historical cosmology as academic subjects, about the nature of biblical revelation, etc., etc. If I am to come to believe that today is Thursday, not (say) Friday, some other beliefs have to go (for example, that I am due to give a lecture today, or that I shall be at home tomorrow), but not so many. The more central beliefs about what kinds of things exist and how they interact determine how the deliveries of sense are interpreted. What you come to believe as a result of stimulation of your sense organs is much influenced by what you already believe; though, once admitted to the system, more peripheral beliefs tend to influence more central beliefs.

Desires interact with the *belief* network. You cannot just desire something; you need some beliefs about it in order to desire it. And any one desire fits well with some desires and beliefs and badly with others. To start with, to have a desire to perform any action at all is to believe the doing of that action to be in some way a good thing. I can't desire to go to London if I *believe* that in all ways it is a very bad thing to do. Secondly, I cannot desire to perform an action, unless I have beliefs about what doing that action consists in; and the more complicated the action desired, the more complicated the beliefs I need to have about it. I cannot desire to fly to London, unless I have some beliefs about what flying is (for example, what aeroplanes are, what the difference between air and land is, what travelling is as opposed to resting somewhere) and some beliefs about what London is (for example, that it is a great city; and to believe that, I need to have some beliefs about what a city is and what constitutes greatness for a city). My beliefs about what there is in the world and what can be done in it give my desires a focus. Thirdly, I desire things because of certain properties which they have. If I desire to be the President of the USA, it will be the applause, the power, the wheeler-dealing, the ceremony, the comfort, or some or all of these which will give rise to the desire, and if I cease to believe that the Presidency involves some of these features, I will cease to desire to be President.

Like beliefs, desires differ in centrality. Some desires, for example, to scratch myself, depend on no beliefs at all; others derive their focus from a whole web of beliefs – for example, the desire to become a priest, gaining its point only from a whole web of theological considerations. The more central ones tend to be both longer lasting and more widely influential.

The most central of his desires and beliefs form a man's character. His most central beliefs include not only the central metaphysical beliefs, such as that there are other people who have thoughts and feelings and the belief that there is a God, or, alternatively, the belief that there is no God; but also his most general ethical beliefs, such as whether one ought to keep promises, no matter what; whether it is all-important to foster a human relationship, to paint great pictures, to keep men alive, to worship God. An agent's most central desires are his inclinations to actions of different kinds in different circumstances, to gamble, to follow a routine, to be generous and thoughtful, or to do his duty, to obey and worship God; and one such desire may dominate the others. These most central beliefs and desires have a structure which forms the agent's character, his general outlook on, and natural response to, the world, and continue to exist for long periods while the agent is giving them no thought. The mental stucture theory of the soul means that we take this analogy of the net a lot more literally than would the moderate theory. For on the mental structure theory beliefs and desires affect other beliefs and desires in virtue of the propositional content of subconscious attitudes, rather than in virtue of the electrochemical properties of the brain states in some sense correlated with them.

My two more detailed arguments in favour of the mental structure theory of the soul rely, respectively, on the two principles basic to all rational inquiry, which I call the principles of credulity and simplicity. The principle of credulity says, start with appearances; in the absence of counter-evidence, believe that things are as they seem to be. For if you don't believe that there is a table in front of you, or that the pointer on the dial is pointing to seven, unless these things are proved from something else, you will never believe in anything at all. Whereas to believe everything which seems to be so, unless evidence is produced against it, will give you a normal system of belief. The principle of simplicity says, take the simplest theory to explain the appearances (that is the one most likely to be true), and if you will get a much simpler theory by supposing that a few of the appearances are delusory, then believe that, but not otherwise. If your simple theory that all metals expand when heated fits all the appearances except one observation which you think you made one Tuesday afternoon, regard the latter as a misobservation. But otherwise stick by the appearances; for it is from them that science begins.

Now my first argument in favour of the mental structure theory is that it does seem to the subject to conform, phenomenologically, to his experience. When we look back at our conduct and thought over a period of time, it seems to us that we have behaved and thought as we have under the influence of a whole system of desires and beliefs which were not in any way in the forefront of our consciousness – desires and beliefs in the sense of subconscious attitudes, not mere brain states.

Suppose that you have been on a long walk from A to B, engrossed in solving mentally some theoretical problem. While giving the matter no conscious thought, you have taken now this path, now that, avoided now this puddle, now that obstacle, until eventually you have reached *B*. Asked to give an account of why you made the series of movements you did, you would say that you *desired* to get to B and *believed* that this route was one which led directly there, that you *desired* not to step in puddles and *believed* that by those movements you would avoid them. It seems to you that you acted as you did because influenced by a whole system of continuing attitudes to which at the time you were giving no conscious thought; that desire and belief affected your conduct in the same way, whether you were conscious of them or not.

Now this view that our conduct and thought are affected by a whole system of subconscious attitudes may, of course, be a vast illusion. But by the principle of credulity, we ought to believe that view in the absence of counter-evidence. There would be counter-evidence if to suppose this led to a much more complicated theory of the world than we would otherwise have. But it does not. It does not introduce a new type of causality, for we have already seen the need to allow a causal role to non-physical events; we have rejected epiphenomenalism on quite other grounds. Mental structure theory merely extends the scope of mental causation. Further, it explains in a very simple way why we make the movements we do, why our beliefs and desires change as they do, and why we have the thoughts we do. All of these things occur because of the connections of reason between the content of our beliefs, desires, intentions, and thoughts.

Take thoughts this time. Suppose that you are attempting to solve some problem mentally – say a murder mystery. You begin by expressing in thought your premises (say, the evidence available to the detective) and then argue to each new step (for example, many of the steps may state that this or that suspect can be eliminated), eventually working up to the conclusion 'Jones did the murder.' Each new step constitutes the expression in judgement of a newly acquired belief. What leads you to acquire each new belief is what has gone before. Normally, however, in such a case each step would not have been taken but for other beliefs which you have but did not express to yourself consciously. Thus you may have moved from 'Smith said that he was in Edinburgh on Wednesday morning and two people claimed to see him there' to 'He was not in London on Wednesday morning.' In the background were a number of beliefs without which you would not have taken this step, for example, 'Edinburgh is 400 miles from London,' 'trains take more than four hours to travel 400 miles,' 'Smith would not travel by air,' etc. The previous beliefs, expressed and unexpressed, lead to the new belief. Now the new beliefs are in general adopted because they follow from, or are rendered probable by, old beliefs, both conscious and non-conscious. You are following a connection of thought, which can be elucidated by the rules of deductive and inductive inference, barring lapses. This simple explanation of why the new belief is adopted is available if we think of the old beliefs as attitudes containing a content expressible by a proposition, and of the non-conscious beliefs as continuing subconscious judgements. What happens is what would happen if the agent had reflected consciously on the content of many of his beliefs and drawn out their consequences consciously. Therefore the simplest explanation of what is going on is that the beliefs are there, subconsciously, influencing the formation of new beliefs in just the way in which they would have done so, had they been formulated consciously.

But if the non-conscious beliefs are simply brain states, we would need a very complicated explanation of how those brain states (those patterns of electrochemical discharge) are such as to guarantee a rational sequence of conscious thoughts; and on the moderate theory, this has nothing to do with the subject perceiving the rationality of that sequence. Among psychologists, no one has taught us better than Freud that the human soul is a structure of interacting beliefs and desires, affecting each other in virtue of their content, some overt and some repressed from consciousness. Materialist though he was in theory, expecting that the mental would somehow or other be reduced to the physical, the result of his own endeavours was to make that task immeasurably more difficult. For no one showed more thoroughly that what makes a difference to a man's desires and beliefs is the content of his other desires and beliefs.

So the twin principles of credulity and simplicity so basic to rational inquiry favour the mental structure theory of the soul over its rivals. The theory may be illustrated by an analogy. Consider an object with a complex shape, whose contours are adjusted to those of a second object so that their shapes fit together, as in Figure 3.1. One object represents the brain, the other the soul. The shape of the soul represents its beliefs and desires; the shape of the brain its electrochemical network of the brain correlates of beliefs and desires. Now it could be that the soul was like a soft cushion, and the brain a hard object; so that the shape of the soul was entirely determined by that of the brain. The mental structure theory maintains, however, that the soul is not totally soft; it has some structure, so that its shape in some parts is determined by its shape in other parts, and its shape to some extent determines that of the brain; for, in determining which new beliefs will be admitted to the system, it determines that the brain states are the correlates of those beliefs. The soul is a continuing structure with enough rigidity to influence the kinds of belief and desire that are admitted to it; and hence the kind of thing which, being removed from one body, could be conjoined to another while retaining that structure.

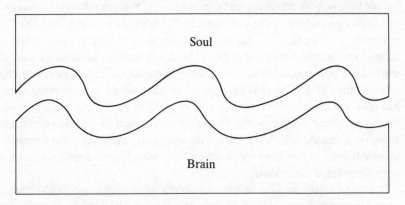

Figure 3.1   Model of the suggested relation of soul to brain

The soul may indeed depend for its present functioning, having a conscious mental life, on being connected to a body; and when that body decays, it will cease to function. But what I have argued in this paper is that what the soul is, is a thing with a structure of belief and desire, a mental outlook against the background of which thought, sensation, and intention occur. Hence if God brings the soul to life again and causes it to function again with some new body or without a body at all, what he will bring to life is a soul with a structure, an attitude or outlook on things.

APPENDIX

In order to forestall possible criticism, I now give a more formal and more rigorous shape to my 'simple argument'. (The formalization resembles that given to a similar argument in *The Evolution of the Soul*, additional note 2.) I use the usual logical symbols: '&' as 'and', ' $-$ ' as 'not', '$\Diamond$' as 'it is logically possible'. I define:

p='I am a conscious person and I exist in 1986.'
q='My body is destroyed in the last second of 1986.'
r='I have a soul in 1986.'
s='I exist in 1987.'
x ranges over all consistent propositions compatible with (p & q) and describing 1986 states of affairs.
'(x)' is to be read in the normal way as 'for all states x'.

The argument may now be set out as follows:

p	premiss 1
(x) $\Diamond$ (p & q & x & s)	premiss 2
$-$ $\Diamond$ (p & q & $-$r & s)	premiss 3

Premiss 2 is as in the text. I understand by my body all the material part of me, and by my soul any non-material part of me. Then premiss 3 is simply a detailed example of the sentence in the text 'If you destroy every part of me, I cannot any longer exist.'

It follows from premisses 2 and 3 that -r is not within the range of x. But since $-$r describes a 1986 state of affairs, it follows that it is not compatible with (p & q). Hence (p & q) entails r. But the addition to p of q, which describes what happens to my body at the end of 1986, can hardly affect whether or not p entails r. So I conclude that p by itself entails r. Hence, from premiss 1, r.

DISCUSSION

RICHARD DAWKINS. I am not impressed by logical argument about the existence of a soul. For example, setting up a parallel argument, it is logically possible that pigs might fly. It would not be possible for pigs to fly unless they had wings or equivalent apparatus. Therefore they do have wings.

SWINBURNE. I did include in my argument a clause, namely, 'whatever else might now be the case with me'. Your argument is not formally similar to mine, because my argument was that it is logically possible that I survive, given that I am a conscious thinking being, whatever else may be the case with me – that is to say, whatever else is happening to my body or otherwise. The mere fact that I am a conscious being, whatever else is the case with me, makes it still logically possible that I will survive. Whereas in the case of your argument, it is logically possible that pigs fly, but if I put in certain other facts about those pigs, such as the fact that they do not have wings or any other device for enabling them to get above the ground, then it ceases to be possible for them to fly.

DAWKINS. But if I were to ask you whether you applied your argument for the soul to cockroaches, would you conclude that cockroaches have an immortal soul?

SWINBURNE. I am *not* arguing for natural immortality of the soul, but only that we each currently have a soul, and that if God so chooses, he can keep it in being. I am not arguing that it continues after physical death from its own nature. Given that understanding of my claim, I am happy to go along with dogs having souls; but I am not too happy about cockroaches, because I do not know whether cockroaches are conscious or not. As we go down the biological scale, we come to creatures about which we are really doubtful whether they do or do not feel anything.

DAWKINS. But as an evolutionist you would have to say that there was a time when an animal did have whatever the soul-property is, whereas its father did not, for I can well believe that consciousness is gradually evolved. But you are talking about logical possibility. Are you going to say that there is some property such that it is logically possible that the son has that property and not the father?

SWINBURNE. Your way of expressing it does not bring out the point. My argument ultimately is that you cannot make sense of the notion of somebody being conscious without supposing there to be two parts of them; their being conscious *entails* there being two parts to them. This means, in your terms, that, somewhere up the evolutionary scale, there came to exist creatures who had two parts to them – namely, those creatures who are conscious. Their becoming conscious consisted in their other part coming into existence. To put it in terms of logical possibility, there came to exist creatures who were such that they were in a state of being conscious; this made it the case that it was logically possible, whatever else happened to them, that they should continue to exist after bodily death.

DEREK PARFIT. About the pig's wings of the first question, you said the difference was that in that case it it only possible that pigs can fly if they do in fact have either wings or some other mechanism enabling them to fly. Whereas you were claiming that it is logically possible that you continue to exist after the destruction of your body, whatever else is true. Will it be logically possible for you to continue to exist after destruction of your body even if you do not have a soul?

SWINBURNE. No, for my words 'whatever *else* may be the case' mean 'whatever else, not entailed by my being conscious, is the case'. My argument was designed to show that having a soul is entailed by my being conscious. I am now conscious. I can make sense of my continuing to exist, and I suggest that I can still make sense of it, whatever suppositions compatible with my being conscious I might make about myself. If it is dubious whether they are compatible with being conscious, then I think one should be cautious about making them.

PARFIT. I thought the argument was: it is logically possible that I continue to exist, whereas that rather misstates it. Your argument is: it is logically possible that I continue to be conscious hereafter, since being conscious entails having a soul.

SWINBURNE. I am arguing that being conscious *does* entail having a soul. That is not my premiss but my conclusion.

PARFIT. Why, if that is not part of the premiss, is it not logically possible that I continue to exist without having a soul?

SWINBURNE. Because there is a further premiss, which I formalized, that I cannot continue to exist unless some part of me continues to exist. Are you wishing to deny my general metaphysical premiss?

PARFIT. I am inclined to accept a lot of the things that you said about what might be the case. There are quite a lot of recent philosophers who argue that the idea of a soul, explained as you have explained it, can somehow be rejected on philosophical grounds. I do not think that those arguments are cogent. So I think the question whether we have souls is to be settled largely, though not entirely, by looking at a whole variety of different kinds of evidence. But I do somewhat share the doubt of the first questioner about whether it can be settled by such an extremely swift argument. It seems to me that it is a very fundamental matter of fact, and I cannot believe that that could be answered so swiftly.

SWINBURNE. My argument is that it follows from being conscious; and if you disagree with the argument, I must ask you whether you accept it as valid and whether you will accept each of the premises as formalized, The second premiss is that is is logically possible that I survive. The third premiss is a metaphysical one, that if anything is to survive, some part of it must survive. The first premiss is that I am conscious. From these premisses it follows, I claim, that I have a part other than my body.

PARFIT. If I continue to have experiences after the destruction of my body, could not my having experiences fill the clause that 'part of me survives'?

SWINBURNE. My having the experience cannot fill the clause that 'part of me survives'. By part of 'me', I mean 'me' as a substance or thing, and what survives must be part of that thing – not an event.

PARFIT. Well, I do not see why. I would have thought that if I was having experiences, that would be enough to count as my surviving.

SWINBURNE. Yes, but it is *me* having experiences, and therefore my metaphysical principle says that part of *me* must survive.

SIR PETER STRAWSON. How can one know that there is just one soul and not, say, twenty inhabiting one's body?

SWINBURNE. I cannot know for certain, but I have good reasons for believing in only one soul, because postulating just one soul connected with this body is enough to explain all behaviour of this body. It is not necessary to believe in twenty souls unless there are twenty different patterns of behaviour which can be explained in terms of twenty different systems of beliefs, desires, and conscious lives manifested by this body.

STRAWSON. So you do not *know* that, say, Swinburne is not the host of twenty souls.

SWINBURNE. Kant was right. I do not know that infallibly, but there are some things we know pretty well, without knowing them infallibly, and the number of souls would be in that category.

STRAWSON. Let us assume that you incorporate twenty such souls. Each one of them would have the impression of uniqueness.

SWINBURNE. Yes, but I think each one would have a justified impression of uniqueness. For if he decides to move his arm and his arm moves, it does not move as part of a co-ordinated system of apparent action except when initiated by that one soul.

STRAWSON. One assumes, of course, that each of the twenty souls has exactly the same mental states and character.

SWINBURNE. Yes. That begins to look like postulating twenty entities to do exactly the job that one is quite capable of doing, and is therefore rightly ruled out by Occam's razor.

STRAWSON. Well, no.

SWINBURNE. Not infallibly, no. Life is full of things that we cannot know infallibly.

STRAWSON. In preference, you individuate souls by individuating people. I only suggest that 'people' will do just as well for all the purposes that you have urged on us from mental structure theory; and that it is to 'people' that we should ascribe mental events and so forth; and that we do not need 'souls' at all.

SWINBURNE. That is quite adequate for this-worldly purposes, but one needs to bring out certain features 'people' have in order to know whether God can raise us up in future. Because if there is nothing more to me than my body, and if every atom of which my body is made turns into energy, so that there is nothing left, then not even an omnipotent being can bring me to life again.

STRAWSON. Can I refer to another difficulty? Why should not your account of the soul be a matter of a structure of connected elements, perhaps of successive elements, but without your requiring a substance?

SWINBURNE. Because such a structure can be duplicated on Mars, Venus, etc. in a hundred other cases.

STRAWSON. It would be a unique structure in that it would be associated in practice with a particular spatio-temporal location.

SWINBURNE. I wish to hold, where the argument starts from, that it is logically possible that *I*, being reincarnated, come to life in some future world where clearly there is no spatio-temporal, basic continuity with the 'me' that has been. The question then arises: if it is possible for me to come to life on some other planet with a life spatially discontinuous with my present life, what would constitute *me* coming to life on that planet? The mere embodiment of a certain system of beliefs and desires seems to me insufficient for that purpose.

STRAWSON. Plus memories, intentions, and so on?

SWINBURNE. Yes, because after all, suppose I had a current duplicate on Mars, and he also is annihilated at the same time as me. Two duplicates come to life in the future world, or perhaps only one duplicate comes to life. So the question is: have *I* come to life? The mere knowledge of which beliefs and intentions are present is not enough to say whether *I* have come to life.

STRAWSON. Of course, given your substantial view, presumably there would be a cut-and-dried answer to it. On the other, different view, there might not be.

SWINBURNE. The argument goes the other way around; that is to say, since it is intuitively obvious that either it is true that I come to life or it is true that my duplicate comes to life, therefore my substantial view must be correct!

MICHAEL LOCKWOOD. I am far from happy with this argument, although I have some sympathy with arguments that are perhaps not very far removed from it, such as those that are advanced by Kripke.[6] I would locate the problem here in your use of the term 'logically possible'. I agree that, in one sense, it is logically possible that I should continue to exist when my body has been destroyed; and this is because, in the same sense of 'logically possible', I think it logically possible that your metaphysical view is correct. Here 'logically possible' means something like 'is not a self-contradictory supposition'. I would prefer to use the phrase 'logically possible' exclusively to mean that. For it seems to me that your argument involves a fatal equivocation between this notion and a quite different one, which I would call 'metaphysical possibility'. Suppose that, as a matter of metaphysical or scientific fact, I am not an immaterial soul. Then, in a perfectly good sense, it is impossible that I should survive in a disembodied form; impossible, indeed, that I should ever have been an immaterial soul. For if my essence is, as a matter of fact, material, then even God could not have made it the case that *I* was immaterial. If I am material, then I am, in this sense, *necessarily* material. Any immaterial being, however like me, could not have *been* me, any more than the shirt I am wearing could have existed and yet have been made (from the start) of cotton instead of rayon. (Assuming that this shirt was made of rayon, no alternative shirt made of something else, however like this shirt in appearance, could have been this shirt.) The problem then is this. Either you mean by 'logically possible' imaginable without self-contradiction, or you mean metaphysically possible – constituting a way things might actually have been, a way some sufficiently powerful being could have made them to be. If you mean the former, then you are not entitled to draw from the fact that it is logically possible for me to exist apart from my body the conclusion that I am actually distinct from my body. If you mean the latter, then just by asserting that it is possible that I exist apart from my body, you are already begging the question in favour of dualism.

SWINBURNE. Well, I do not agree with the distinction between the 'logically possible' and the 'metaphysically possible'.

LOCKWOOD. The 'consistently imaginable' and 'metaphysically possible' is the distinction: that which it is not contradictory to deny and that which is a genuine way things might be, two quite distinct concepts.

SWINBURNE. My view is that what you call 'metaphysically possible' is analysable straightforwardly in terms of logical possibility. To take one of Kripke's examples, it is not 'metaphysically possible' that this lectern should be made of ice (or whatever). Given the lectern that it is, made of wood, it is not both logically possible that the lectern was originally made of ice and now that it is not made of ice and that it is the same lectern.

STEVEN COLLINS. I find the remark that it is 'logically possible' that *I* survive even if my body is destroyed to be entirely opaque. It happens often that some special – and mysterious – significance is given to the word 'I', either, as in your presentation here, by a special tone of voice, or in print by italicized typography. But tones of voice and typography cannot stand in for philosophical argument. While it may be true that I can imagine, for example, that my consciousness might be carried by different bodies, or even perhaps, that 'I' might exist as a collection of disembodied memories, I do not think that tells me anything whatsoever about what 'I' I really am.

SWINBURNE. I think it is obvious what I mean by 'I', and I suspect that that holds for you too. If we were not discussing this particular issue, it would be pretty obvious to you what you meant by 'I' in any normal sentence you would utter. I cannot define 'I' and you cannot, but then we all have to start with some undefined terms, whose conditions of application are self-evident, or are at least more evident than any other terms. We must just start off supposing that we understand what we mean by them.

PARFIT. Would you mean the same as Professor Strawson, since he uses 'I' to refer to the person?

SWINBURNE. Yes, I do, for 'soul' is a technical term introduced at a later stage in order to bring out what is involved in the notion of the 'person' with its two components. That is a defined philosophical term. We have a primitive understanding of how to use the word 'I', what we are saying by and what is entailed by our statements in which we use it.

COLLINS. The indexical 'I' is used to perform a large variety of different tasks, most commonly to refer to this organism with its conscious states. This is a capacity that this organism has, and it is a skill which is learnt, given all sorts of linguistic, cultural, and other practices. Therefore I do not think that the simple use of it tells me anything whatsoever. Unless you unpack your second premiss a very great deal, it seems to me that I simply cannot follow it at all.

SWINBURNE. That argument you have used, you would not use for any other word but 'I'. Of course, we are conditioned by social practices, by our education, etc. But by these we have come to have a grasp of what we are saying, and have learned the skill of using the word 'I', just as with the words 'brown' or 'table' or any other word. Why be sceptical about 'I' when you would not be about all these other words that you have learnt? I think that it is because you are worried that certain philosophical conclusions follow. This is a word we use so commonly, so frequently. Children can understand it in simple stories: 'I will do this,' 'I will do that.' They understand the fairy stories of 'me' being turned into a frog or a prince. It all comes over very clearly. Therefore there is every reason to suppose that we can operate with, understand, have a grasp of 'I'.

JILL ROBSON. I think it is related to the business of who 'I' am. I am unhappy about your example of the two hemispheres. I cannot see how you can take a cerebral hemisphere and still have anything that is anything like a conscious human being. What happens if you divide it and put it in two separate skulls?

SWINBURNE. This is much discussed in philosophical debate. It is supposed that it can be done, so that the question arises as to how we interpret it. That is to say, let's suppose we can transplant the hemisphere and would get a conscious human being. What does one say about it?

GRANT GILLETT. I am always amazed by the way that an intuition that one can perhaps imagine something clearly seems to bear tremendous weight in such arguments. Taken in conjunction with the fact that intuitions differ, it seems to make the whole enterprise slightly dubious. For instance, we are supposed to know what it is like to be a 'person' with a single cerebral hemisphere. Having met patients with much less serious brain defects, I do not find such situations at all clearly imaginable or intelligible, and I just wonder how such a vast weight of philosophy should turn on such vagaries of individual intuitions.

SWINBURNE. All philosophy turns on just this sort of imagination in my view. Take any well-aired philosophical discussion about metaphysical or ontological matters. 'Imagine my brain removed and in a vat,' says one philosopher. 'Not at all,' says another, 'I cannot possibly imagine it being *my* brain that is in the vat, because there are certain incoherences, difficulties, and so on, involved in that.' Any philosophical argument is designed to show that certain states of affairs are or are not 'logically possible'. The point is to draw attention to what we are saying about *actual* states of affairs, what we are ruling out and what we are not ruling out. In order to understand what is entailed by them, we need to see what is compatible or incompatible with them. To understand *that*, we need to see what states of affairs are 'logically possible'. Take an example which goes against myself. People say to me, 'I can imagine going back in time to the Egypt of the pyramids.' Now *I* do not think that is logically possible. So here you have a counter-instance to my argument. How does the argument get started? It starts by showing that if somebody makes such a supposition, then one can show that some sort of in-consistency is involved in that supposition; in which case his initial supposition, that the state of affairs is 'logically possible', is shown to be logically false. If, on the other hand, he can spell out in a lot of detail what it would be like for him to do this in some consistent way, then he is vindicated.

JANET SOSKICE. With regard to the brain-transplant thought experiment, you said that the resulting person, were the transplant successful, would be you. Of course, the resulting body would be you, too, because, if you survived, you would refer to the 'new' body as we do to our present bodies. We use 'I' self-referentially, including our bodies as ourselves. Now if this is so, I do not see any reason why we need a 'soul' to believe in life after death, a belief I actually share. Because, given that we know that the material framework we have, the tissues and cells themselves, are continually exchanging with new material, I do not think it would be difficult for God, given the kind of powers which Christians attribute to God, to re-create a physical entity, a 'body' of some sort which retained the memories and the character which would suffice for personal identity. I do not see why that is any more problematic for God than him calling up the 'soul' to give it another body.

SWINBURNE. A body, which is an embodied person, could be created, and that embodied person could have the same beliefs, the same apparent memories, and the same desires as me. But my earlier argument was that that is not enough to make that person me.

ARTHUR PEACOCKE. I would like to take up the evolutionary point raised earlier. The history of this planet exhibits a range of creatures, from those with the most elementary nervous systems and often highly mechanized behaviour to the higher primates and ourselves, with various levels of consciousness. Consciousness seems to be an emerging attribute which develops as time proceeds. I find it very hard to see why that functional property coded in a certain complex physical structure requires a new entity to be invoked, of an entirely different kind, to appear on the scene to ensure its emergence. How could something substantial, some substance or some other entity different in kind from that which has been evolved so far, suddenly come in to the evolutionary, temporal sequence? One can postulate that only if one has some presupposition about an intervening God who does it for some special purpose. We can otherwise have no idea how such a 'soul' could arrive naturally, as it were.

SWINBURNE. In my sense, animals do have souls, but they have a different kind of mental life and different capacities from humans. So even if animals have souls, they are different from human souls, the former 'sensitive', the latter 'intellectual', to use the distinctions made in the Middle Ages. It was Descartes who postulated that only creatures with reason and reflection have souls. At some stage there was a first conscious creature, and there is therefore at that point a clear and enormous qualitative gap. I am simply describing that qualitative gap in my terms. There are gaps, and there are moves up the scale. The soul comes in fairly low down the scale.

STRAWSON. Would a computer have a soul?

SWINBURNE. The answer to that is certainly that modern computers do not, but that in the next century, computers might. That would be a guess on my part. It would be justified to the extent that the computer resembled me, not merely in its patterns of response to outward stimulus, but also in terms of the kind of organic molecules it was made of. I really do not know the answer.

STRAWSON. But it is open for computers to have souls on your cosmology?

SWINBURNE. Yes, I am not defending the doctrine that souls only come into existence as a result of the sexual process. That is the normal way of things now, but there could well be other means.

4

The Person as Object of Science, as Subject of Experience, and as Locus of Value*

DAVID WIGGINS

1. On occasion, almost everyone feels difficulties in holding in a single focus three very different ideas:

  (a) the idea of the person as object of biological, anatomical, and neurophysiological inquiry;
  (b) the idea of the person as subject of consciousness; and
  (c) the idea of the person as locus of all sorts of moral attributes and the source or conceptual origin of all value.

* This is a reconstruction of a talk before a mixed lay and theological audience, given at the behest of Dr Arthur Peacocke, Director of the Ian Ramsey Centre, Oxford, in a series dedicated to differing conceptions of the person and their legal and ethical implications. Overwhelmed by the difficulty of proving anything about personhood, let alone its implications, and having always preferred to manage such questions by indirection or by unkind criticism of the efforts of others, but unable also to disentangle myself from the demand to speak on this theme, I decided to postpone all legal, medical, and other problems of gestation, birth, ageing, and death, in order to begin at the beginning. And, once there, I had necessary recourse to a blend of undemonstrated assertion, self-plagiarism and self-explication. I wish I could have provided a securer foundation for the pursuit of these further questions.

For the original source, see *Sameness and Substance* (Blackwell, Oxford, 1980), especially chapter 6 and Longer Notes 6.14 and 6.36 (also the *Errata* to be found on the inside of the back cover of the 1981 paperback).

Substantial debts to Hidé Ishiguro, John McDowell, and Peter Winch are acknowledged at the relevant points, *ad loc.*

The reconstruction was made while I was a Fellow at the Center for Advanced Study in the Behavioral Sciences, Stanford. I am grateful for the financial support of my fellowship there, provided by the Andrew W. Mellon Foundation.

2. We see people in all sorts of ways and under all sorts of aspects. But on the most fundamental level of singling out and individuation, what really is a person? Well, someone may say, whatever truths there may be to discover about this, the expression 'a person' obviously doesn't mean the same as the expression 'a human being'; and neither means the same as 'a self': so being a person isn't the same as being a human being or being a self. These are different concepts. And so, he may say, moving straight up to the higher or more transcendent ground, '*x* can be the same person as *y* without being the same human being as *y*, and *x* can be the same self as *y* without being the same human being as *y*.'[1]

The conclusion does not follow. But the swiftness with which we reach something so interestingly extravagant suggests that, even at the most elementary level, attention needs to be paid to certain sorts of detail. As soon as even the smallest modicum of theory or construction enters into this area, it seems that we need to make the distinction between sense and reference.

3. Figure 4.1 gives a picture of the connections between sense and reference that was drawn by Frege for Husserl in a letter dated 24 May 1891.

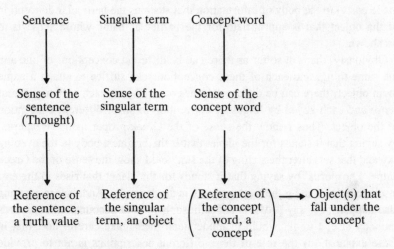

Figure 4.1 Sense and reference

Concentrate first on the middle column and the relatively familiar case of a name or name-phrase. We have the name or name-phrase at the top, connected via its sense, given in the middle line, to the thing that the name or name-phrase stands for, given on the bottom line. We might try to bring this to life by saying that to know the sense of the name 'Socrates' is to be party to a linguistic practice that makes it possible to utter a sentence like 'Socrates is

58   *David Wiggins*

wise' significantly and that provides for one to mean by this something that renders the utterance of the sentence answerable for its correctness to how matters stand with Socrates in particular (with Socrates in distinction from everything else) in respect of the property that is in question (namely, in the case of this sentence, wisdom). To be party to that practice, one must know what 'Socrates' means, and one cannot fully know that without knowing who Socrates is (in the normal sense of the elusive but useful phrase 'knowing who Socrates is').

To know the sense of a name, then, is to know what (which thing) it is that the name stands for – that is, to know what its reference is. But, given a particular name, not just any old way of saying what that reference is will impart or show equally well the sense of that name.[2] Different names with different senses may be expected to correspond to different *conceptions* of that item of reference, or to different ways of thinking of it. It follows that, in order to explain the sense of a name and to attach to it the right 'mode of presentation', what is needed is for the explainer to use the appropriate way of saying which item the name stands for. And whether to give or to receive (come to understand) such a mode of presentation, one must be party (or be made party) to the body of information that sustains the particular conception of the object that is appropriate for the particular name whose sense is to be shown.

Obviously, then, in so far as there can be different conceptions of one and the same thing, and each of these conceptions can suffice to attach a name to an object, there can be different names of an object, each with a different sense and each keyed by linguistic convention to some different conception of the object. Thus I show the sense of the Greek proper name 'Hesperus' by saying that it stands for the planet that is the brightest body in the evening sky and that sets after the setting of the sun: and I show the sense of the Greek name 'Phosporus' by saying that it stands for the planet that rises in the east just before dawn and is the brightest body in the dawn sky. And, before anything else happens, let any professional philosophers who encounter these words (nobody else, I think, would misunderstand them) take careful note that in these explanations the role of these different descriptions is not to provide different *synonyms* for the two different names – indeed, that is not the point at all – but only to pick out the reference in the appropriate way. The role of these descriptions is to draw upon a certain body of information to steer or hold thought onto the right item in the right way.

4. The sense of names is not the case we are finally interested in. It is just the case that is usually found the clearest, and by analogy with which we can now understand the expressions that we are concerned with. So now let us

look in Figure 4.1 at the right-hand column, which comprises verbs, adjectives, and substantives like '[a] person', '[a] self', '[a] human being'. In Frege's scheme these are expressions that stand for properties, or (better) for concepts. Just as to know the sense of a singular term and its contribution to the meaning or truth conditions of a sentence is to grasp the mode of its presentation of the object that it stands for, so to know the sense of a predicate and its contribution to the meaning or truth conditions of a sentence is to grasp the mode of its presentation of the concept that it stands for. Thus we say what the predicate's sense is by saying what concept it stands for.[3] In the case of a singular term, we can show one sense in preference to another by exploiting one mode of presentation rather than another to say what the object of designation is; and I claimed that, if we need to amplify our identification of the object, we should draw upon and expound one body of information rather than another, carefully preferring the information that sustains the particular mode of presentation we are bent on conveying. For the sense of a predicate, the procedure can be the same. We convey the sense of 'horse' in preference to the sense of (say) *Equus caballus* by exploiting a suitable everyday account of the concept rather than a less suitable scientifically based account to say which concept the predicate stands for. To explain the sense of the ordinary substantive 'horse' and convey the reference of that, we draw upon and then expand *ad libitum* an everyday body of information such as 'a horse is an animal that has a flowing mane and tail; its voice is a neigh; and in the domestic state it is used as a beast of burden and for riding upon', preferring this account of the animal to the zoological account that might be appropriate for *Equus caballus*. By contrast, the appropriate account for *Equus caballus* might make reference to the criteria for classification of animals as perissodactyl quadrupeds, locate their species within the genus *Equus* and the family *Equidae*, and then dwell upon the other anatomical and evolutionary marks of the species.

5. In the special case I am using for purposes of illustration, where the terms 'horse' and *Equus caballus* depend for our understanding of their meaning on our getting to know which natural things they are true of and on our mastering some recognitional stereotype, there has to be something in nature that these explanations are answerable to. But of course the same is true of 'human being', 'man', 'homo', 'ἄνθρωπος'. Here too there is something in nature of which there might be different conceptions. And so, just as differing conceptions steer the different substantives 'horse' and *Equus caballus* with their different senses on to one and the same item, namely, the same concept, so it *may* be that the expressions 'person' and 'human being' are steered, by differing conceptions of something in nature that they stand for, onto one and

the same concept – and onto the *same* thing in nature. If so, the situation we have encountered could be represented as in Figure 4.2.

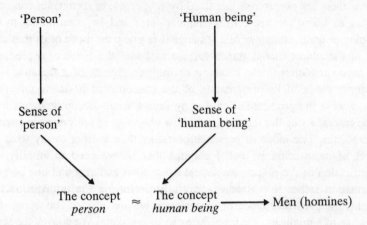

Figure 4.2. Referential convergence of distinct predicates with distinct senses.

Note that if things are as in Figure 4.2, or if the references of 'person' and 'human being' were *theoretically discernible but they determined the same principle of individuation*, then the undoubted difference between the senses of 'person' and 'human being' could not show anything like what it was required to show in the argument from which we set out in §2. It is perfectly consistent with all the differences we hear between 'person' and 'human being' that it should be an illusion – an almost but not perhaps utterly irrepressible illusion – that we are able to find an autonomous, self-sufficient sense for the word 'person' that does not lean secretly for its support upon our understanding of 'human being' and our empirical notions of what a human being is.

6. Having disarmed one sort of misunderstanding, then, and having suggested the possibility that the relation of the concepts *person* and *human being* is one of either dependence or identity, our proper task is to go back to the question of what a person is and the problem of finding a single focus in which to hold the idea of person considered as object of scientific inquiry and the idea of person considered as subject of consciousness. Before I engage with that, however, I need to recapitulate, in order to develop it further (§7), what I have said about what I called 'conceptions'.

First, a conception of an object such as the planet Venus or of a concept such as *horse* or *human being* was something that depends on there being a body of information (or misinformation) about the item the conception is the conception of.

Second, this conception was what we grasp when we grasp the sense of an expression and its mode of presentation of something. In grasping that, I learn what the conception is a conception of, and something about the item that the expression presents.

Third, it is necessary to contrast the concept and the conception. The conception was a way of thinking about something, either an object or a concept. Whatever the differences between an object and a concept, the concept *human being* resembles an object like Venus in respect of being the sort of thing that such *de re* thinking can be the thinking of.

Finally, both conceptions of objects such as Venus or of concepts such as horse or human being and the bodies of information that make these conceptions possible can be better or worse, correct or incorrect. (If a conception were gravely or totally incorrect, no doubt that could subvert its claim to be a conception of this or that object or concept: but this is not to deny that a conception can be mistaken in various ways without detriment to its having that status.) Where there is error, the conception in question is not only a conception but also a misconception of its object. The misconception can be a public or shared one, in which case the correction of error may result in some change in the sense of an expression. (Or even, consequentially, of the reference – but that is rarer.) Alternatively, the misconception may be the property of some particular thinker – and in that case he will have simply failed to catch on completely to the received sense or acceptation of a word, a failure which in no way excludes his having a partial and improvable grasp of it and does not exclude his having a *de re* thought of the object or concept it is a misconception of. (Nothing excludes degrees of understanding here.)

7. Now there are two different ways in which the sense-sustaining conception can relate to the reference of a predicate.

Sometimes understanding a word correctly simply consists in conforming one's use of it with a certain publicly agreed stipulation. An oculist is an eye-doctor; a house is a shelter against destruction by heat, rain, or wind (Aristotle). Similar definitions are no doubt possible – 'analytic' definitions, as one might say – of 'vicar', 'train-driver', 'infantryman', 'footplateman', 'surgeon', 'tenant', 'citizen', 'metic', 'minor', 'patrial'. Here an explicit verbal definition is possible, and a correction can be necessitated only by the need to find a stipulation that better explains speakers' use of the word or by the need to respond to changes in social organization or technology or the law. (In the latter case, we need not be surprised if the word taken in the new sense has a different reference and a different extension from the word taken in the old sense.)

That is one case. The other case – and 'human being' and 'horse' clearly belong in this second class – is where there is no non-circular definition or illuminating potentially explicit necessary and sufficient condition for the application of the term. The only thing that can be had then is an explanation or elucidation that depends on our singling out the reference *in rerum natura*, and where understanding of the reference depends on the possibility of recognizing that which the name stands for, or catching on to a stereotype by which one may recognize the things or specimens that fall under the concept (the things or specimens belonging in the extension of the predicate, which Frege draws horizontally to the right in Figure 4.1, and justly insists on distinguishing from the reference). Here the conception is answerable to experience and may have to be further developed and constantly corrected against experience. It is extension-involving, one may say.[4]

Before engaging with the more controversial predicate '[is] [a] person', I want to dwell for a moment more on some uncontroversial instances of this second case. When we call something a horse or a human being, we are subsuming it under a general term whose sense is kept in being by a publicly shared conception, and the conception is answerable to what actual horses or people are like. It is an a posteriori conception. If someone claimed he really didn't know what the label 'horse' or 'human being' meant, we could only lead him by the hand back to the world itself or remind him of what he already knew, conducting him again through the relevant stretches of living experience.

This is obvious for 'horse' and 'human being'. It is less obvious for 'person'. But what I shall hope to do is to bring the concepts *human being* and *person* closer and closer together by inquiring into what is involved in the attribution and the exercise of the faculties that are distinctive (equally distinctive?) of persons and human beings, and by looking at what lies beneath the surface in the process of interpretation by people of people. As I have said, my chief concern will only be to exhibit the philosophical and ethical consequences of likening the reference of 'person' to that of 'human being', and the speculative advantages that accrue to us if we understand the predicate 'person' as needing to stand for something no less empirical than 'human being' stands for.

8. Let us now focus on *person* itself. Beginning with the least controversial part of the case for your trying out the assimilation I am recommending, I begin by noting that, just as in the cases of 'horse' and 'human being', there is no good reason to expect to find any pure a priori analytic definition of 'person'. In practice we recognize persons without recourse to a definition; and I submit that, in spite of the differences of sense already conceded, the way in which we actually do this is by making use of our stereotype for 'human being'. If there is no alternative to our actual practice, then it seems that our grasp of the term 'person' is just as extension-involving as our grasp of 'human

being'. Secondly, I note that 'person' is conspicuously unlike 'chairman', 'vicar', 'president' – titles that are conferred formally or in accordance with a procedure on something already singled out in another way – and almost equally unlike 'friend' (an epithet whose application can involve an element of voluntary or semi-voluntary decision, or of 'aspect-seeing').[5] Finally, the concept *person* had best not be like the concepts of various kinds of executant, or like concepts that have to change in response to technological progress such as *surgeon* or *infantryman* or *footplateman*, or like legal concepts that we may decide at any moment to modify, such as *tenant, citizen, metic, minor*, or like legal concepts that we simply invent, such as *patrial*. Whenever x is one of these sorts of things, there is always a more fundamental answer to the question 'What is x?'. 'Person' looks like a fundamental or basic sort of classification. What is more, any comparison of these terms with 'person' seems to make a mess of what we mean by 'a good person' (a point familiar to readers of Aristotle, if not to Aristotle).[6]

9. So much for the more or less uncontroversial background to what we ask when we ask what the word 'person' means and what the concept is that it stands for. Against that background I now consider a well-known suggestion that bears on our question.

In his book *Individuals*,[7] P. F. Strawson claims that the concept of *person* is primitive. To interpret this claim, we need to say what the primitiveness is relative to. I interpret Strawson as saying that *person* is primitive relative to the concepts that can be picked out in a language that has all the expressive resources needed to speak of no matter what events, processes, and substances – provided that the events or processes are not singled out in this language as events or processes that involve conscious subjects and the substances in question are not singled out as conscious subjects. If this is right, then Strawson's claim is that, if you did not have the idea of a person from the start, then you could never build up to it from any combination of ideas like those of experience, material body, and causality. It is important though that the fact that you cannot build up in this way (and probably cannot build up in any other way from any other starting-point that doesn't already contain ideas like that of person) does not entail that you cannot say anything at all in explanation of what a person is. Indeed, in the course of a famous argument in this chapter of *Individuals*, Strawson does say a great deal about what sort of idea the idea of person is. What the claim of primitiveness prepares the way for, rather, is this: that a person is, *par excellence* (and as a presupposition of all the traditional questions in the philosophy of mind), the bearer of *both* M-predicates *and* P-predicates, where M-predicates are predicates that we could also ascribe to material objects and P-predicates are predicates that we could not possibly ascribe to material objects and comprise such things as actions, intentions, thoughts, feelings, perceptions, memories, and sensations: and that 'a person is a type of entity such that both predicates ascribing states of consciousness and predicates ascribing corporeal characteristics are equally applicable to an individual of that single type'. It is a disservice to Strawson to see this as intended as a definition. (There are several reasons why it cannot be that: one of them being that it is probably insufficient, and another that the ideas of the relevant types of experience are coeval with the ideas of person, consciousness, and conscious subject themselves and are simply not available for an old-fashioned non-circular definition.) Rather, the claim has the status of an elucidation – or a reminder, helpful only to those who already know what a person is, of *what* it is that they already know.[8]

It is a good reminder. But to put it to further use, I need to make the case for an emendation. This arises out of the objection that, as they stand, Strawson's definitions are *creative*.[9] They are not neutral with respect to the question 'Are persons material objects?'. That question is a substantive one (however it is interpreted). Mere definitions of M-predicate and P-predicate ought not to settle it.

To attend to this point, let us characterize the two ranges of predicate separately and positively as follows:

(i)   M-predicates are predicates that are matter-involving;
(ii) P-predicates are predicates that are (directly or indirectly) consciousness-involving, in the way in which action, intention, thought, feeling, perception, memory, and sensation are consciousness-involving.

And what happens now? Well, the possibility becomes fully visible that almost all P-concepts may turn out to be M-concepts. In its full generality, I do not aspire to prove this. But I think I can make it plausible and try to relate it to the problem of holding bodies and conscious subjects in a single focus.

10. First consider the P-concept (or P-property) of remembering.[10] Suppose Henry plants a tree. For Henry to remember planting the tree, his subsequent recall of his planting must be related in the right sort of way to the incident. For, even though he did plant the tree, Henry's simply thinking he remembers planting it is not sufficient to establish that Henry really remembers doing so. He may have forgotten the actual planting. If someone has told him about it later, then Henry may have imagined the planting; and, even as he imagined it, he may have forgotten that he knew about the action only from another person's account. This is a real if remote possibility. What is required then, in addition to the right kind of agent-centred inner representation on Henry's part, is that there should be a causal relation between his planting the tree and his subsequent memory representation. So far this is a sufficiently familiar

point and still consistent, it might be said, with the P-property of remembering not being an M-property. What is more controversial, but seems almost equally certain, is that it is impossible to say what the right sort of causal connection between an incident and the memory representation of it is without having recourse to the notion of something like a memory trace.[11] If this is right, then a purely conceptual (though not necessarily purely a priori) inquiry discovers to us that the P-property of remembering is necessarily also a rather particular M-property.

Now this argument about the P-property of remembering has important parallels when we consider other faculties that are distinctive of persons. Consider the P-property of perceiving. For there to be a perception of *x*, something would have to be able to count as a misperception of it. But what is the difference? If we are to make the distinction we need, then there has to be something independent of what is subjectively given in perception. But then we must mark the position of the perceiver. There must be such a thing as an answer to the question of where the perception is *from*. Otherwise there is nothing that the perception is answerable to. And what else can fix where the perception is from but the body, head, and eyes of the perceiver? So again, a P-property, here the P-property of perceiving, turns out to be matter-involving. It is an M-property, and on further investigation it might turn out to be a rather particular one – just as experiential memory turned out to be inconceivable without the kind of matter on which a trace or systematic change can be imprinted by the original incident and which can carry the resulting state forward to the time when the person involved recalls that event.

Once we get a feel for how P-properties can turn out to be M-properties, we appreciate the possibility of a kind of alliance between conceptual and post-conceptual modes of inquiry, each being partly a posteriori, the first being philosophical and the second post-philosophical or scientific. It is a recognizably philosophical (even if not wholly a posteriori) discovery that a disposition is the sort of thing that can rest latent, be revived and refreshed and is at the disposal of its owner to use under all sorts of different circumstances or not to use, and that it is impossible to conceive of memory causality by analogy with action at a distance as a transaction over a matterless gap between the external world at one time and a mind at a later time.[12] And it is a recognizably philosophical discovery that there has to be something that will count – independently of the content of a perception – as where the perception is *from*. It is a post-philosophical inquiry how exactly these specifications are realized (even if, in practice, post-philosophical or scientific inquiries constantly draw our attention to oversights and points that philosophy itself had a prior obligation to register).

11. How far will this sort of argument run?[13] It may seem that no argument of this kind will be possible for the case of abstract thought. And perhaps it is not – except in so far as the process of thinking involves (for example) experiential memory. But before we make too much of this point (if it is a point), we must ask: Can we really envisage a person *simply* as a disembodied thinker, without experiential memory as we have described it, without perception or feeling, without pleasure and pain?

I put such questions in order to prompt you to try envisaging *all* P-properties as M-properties. My suggestion is that, if you push a serious account of what each P-property is as far as it will go, you will always find something matter-involving. What happens then? Well, it may seem for a moment that this subverts Strawson's original claim about the primitiveness of *person* relative to the language of physicalism. But, if you are troubled by that point, then remember that, in the sense of being the reference of a predicate that is *reducible* to anything expressed in the language of the sciences of matter or the language relative to which the primitiveness of the concept of a person was being claimed, no P-property is manifestly material or physical. What we are concerned with here is not the reducibility of psychological concepts to concepts that pull their weight in the sciences of matter, but rather with the fact that the elucidation of psychological concepts seems to be essentially *matter-involving*. If an inconsistency seems to have emerged, it is only because it goes unnoticed that there are at least two distinct senses in which the words 'physical' and 'material' are used inside and outside philosophy. The two senses seem to be:

(1)   *x* is material if and only if *x* falls under a concept whose elucidation is matter-involving;

(2)   *x* is material if and only if (a) *x* falls within the extension of a predicate *P* that is reducible to predicates that pull their weight in some physical theory or science *of matter*, and (b) it is possible to say in terms of *P* what *x* is.

Insisting on this distinction, what the M-hood of all P-properties suggests is that persons are material or physical things in sense (1), something that it may be morally important in certain connections to insist upon; but that, in sense (2), it may prove equally important to insist that they are not material.[14]

12. Let me hark back now to the three ideas I said that we have to try to hold together in focus. These were the ideas of

(a)   persons as objects of biological inquiry,
(b)   persons as subjects of consciousness,
(c)   persons as the locus of value.

What I have claimed so far is that there is no hope of building up from (a) to (b). But note that the impossibility of building up from (a) to (b) leaves it perfectly open that you can still build down from (b) to (a). And that is the first of the two suggestions I promised. Seeing the concept of *person* as primitive relative to concepts that pull their weight in the sciences of matter, and as primitive relative to the concept of a human body, and understanding better what a living person is, we may define the body of a person as that which realizes or constitutes the person while he or she is alive, and will be left over, when, finally succumbing to entropy, the person dies. And we may say that what anatomy and neurophysiology are concerned with is a kind of abstraction.[15] Starting with *person*, one abstracts to the living body; and from that, one abstracts to an object whose processes can be subjected to biochemical and anatomical research.[16] If these latter processes come to be described in ways from which full descriptions of P-processes and P-properties can be recovered, that will be a signal scientific achievement. But, even though we know that without the M-processes that scientists describe, life and consciousness would not exist at all, we do not need to *expect* this scientific achievement. I am not even sure whether we ought to be anxious to assert that such a scientific achievement must in principle be possible (in any honest sense of 'in principle'). We begin with the world as it presents itself to us, and with ourselves as we know ourselves. Philosophical reflection suggests that all P-properties are M-properties, and may even suggest that outside the realm of mathematics and logic there is a general difficulty in the idea of any property that is not an M-property. Then we learn more and more about the exact ways in which the properties of the things in the world that we know, including the properties of ourselves, are matter-involving. We learn the further M-marks of these properties. (By the marks of a property F, I mean the properties G such that if anything has F, then it has G.) It is inevitable that the possibility will then present itself of accounting somehow for all the marks of *every* property in terms of the marks that can be discovered by what is recognizably physical science. That is a fairly clear programme. The thing that is obscure is why we should expect that this possibility *must* become actual. Indeed, on second thoughts, is there not reason to expect that, if the scientific world-view is to explain absolutely everything, including how things are for conscious experience, then it must itself give hospitality to the ideas of conscious experience and subjectivity themselves? But then either the clear programme is bound to be difficult to complete – or it must become much less clear. Or rather, both. Surely we must reconsider our first ideas about what can count as a science, and consequentially, we must be ready to adjust our ideas about what an explanation is.

13. Let us go back now to the three ideas (a) (b) and (c) of §1. Seeing (a) and (b) together in the way just described, let us try next to relate them jointly to (c). To begin on this part of the inquiry, I want to consider an older and equally celebrated account of personhood. In his *Essay concerning Human Understanding* (II. xxvii), Locke describes a person as

> a thinking intelligent being that has reason and reflection and can consider itself as itself the same thinking thing in different times and places; which it does only by that consciousness which is inseparable from it.

> Wherever a man finds what he calls himself, there I think, another may say is the same person. It is a forensic term, appropriating actions and their merit, and so belongs to intelligent agents, capable of a law and happiness and misery. This personality extends itself beyond present existence to what is past only by consciousness; whereby it becomes concerned and accountable, owns and imputes to itself past actions, just upon the same ground and for the same reason that it does the present. All of which is founded in a concern for happiness, the unavoidable concomitant of consciousness: that which is conscious of pleasure and pain desiring that the self that is conscious should be happy.

In my book *Sameness and Substance*, I deprecated the suggestion that 'person' is only what Locke calls a 'forensic term'. And I deprecated the idea that 'person' is any other sort of functional or role term. But I supposed that the claim might be seen as only a mistake of emphasis on Locke's part, just as I supposed that one might prescind from the various other features of Locke's account of personhood. I formulated what I claimed was a neo-Lockean account as follows:

> *x* is a person if *x* is an animal falling in the extension of a kind whose typical members perceive, feel, remember, imagine, desire, make projects, move themselves at will, speak, carry out projects, acquire a character as they age, are happy or miserable, are susceptible to concern for other members of their own or like species. . . . conceive of themselves as perceiving, feeling, remembering, imagining, desiring, making projects, being susceptible of concern for others. . ., who have and conceive themselves as having a past accessible in experience – memory – and a future accessible in intention. . . . '

Surely this cannot be very badly wrong. But what particularly interested me at this point was the constant need for *aposiopesis* – the essential incompletability of the statement, the incompletability that is registered by the dots. Certainly this is not an analytical definition like 'oculist = (df) eye-doctor' or a stipulation answerable to nothing in experience except the decision by English speakers to abbreviate some longer formula by the word 'person'. What the neo-Lockean statement really represents is the attempt to transcribe the marks of being a person from our own knowledge and experience of persons and our own as yet unexplained sense of what is important and what is not important about that status. But note that this is the experience of human beings; that the marks we arrive at in this way are as much a posteriori marks of human beinghood as of personhood; and that it seems the task of transcription must be an *open-ended one*. Much more needs to be said about the basis on which we began upon it. What was the principle on which we got as far as this? What is the principle we understand when we think we understand how to continue the task? No doubt we grasp some stereotype. But what makes up this stereotype? Are the constituents of the stereotype organized by anything substantially different from the reference that holds together the stereotype for 'human being'?

14. The first thing we need here is some principle that generates the list and by reference to which it seems we supply extra marks of personhood where the dots have been left. Perhaps this will show *the point* with which we apply the word 'person' to a creature. In *Sameness and Substance*, one of the principles that I suggested we need for this purpose was 'x is a person if and only if x is a living animal (or belongs to a kind of living animal) that we have no option but to account as a subject of consciousness (or potentially such) and as an object of reciprocity and interpretation'. I should still claim some plausibility for this as conveying the principle of our *de re* grasp of what a person is. But note that this was not a definition and that this plausibility is partly owed to a certain relativity that was not made explicit in *Sameness and Substance* and had better now be signalled and clarified.[17] The relativity consists in the fact that it is *for us* to make sense of this creature – never mind the duties or obligations of other intelligences. The sense of the word 'person' is not, however, relative in a way that makes it significant to speak of x's being a person 'for us'. That is not what either the elucidation or the claim of relativity is meant to suggest. Rather, the sense is relative in the sense that the marks of personhood are the marks that are presupposed to the actual ability to arrive at fine-grained interpretations that is our ability.

Now that I draw attention to this relativity, it may seem like a weakness, and perhaps in some way it is. But I want to persuade you that it is also a strength. If I succeed in persuading you of this, then I believe that the effect of this will be not only to strengthen any case that I have made for super-imposing (b) upon (a), but also to show a way to superimpose ((b)-superimposed upon-(a)) upon (c). It will become apparent that to understand fully what it is for us to make sense of another creature as a person will be to understand what forces us to account that creature not only as a subject of consciousness and a subject for interpretation but also, consequentially, as an object of reciprocity, or (in more Kantian terms) as a member of the kingdom of ends.

15. What is interpreting? Interpreting x is making sense of x (something of which making sense of x's speech is just one special case).[18] When we make sense of others we have to have at our disposal at least three kinds of predicate of human subjects and the environment in which they exist:

(i)   predicates of conscious subjects, like 'x believes that . . .', 'x wants this', 'x strives to A', etc.;

(ii)   predicates of the world that impinges upon conscious subjects;

(iii)   predicates by the application of which we attribute not only actions but also intelligible speech to conscious subjects.

In trying to make sense of people, what we have to do is to draw upon this full store of everyday predicates of human subjects and the objects and events that impinge upon them and find a way of describing others that distributes these interpretive predicates over subjects at times in such a way that (a) the propositional attitudes that we ascribe to subjects are intelligible singly and jointly in the light of what we see as true descriptions of the reality to which we take the subjects (or their informants) to have been exposed; and (b) the actions that we ascribe to the subjects are intelligible in the light of the propositional attitudes that are ascribed to them.[19] (More may be required, but at least this much is.) Obviously we find such a distribution of predicates by a process of approximation, and the suitability of any one description may depend on the suitability of indefinitely many others. Much needs to be said about how we can find an entry point, and how an alien theorist might recapitulate the process by which we so naturally and readily do this in real life. It is a hard question too whether there is a unique description that best satisfies these requirements. What is certain is that absolutely every way in which we can ever do this will involve our seeing others as subject to a substantive norm of rationality that we see ourselves as party to and that we can draw upon from within ourselves. (By calling such a norm a 'substantive norm' I mean something that implies the possibility of agreement between inter-preter and subject about ends, for instance, and also about the fit of means with ends and ends with means.) As interpreters we begin where we have to begin, with the supposition that others are attuned to the same reality as the one that we are attuned to, that they are impinged upon by the same features as we are, that (normally) they are interpreting us even as we interpret them, and that they are susceptible to the very same sort of practical and evaluative considerations as we are. We can modulate the supposition point by point, piecemeal, trying always to keep to the minimum the unexplained disagreements that our interpretations involve us in. The net is drawn tighter, and the two theoretical requirements (a) and (b) become ever more precise and exigent (and by being more precise and exigent, ever more fruitful) when language enters into the picture and the beliefs and concerns one person projects upon others become more and more detailed and specific. It is to be expected that the conception of the task itself will shift and develop; but one assumption that we need to make is constant, namely that there is always the *uncircumscribed possibility* of agreement. Or, more precisely, the assumption we need to make is that, with respect to everything and anything, either there is the possibility of total agreement, or disagreement must be intelligible. No wonder then (if the *Sameness and Substance* elucidation of *person* was correct) that, in the interest of our securing and vindicating our mutual attunement, the Lockean elucidation of 'person' grows and grows. For there is no clear limit to what concerns and capacities and perception and feelings... we shall have to credit our fellows with if we are to make sense of them. (This is not yet to say that all the marks of 'human being' belong in the class of marks of the concept *person*. What we are experimenting with is an assimilation of these concepts, not yet an outright identification. As the assimilation becomes closer, and more of the marks of human-beinghood are seen as marks of personhood, it will simply not matter whether the concepts finally coincide. Their actual extensions will coincide, and it will be no accident that they do.)

If you still think it is just obvious that there are non-human persons, then see whether you can describe, up to any required level of detail, how we should make sense of non-human creatures, become attuned to them, or be in a position to treat their feelings as if they were our own; or see how you imagine making sense of these creatures *without* doing that. On the picture I have been suggesting should be given its trial, what sustains the idea of a person is the idea of interpretation and the innumerable P-properties of human beings that the process of interpretation forces one to assume one can project upon others. People are the subjects of fine-grained interpretation *by* us and are the would-be exponents of fine-grained interpretation *of* us. But, as I have said before, this is not the definition. And now I can say why. If it were a definition, we should have to ask: does it mean that x is a person if and only if *there is a z* such that x is a subject for interpretation *by* z? Or is x a person if and only if x is a subject for interpretation *by us*? If the first, then most animals are persons, given our definition of interpret (for animals too have to make sense of one another). If the second, why does not '*x* is a person for us' make sense? The status of the *Sameness and Substance* suggestion was only that of a conceptual direction – a direction how to supply extra marks to the neo-Lockean statement of what a person is – and of an explanation of the point of that statement.

16. Presented with the human form, we immediately entertain a multitude of tentative expectations, unless something inhibits or perverts this response: and that is how it has to be. But faced with a Martian or an automaton, unless this is a creature synthesized by procedures that would somehow carbon-copy the contingencies of human frame and human constitution, we should have to be mad to entertain any of these expectations. What we face is at best an alien intelligence whose sources of satisfaction are inscrutable, except in so far as we can make sense of them by imagining ourselves in its place – but that is the way of proceeding which is excluded by the hypothesis that what we confront is a Martian or automaton. An alien intelligence is not a person. A person is a creature with whom we can get onto terms, or a creature that is of the same animal nature and psychophysical make-up as creatures with whom we can get onto terms, there being no clear limit to how far the process can go. (Though that is not how we define 'person', but simply the consequence of a certain method of elucidation.)

17. I began by promising to make two suggestions about how three ideas could be held in a single focus. It will bring me within reach of completing the second and last suggestion if I illustrate the contrast between the human and the alien with two notable philosophical texts (not deterred by the fact that the first is *en route* to becoming the most hackneyed of twentieth-century philosophical assertions, or by the fact that the aptness of the second was suggested to me by an article that was intended as a critique of the same opinions I am defending here).[20]

If a lion could talk, we could not understand him.

L. Wittgenstein

Anybody who is in our vicinity exercises a certain power over us by his very presence, and a power that belongs to him alone, that is the power of halting, repressing, modifying each movement that our body sketches out. If we step aside for a passer-by on the road, it is not the same thing as stepping aside to avoid a billboard: alone in our rooms we get up, walk about, sit down again quite differently from the way we do when we have a visitor. . . . But this indefinable influence that the presence of another human being has on us is not exercised by men [such as one's adversary in Homeric warfare] whom a moment of impatience can deprive of life, who can die before even a thought has a chance to pass sentence on them. In their presence people move about as if they were not there.

Simone Weil

At one pole, what Wittgenstein seeks to dramatize is the interpretative divide between intelligences between whom there is scarcely the beginning of agreement in responses, let alone the uncircumscribed possibility of agreement. At the opposite pole, what Weil describes is what it *is* to treat an entity as an object of interpretation and as a subject of consciousness as we know it, or as potentially one of us – an object of reciprocity, that is. To be ready to take a person *as* a person, what I have to be ready to do is to explore that uncircumscribed possibility. To treat a person like a thing (like a billboard), what I have to be ready to do is to suspend all the impulses on which that uncircumscribed possibility precisely depended.

Consider willful killing. Consider what we have to lay aside even to contemplate the actuality of this. Where there is danger from a mortal enemy, someone may kill the enemy intentionally and without a further thought. There may be no time to have a further thought. The to-and-fro of ordinary interpretive intercourse in which we are normally caught up has already been conspicuously suspended. (For some people, it takes a great deal to put that into abeyance. How slow some are with a gun precisely shows how much it takes to make them do so – a fact clearly recognized in all systems for the basic training of military recruits and conscripts.) But where nothing has put the to-and-fro of ordinary interpretive intercourse into abeyance, consider how much, how many habits of mind and feeling, you then have to put aside coolly to contemplate simply cutting off, simply 'taking out', another person. Obviously, all these things can be laid aside. But the point is not that they *cannot* be put aside, but the psychic and visceral cost – and the prima facie irrationality[21] – of doing so. (A Humean variant of a Kantian contention.)

An explanation of what is wrong with willful killing or wanton cruelty or repaying good with evil that started from here might seem to be unable to rise above the superficial. But, if anything is superficial here, it is the opinion that this sort of explanation is *bound* to be superficial. There is no reason at all why an interpretive-cum-subjective explanation of this sort should not be developed into an explanation as deep as the moral facts are.

17. If this were the right place, I should now try to show how an analogous explanation of the *origin* of all value could have subjective responses as its starting-point, how it could graduate to a level at which values emerged as

objective as well as subjective,[22] and how the account that it suggests of moral concerns and moral qualms vindicates the claims of these attitudes to be manifestations of genuine moral disinterest. But the time has come to return once more to the problem that we set ourselves in §2. That was how to hold in a single focus (a), (b), and (c) – the biological, the mental, and the moral aspects of personhood. We reached (a) by abstraction from (b). But now we reach (c) by understanding more and more fully just what it takes for x to count as the bearer of the properties by virtue of which x counts as the bearer of P-properties *and* M-properties, as a subject of consciousness and as an object of interpretation. We reach these marks of the person not by an unprincipled transcription of all the marks of being a human being no matter what, but by letting our conception of human being and our conception of person come together so that each will supply the conceptual lacunae in the other. Our grasp of what it is to be a human being gives matter and substance to our conception of persons and the faculties and other P-cum-M-properties that are distinctive of them; while our conception of persons, and our apprehension of persons as subjects of consciousness and objects of reciprocity and interpretation, is what directs and animates our search for those marks of human beings in virtue of which we have to see them as the bearers and sources of value. This is a search for which the idea of human being furnishes the actual materials – the precipitate of all sorts of evolutionary, biological, historical, and cultural facts. These are the contingencies upon which the concepts to which we address our actual conceptions of personhood must depend for their nature and being.

5

Reasoning about Persons

GRANT GILLETT

> If you know you are yourself, you know that you are not somebody else, but
> do you know that you are yourself? Are you sure that you are not your own
> father – or, excuse me, your own fool? Who are you, pray?
>
> George MacDonald, *Lilith*

I wish to examine the idea, recently championed by Derek Parfit, that a set
of psychological states and the relations between them will serve as a
perspicuous analysis of the concept of a person and/or what matters about
personal identity.[1] This is usually called the 'bundle theory'.

In a discussion of personal identity there are two approaches that we might
take. We might explore the 'grammatical' or conceptual relations which determine the concept of a person, and see what they tell us about the nature of
persons as identifiable and re-identifiable particulars of a given type. Personal
identity is central to this project. Or we might describe the causal and social
conditions which are necessary to the existence and activity of a person. Once
we have decided what we mean when we speak of persons, these can be
elucidated. These conditions belong to what Kant would call 'the de-facto mode
of existence' of persons, and thus are not necessarily part of the conceptual
analysis of the concept *person*. Whether these conditions are important in
considering the metaphysical nature of persons can be considered later. For
the moment our concern is to understand the realities involved in a coherent
concept of a person and his mental life.

To the bundle theorists' suggestions I will offer three counter-arguments.
First, an account of personal identity in terms of mental connectedness and
continuity cannot be philosophically motivated (this argument will seek to
undermine the basis on which a reductive account is thought to be required).

Second, there must be a principle of actual unity, in terms of a personal subject, underlying our thought life. Third, in defining myself and developing as an individual, I show myself to be more than a collection of mental phenomena.

THE BUNDLE THEORISTS' CASE

To take the first argument, 'brain bisection' data are often taken to require a revision in our traditional conception of personal identity. Nagel has remarked: 'The ultimate account of the unity of what we call a single mind consists of a enumeration of the types of functional integration that typify it.'[2] He concludes: 'It is possible that the ordinary, simple idea of a single person will come to seem quaint one day, when the complexities of the human control system become clearer and we become less certain that there is anything very important that we are one of.'[3]

Parfit argues that what is important in our concept of personal identity is just mental continuity and connectedness. 'We might now claim, as a first approximation, that the truth of statements about personal identity just consists in the truth of certain statements about psychological and (perhaps) physical continuity. The fact of personal identity is not a further fact, apart from certain facts about these continutities.'[4] Although he is often taken to be claiming that he is concerned only with what matters about the lives of persons, he also writes:

> We could therefore redescribe any person's life in impersonal terms. In explaining the unity of this life, we need not claim that it is the life of a particular persons. We could describe what, at different times, was thought and felt and observed and done and how these various events were interrelated. Persons would be mentioned here only in the content of many thoughts, desires, memories, and so on. Persons need not be claimed to be the thinkers of any of these thoughts.[5]

Parfit draws on two sources to support these claims: (1) findings in human beings with brain bisection; and (2) the imaginative consideration of various scenarios involving grades of mental and physical discontinuity. I shall argue that brain bisection data do not support his interpretation and that the thought experiments are not valid.

Brain Bisection

In the operation of sectioning the *corpus callosum*, most of the fibres between the two hemispheres of the brain are divided. From patients who have had such an operation, it is possible to elicit disparate responses to information delivered separately to each cerebral hemisphere. Because each half of the visual field and each hand is linked predominantly to the opposite cerebral hemisphere, the two hands can be made to respond differently in certain tasks by selective presentation of information to one or the other hemisphere. The tasks show a degree of informational complexity such that normally the behaviour produced would be considered the conscious performance of an intelligent person.

In everyday life, as distinct from the test setting, 'split-brain' patients showed no noticeable disabilities apart from rare occasions on which different tendencies were evinced by left and right hands to the same external object. In one case a man embraced his wife with one hand and pushed her away with the other. In another a patient had occasional difficulties because his right and left hands chose different clothes for him to wear. In general, it was noted that, even in an experimental situation (where information was carefully split between hemispheres), the patients would often tip themselves off so as to achieve correct responses. For example, if the patient was asked to perform an 'object choice' with his right hand, the information for which had been given to his right hemisphere, he might grimace each time the right hand tended toward an incorrect object and smile when it finally chose the correct object. The patient thus clearly attempts to integrate information which has been fragmented due to the disruption of the causal conditions which normally enable him to take full cognition of it. Sperry says: 'Everything we have seen so far indicates that the surgery has left these people with two separate minds, that is, two separate spheres of consciousness.'[6] Parfit accepts this suggestion uncritically, but I will argue that it requires scrutiny.

Sperry himself remarks on the tricks used by the patient to try to overcome his difficulties.[7] We might, therefore plausibly ask: 'Is there a single subject of experience who is making and is aware of making these mistakes?' rather than 'How many separate streams of consciousness are these here?'

The Russian neuropsychologist Luria writes about a man who survived a penetrating missle injury to the brain which left him with severely fragmented thoughts and says: 'I had a chance to witness his long, relentless fight to recover the use of his damaged brain.'[8] This is the model I would favour, that of a person attempting to overcome the effects of damage to a part of his body, rather than that of a complex of conscious entities which can come apart.

However, in the brain bisection cases we do have a problem for our conception of a person as a unitary conscious subject and a 'rational' agent. The patient receives information, and in the light of it may form two different intentions. To take a simple case, after receiving a visual 'message' in which shapes of different colour are flashed in each half-field, the left hand of a patient picks out a red object and the right hand a blue object. Although we can give an explanation of these events in terms of brain function, it is far from clear what can be said about what the agent is thinking in this situation. He can select a red object but not say that what he has selected is red. On the other hand, he can both select a blue object and say that it is blue. What thoughts can be attributed to him? At this juncture, several points need to be made. First, in everyday life, not everything that I do forms part of my conscious thought. Second, a person's thought content shows certain structural patterns (or 'generality constraints') and inferential connections. The concepts involved enter a variety of structurally related thoughts, and the thoughts themselves are used in a variety of ways. Thus, if I grasp the concept *red*, I can grasp, in part, the thoughts 'the paint is red,' 'the chair is red,' 'that is red,' and so on. If I grasp the concept *house*, I should grasp in part 'the house is blue,' 'the house is red,' 'the house moved,' and so on. Later, I will consider certain conceptual requirements imposed by these ascriptions, but for the moment I wish only to note that these conditions must be met before we can know what it means to ascribe, or self-ascribe, a given thought. As stated, the conditions seem to be linguistic; hence it might be argued that since the right (or non-dominant) hemisphere can think but has no language function to speak of, these conditions amount to a stipulation against it. Luria, Vygotsky, and Davidson have all remarked on the intimate connections between thought and language. Davidson in particular has argued – I think correctly – that where there is no language for its expression and elaboration, we cannot ascribe a full human range of thoughts with propositional content.[9] Third, it is only as a subject of thought ascriptions that a person is a conscious rational thinker. In these experiments the subjects are not only conscious, but are often conscious of an internal conflict which they try to overcome by various tricks and, by succeeding, make some ascriptions secure. Because they do try to reintegrate the information they receive, they can properly be said to be struggling with certain cognitive difficulties from a unitary standpoint, rather than to have become two mutually independent streams of consciousness only contingently related to each other. In other words, the subject considers himself to be a single, conscious albeit handicapped subject.

Sperry's data warrant certain cautious conclusions. First, human cognition is dependent on the intact function of the brain, and is not carried out in some immaterial mind, cognitive substance, or inner self. Second, our conception of a person, and his thought life draws on our experience of intact human beings.

Even after a brain bisection, a person tries to perform the tasks he is assigned; he makes mistakes and is conscious of so doing. The person, 'he', and 'his' here point to the real identity or unity which remains intact in this situation, despite disrupted brain function or disorders in the 'complexities of the human control system'.[10]

Thought Experiments

Parfit supports his interpretation of split-brain cases by reference to certain fantasies or thought experiments. These involve the replication of persons (for example, in a teletransporter), graded mental and physical discontinuities of personal constitution , and the 'fission' and 'fusion' of persons.

In the first of these scenarios, I am in some way replaced by, or made to give rise to, a fully-fledged psychophysical replica of myself, complete with memory and character. I am asked whether this would be me, or, even more suggestively, whether I would consider myself to be myself after such replication. I am then asked to consider what would happen if two such replicas were produced. It is argued that, if identity is what is important in the first case, then the production of a second replica would completely confound what is important, because I could not be identical to two individuals who would subsequently lead separate lives. From this Parfit concludes that identity is not what matters, because, although the outcome for me is no worse in the second case than the first, I do not have a one-to-one identity relation with either resulting person.

In the second set of scenarios he considers a range of cases in which I am replaced piecemeal, either mental link by mental link or nerve-cell by nerve-cell, so that, in the limiting case, I lose all resemblance to my original self. Parfit contends that we could not draw a line and say that identity was preserved up to such and such a point but that thereafter it changed. If identity resided in a single mental essence in each person, such a line could be drawn. What is claimed is that there is a degree of psychological continuity and connectedness which captures all that one can only try to grasp using the concept of personal identity. The identity of a person is said to reduce to a matter of the relation between various 'experiences' or mental states.

In a third scenario, that of fission, my brain is divided and placed in two different bodies, each of which lives a normal life. Again, I am unable to claim one-to-one identity with either resultant person, although I have an important connection with both. But living as two people is not the same as dying, so again it must be mental connectedness and continuity and not identity that matters.

To these arguments I offer two objections, one attacking Parfit's license to use certain concepts in describing the cases and framing his conclusions, the other claiming that he describes the cases in such a way as to beg the question. Seddon[11] and Wiggins[12] have both argued that questions of possibility and the nature of certain concepts cannot be settled merely on the basis of what we think we can imagine, but must take note of the conceptual connections involved in our ordinary linguistic practices. Seddon's examples include a bar of iron which floats and carnivorous rabbits on Mars. We may think we can conceive of such entities, but yet be deceived.

Consider the bar of iron. We think that what we are imagining floating on the water is iron, but is it really iron? What is the atomic number and configuration of the stuff that is floating? How do these facts relate to its crystal lattice structure and density? Does it have the same physico-chemical relations to other elements as iron? But if it has all these characteristics of iron (and how else do we know that it *is* iron with which we are dealing?), how can it float on water, since these properties logically entail that it does not? We might respond, 'Surely we can imagine the density as being different and the other properties remaining the same.' But how can that be, when the density is an outcome of all those other things? These imaginings lead us into a tangled web in which we do not know what to think.

Wiggins makes similar points in relation to the identification and re-identification of particulars under sortal concepts. The concepts according to which we identify something as being the thing it is involve an idea of the way that the kind of thing concerned behaves and the kind of life history that it has. He mentions frogs. Imagine that I have been given a tiny tadpole and, because I have been told that it will grow into a frog, have called it 'Freddy'. Given it on my seventh birthday, I take good care of it, and am the proud owner of a tiny frog by the time I turn eight. But now imagine a different version of the story, in which I neglect my tadpole, whom I call 'Freddy' but do not know is destined to become a frog. Fortunately the stagnant pond in which I deposit it contains many mosquito larvae and midges and, unbeknown to me, Freddy still becomes a frog. One day I go out to see my little tadpole and find instead a greenish-brown amphibian. I conclude that the 'new' creature has eaten Freddy, and I know not where his little soul may be. (One can imagine a world in which this train of thought would be appropriate, a world in which tadpole-like creatures never become froglike creatures at all.) It is clear that an adequate conception of Freddy, which would allow me to re-identify the particular I have named 'Freddy', can only be achieved when I take cognizance of the natural history of frogs. We might similarly contend that an adequate concept of persons needs to take account of the facts about human beings. We need not identify persons extensionally with human beings, but need only adduce the fact that our concept of a person and the ascriptions we make to persons are paradigmatically based on our dealings with human beings.

Human beings are born with a certain constitution and, through the many and varied experiences that they undergo, develop into adults with a certain conceptual repertoire, character, set of memories, self-image, emotionality, aspirations, abilities, eccentricities, and so on, all of which are holistically interconnected. To call a human being a 'person' is to refer to him as an entity whom we implicitly take to be this way. Our concepts and thoughts have meaning in so far as we acquire and use them within this process of maturation. The nature of this process and the complex interrelation between personal history, brain structure, and mental function means that a person cannot simply be replicated, replaced, or divided. Both personal identity and mental ascriptions are determined within the framework of these conditions.

Consider now the fusion of persons. Parfit writes: 'We can imagine a world in which fusion was a natural process. Two people come together. While they are unconscious, their two bodies grow into one. One person then wakes up.'[13] I maintain that it is not at all clear whether we *can* imagine what is described here. What are we supposed to imagine? What happens to the brain as all these neural interconnections are altered? What about the intricate connections by which the higher functions are integrated with the more primitive centres serving basic needs and attention. If we take just one concept used in everyday life and consider the many different interactions and experiences which have secured its role in our conceptual system, what are we to say about the use of this concept in the 'fused' individual? The mental function of a person is normally built as the brain changes its microstructure and function in response to experience; but in the fused individual this has all been knocked cock-a-hoop. The integrity of brain function essential to the grasp and use of a given concept has been disrupted. When we pursue this putative notion of fusion, we do not even know what we are saying.

Such indeterminacy is found in every situation that Parfit urges us to imagine. To move from highly circumscribed anomalies in the neuropsychology of patients who have suffered hemispheric disconnection to a discussion of persons dividing and fusing is to take leave not only of the constraints of actuality, but also of the determinacy of content which ensures our grasp of the concepts concerned. As for my second objection, that in each of the ingenious thought experiments devised by Parfit the case is described in such a way as to force a certain conclusion, consider the following:

At the beginning of my story, the scanner destroys my brain and body. My blueprint is beamed to Mars, where another machine makes a replica of me. My replica thinks that he is me and he seems to remember living my life up to the moment when I pressed the green button. In every other way, both physically and psychologically, my replica is just like me. If he returned to Earth, everyone would think he is me.[14]

But would he be me? Would he think as I think? I cannot tell. Nor is it clear what should be said here, for normal concepts lose their grip. What is clear, however, is that the way things are described, a certain conclusion is thrust upon us. 'I press the button. As predicted, I lose and seem at once to regain consciousness, but in a different cubicle. Examining my body, I find no change at all. Even the cut on my upper lip, from this morning's shave, is still there'.[15] Here, what matters is clearly preserved, for I am the same person; my identity has been preserved, but *that* is precisely what is at issue. In the same way, Parfit imagines me sitting a physics exam in which I divide into two streams of consciousness. But in each 'stream' Parfit goes on using the word 'I' in such a way as to ensure that everything that could matter is preserved. He never tells us which hemisphere uses the reticular formation, 'motivational' centres, and other 'attentional' mechanisms that have never been split in a living human being but that seem to be involved in all coherent mental activity.

In talking of 'my division', he imagines two half-brains functioning in two individuals into whom they have been transplanted. But again we must waive our constraints on possibility, and again the question is begged. Each person has the mental integrity characteristic of a human being, which is dependent on the activity of a fully functioning brain. We just do not know what the mental lives of entities without this integrity would be like.

What is astounding in Parfit's cases is that, having seen the rabbit put into the hat, we are nevertheless impressed when he draws it forth again. In each case what is said to span the gap between the initial person and the final person is just psychological continuity and connectedness, but each description involves the preservation of a strong sense of personal identity and an integrated viewpoint on the world. Whether a connected bundle of 'experiences' could preserve this is what is under debate.

I shall now turn from this indirect attack on the evidence adduced in support of Parfit's theory to a direct attack on its content and that of related theories. I will claim that the theory neglects two important, constitutive features of the mental life of persons. Both features imply the existence of a mental subject who is unitary in all his experience and not merely the relation of that experience to a physical or causal substrate.

THE UNITARY PERSONAL SUBJECT

Both Hume[16] and Kant[17] argue that there is no empirically discoverable self present in experience. None the less, two facts suggest that there is a unitary subject of experience and conscious thought. First, I am capable of conceptual thought (by this I do not mean to imply that there may be other kinds). Second, I ascribe mental and physical predicates to myself without recourse to evidence for those ascriptions.

Conceptual Thought

Conceptual thought requires that a given event be correlated and compared with other events so that similar and contrasting features can be recognized by the thinker. Particular experiences are described in terms of universals, and can only be described thus through the application of concepts. This involves a rational subject 'working over' the events in his life.[18] Similarities and identities are recognized, contradictions are detected, and puzzles are noted so that, at some stage, they may be recalled and relfected on. This requires what Kant calls the 'transcendental unity of apperception', a formal principle stating that one conceptualizing rationality must think the diverse, particular thoughts ascribed to a subject. Without this unity, conceptual thought would be impossible, and mental states could not be ascribed to a person in the way they are.

Any concept functions by means of its place in the network of terms and practices in which it is embedded. Wittgenstein has also observed that a 'dictionary in the mind' is no dictionary at all;[19] conceptual terms must be part of a normative practice of reference and use. There must be normative constraints on the use of a term other than its seeming right to the user. This means that the source of the standards which a thinker's performance aims to meet must be independent of that performance; thus, the person concerned must be an entity in an objective world with which he interacts. Practices regulate (or provide the normative constraints for) our conceptual usage and hence our thought in general. A single individual must be the same thinker who uses a term now with a given intent and also at other times and places, if that term is to come under the rules or normative constraints which ensure consistent use. He must be aware of the conditions under which use of the term is appropriate, and, as he conforms his practice to the rules, come to a mastery of the concepts in which he thinks of the world and his own mental life.[20]

I may have no experience or 'impression' or 'intuition' of an 'inner me', but I can be sure, nevertheless, that there *is* an essential unity in all my thought. My thought, to be coherent, must be the thought of a persistent rational being subject to independent normative constraints on his thought content.

Self-ascription

Any person is capable of ascribing both mental and physical predicates to himself without appeal to criteria of personal identity.[21] If I say 'I have a stomach ache' or 'I have just come in from the back garden,' then, under normal circumstances, the questions 'What evidence have you for that statement?' or

'How do you know that?' would be nonsensical. To be able to say such things reliably is part of what it is to be a human being who has learnt a given language.[22] If a person regularly went wrong in saying such things, we would not know what to make of his thought, and I do not see how he could be any better off himself. Similarly, there is a close relationship between the fact that the same thinking subject must make judgements at different times in order to grasp the normative constraints on those judgements, and the fact that I have criterionless or non-inferential access to thoughts that I have had on different occasions. Evans notes: 'This features of I ideas means that they span past and present in a novel way (and expectation will bring in the future).'[23] The use of 'I' depends on there being a particular who is re-identifiable by self and others over time. Many propositional attitudes which constitutively enable a thought life to make sense (most beliefs, desires, expectations, moral convictions, and so on) are not things that can be manifest at just one time, or that could be ascribed sensibly to a ten-minute 'slice' of a person's life; they have rich conceptual relations to past and future, because they presuppose that the thinker to whom I now ascribe them was the thinker of past thoughts and will have related thoughts in the future. I observe the same constraints when I ascribe both mental and physical predicates to myself. The latter may have 'subjective', or phenomenal, features. I ascribe predicates which have both phenomenal and objective features, and thus I assume that the individual to whom these predicates apply is both a subject of experience and an objective entity. In the first-person case, it emerges that there is no 'deep' or 'inner' self which serves as a referent for 'I'. The 'I' to whom I refer and the person to whom others refer is the same entity. This entity is the subject from whose vantage-point I view the world, but also is an object to whom others refer. In thinking of myself and my relation to the world, I draw on my own conceptual resources, but also depend on a mastery of first-person locutions achieved in a public set of practices. Some of these locutions will be avowals which I make in the appropriate circumstances; some will involve self-reflexive judgements in which I use concepts that others also use to make judgements about me (thus applying them to myself).

Consider a memory claim such as 'I remember seeing X yesterday.' This also is made on the basis of the capacity to use concepts consistently over time. Just as the mental subject who uses a term today must be the same subject who has previously grasped the use of the term, so he is the subject who has criterionless access to his own memory. Parfit and all the other bundle theorists neglect the first of these facts about the structure and coherence of conceptual thought; they are then left with a problem in that they rely on *memory* as a principal component of mental continuity and connectedness. But that faculty presupposes, in its conceptual structure, that it is the same subject who now remembers what he says he remembers that he experienced. Construction of identity in terms which rely heavily on memory is thus tightly circular. For this reason, Shoemaker, Parfit, and others seek to replace the normal conception of memory, which is clear and workable, with a notion of 'quasi-memory' (Q-memory), which Parfit defines as follows: 'I have an accurate quasi-memory of a past experience if (1) I seem to remember having an experience, (2) someone did have this experience, and (3) my apparent memory is causally dependent, in the right kind of way, on that past experience.'[24] We shall overlook the problems raised above about the implausibility of separating the condition 'causally dependent in the right kind of way' from the normal conditions of human existence, although it is susceptible to exactly the objections raised with regard to fusion and brain function: namely, that the right conditions entail the fact that I am a subject who retains personal identity over time. We are invited to imagine a case in which a person has a few of someone else's memories. Again, we must relax our constraints on possibility, but let us do so, and then force a wider application of this suggestion.

Let us imagine that, in general, people have Q-memories some of which have been transpersonally induced. Consider the statement 'I remember seeing X yesterday.' Do I? A flood of doubts call into question the coherence of my thought. Who do I mean by X here? I cannot be sure whether it is someone I have met or whether it is somebody whom I have a Q-memory of meeting. Can I trust my inclination to call him 'X' or to call that day 'yesterday'? And who do I mean by 'I' here? Am I really me, or just someone I have a Q-memory of being? What name do I give myself? I cannot definitively answer any of these questions, and there is no point in others trying to put me right. Not only are they in the same boat, but I might not remember the clarification that they offered to me as being pertinent to *me*. I might be muddled about the context in which it originated, what led up to it, who it was who was muddled, or what the nature of the muddle was. Here we experience the peculiar vertigo that sets in when our concepts come adrift, and we no longer know what we are really thinking.

Wittgenstein remarks: 'There is a lack of clarity about the role of imaginability in out investigation. Namely about the extent to which it ensures that a proposition makes sense.'[25] We only think that we can imagine what Q-memory is; but when we examine it, we realize that we do not even know what it is that we are imagining. We might seek to overcome this objection by admitting that Q-memory is incoherent as a transpersonal possibility, but claiming that people have Q-memories of their *own* experiences. However, we would then find ourselves back in the circularity we sought to escape.

I do not know whether it would be possible for some psychological entities to have something like Q-memories (a decision will have to await a coherent description), but in speaking of such entities, we would no longer be talking about people and the type of mental life that they have. People are beings who refer to themselves as bearers of certain predicates and have memories; they thus show themselves to be objective entities whose nature spans the mental and the physical. They are subject to certain principles of individuation and identification over time which take account of what a person is. The identities of persons can be decided only when such facts about the nature of persons are kept clearly in mind. Wiggins attempts to capture these considerations in his definition of a person: '...a person is any animal the physical makeup of whose species constitutes the species' typical members thinking intelligent beings, with reason and reflection, and typically enables them to consider themselves as themselves the same thinking things, in different times and places'.[26] The relation between the experiences which make up a given person's mental life is not irrelevant to personal identity, but neither will it serve as a reductive analysis of the concept of a person. A person is a creature with a physical constitution, but he is also a mental subject with continuity in time, who thinks conceptually, has propositional attitudes, makes avowals and first-person judgements, and remembers his past experiences.

Defining Myself and Developing as a Person

An important feature of our lives as persons is that we can observe, narrate, and comment on our mental lives. This reinforces our conclusions about personal identity. First, we note that as people develop in their thinking, so their understanding of people in general becomes more informed. What they come to believe about people, including themselves, draws more and more on the wealth of experiences and interaction which give content to concepts of *human being* and *person*. Birth, growth, maturation, mortality, emotional sensitivities, human abilities, social interactions, culture, beliefs, and so on are part of this experience. As a person's identity becomes defined, so the kind of story he tells about himself takes on a richness and depth which draw on his cumulative experience of life. That he *can* tell such a story suggests that his life and identity is more like a painting or a novel than a heap of sand or a string of contingently connected events. The resulting composition is not merely a 'stream of consciousness' liable to all the twists and vagaries found in dreams or reveries, but is profoundly influenced and formed by the empirical nature of persons and by their relations to an objective world of which an important constituent is other persons. The principles of identity and cohesion which regulate our 'internal life' are principles which incorporate all the things we know to be true of people, and therefore involve just those facts to which Wiggins and Seddon have drawn our attention.

Second, the fact that it is a person, replete with a biography, a holistically constituted mental life, and interactions with the world, who is not only telling the story, but also reviewing, anticipating, criticizing, and making resolutions about his developing narrative, indicates that a relation between mental states is far from being an adequate model for describing what matters. Mental states do not pass judgements and assume attitudes to each other. If they did, it would be fascinating to catch them at it sometime; I suppose it would be a psychological version of the 'Magic Toyshop'. But in my autobiography, a *person* is active; self-scanning mechanisms will not fill the bill. When we talk about a person, we are talking about a conceptually sophisticated being who can both tell and appreciate a story, and who can, to a certain extent, hold himself aloof from his own experiences and regard himself with a critical eye, informed by all that he knows of life. The mental life of a person can be understood only with the aid of a substantive concept of a person as one who has an identity and an interest in that identity.

In summary, a bundle theory of personal identity is inadequate. It is not supported by neuropsychological data, and is given credibility only spuriously by thought experiments which ignore the conceptual constraints on the terms used to describe them. Further, such theories neglect the fact that our thought life, to have the conceptual structure and quality that it has, must be seen as the mental activity of a unitary, continuing subject of psychological ascriptions who makes conceptual judgements. Finally, the self-narration which characterizes our thought life is incompatible with a notion of personal identity involving anything less than a fully self-reflexive, concept-using subject of experience.

Contra Parfit, I would claim that a person's life cannot be 'redescribed in impersonal terms'; it must be seen as the life of a particular person, otherwise we could make no sense of, nor ascribe any content to, what was thought and felt and observed and done, and how these events are interrelated. Persons must be acknowledged to be the thinkers of their thoughts, or our grasp of the nature of our thought lives will slip away completely.[27]

And so, finally, to ethics. It would seem that my consideration for, and involvement with, persons is not only the basis of my thought life, but also the natural milieu in which the continuing individual who is me develops and refines his own personality. Thus I, as a subject-agent, as the mental being who unifies my thought and experience, have an essential engagement with others as continuing mental and physical subject-agents, and am affected by their thoughts, feelings, and relationships. In this web of interactions, I empathize with them and appreciate their and my concern for the future and for our mutual vulnerability as flesh-and-blood creatures. I appreciate my own pain, joy, longing, hope, and distress by acquiring the terms and associations in which to understand these common human experiences. I appreciate myself and the unfolding story of my own life in and through my interaction with others. I appreciate it as a life in process of creation, over which I have certain powers and for which I have certain responsibilities. Having said all this, I seem to have said that I am an inescapably ethical being, so there I will rest my case.

A Response – DEREK PARFIT

Dr Gillett's paper is so full of ideas that I can't hope to respond to more than just a few of them. First, as Dr Peacocke suggested, I shall sketch parts of my view about the nature and significance of personal identity. I argued three things: that most of us, even if we are not aware of this, have certain strong beliefs about what is involved in our own identity – or continued existence – over time, that these beliefs are false, and that, if we gave up these beliefs, this might affect some of our emotions and moral principles.

Part of my argument for these claims appealed to various imaginary cases of the kind found in science fiction. I agree with some of Dr Gillett's objections to the use, in philosophy, of bizarre examples. If we imagine away the scaffolding of natural facts which are presupposed by many of our concepts, it may be pointless to ask what we would then say, since our concepts may simply fail to apply. But I used such cases to throw light, not on our concepts, but on our beliefs. When we imagine ourselves in these cases, most of us are not merely baffled. We have certain definite convictions about what either might or must be true.

Dr Gillett argued that some of these examples are hard even to imagine, especially my case of fusion, in which two different persons join together, and become one. I agree that this case raises many doubts. For this reason, I gave it little more than a glance. A simpler kind of example, which I dicusssed at length, involves what I called Teletransportation. If this process happened to me, a Scanner would destroy my brain and body, while recording the exact states of all my cells. My blueprint would then be beamed, at the speed of light, to some place like Mars, where a Replicator would create, out of new matter, a brain and body just like mine. To some readers of science fiction, Teletransportation seems to be a way of travelling; others think it a way of dying.

In describing such a case, I assume that such a Replica of me would be, not just physically, but also psychologically just like me. He would have my character and intentions, seem to remember living my life, and so on. It is not hard to imagine that this might be true. Nor is the process of Replication hard to imagine. It will obviously remain impossible to make an exact copy of someone's brain: but this seems to be merely technically impossible. This imagined case is not deeply impossible, like the floating iron which Dr Gillett discussed. Professor Swinburne mentioned a similar case, when he mentioned the difference between its being he, or merely someone else who is like him, who might be resurrected after his death.

I then turned to the version which I called the Branch-Line Case. Since the New Scanner does not destroy my brain and body, I am able to meet my Replica. While we are talking, I learn that I am about to die. My Replica tells me not to be concerned. Since he is exactly like me, he will take up my life where I leave off. He will look after my children, and write the book that I have planned. Perhaps my friends and relatives will not even know that he is not me.

In such a case, would I have a reason to be concerned? On the 'Reductionist' view about personal identity which I and others defend – and which is close to the Buddhist view that Steven Collins discusses in his book *Selfless Persons*[28] – on this view, I should say: 'My prospect is about as good as ordinary survival. What it is rational to care about are the various psychological connections which, in ordinary cases, unify a person's life – the connections of character, memory, and the like. Since I am connected to my Replica in all these ways, I have no reason to be concerned.' But, though I accept the reductionist[29] view, I would find these claims hard to believe. It would be far easier to believe that what matters is that, soon, there will be no one living who is me. On this more natural view, though it may be some consolation that I shall have a Replica, my prospect is nearly as bad as ordinary death. This is what, in such a case, most of us would believe. We would think that personal identity is what matters.

In the Branch-Line Case, because my life overlaps with that of my Replica, it is fairly clear that he is not me. It is therefore fairly clear what would happen to me: I would be about to die. I also discussed several cases in which it would be much less clear what I should expect to happen. One example is what I called the Physical Spectrum. This is a range of different possible cases, in each of which some future person would have some proportion of the cells in my brain and body. This proportion would, in the different cases, range from all to none. Since my other cells would be replaced with exact duplicates, the resulting person would in each case be just like me. Once again, these cases are only, though they will always remain, technically impossible.

At the near end of this range, where only 1 per cent of my cells would be replaced, the resulting person would clearly be me. (I remark in passing that scientists have begun to transplant cells from one mammalian brain to another, and that the transplanted tissue does not, like other transplanted organs, provoke rejection by its new body.) In the case at the far end, which is Teletransportation – with complete 'replacement' – most of us would think that the resulting person would not be me. (If this is not our first reaction, we can be pushed towards it by considering the Branch-Line Case.) But, in cases in the middle of this range, what should I expect to happen? Suppose I know that before tomorrow half my cells – or three-quarters, or nine-tenths – will be replaced with exact duplicates. The natural question is, 'Would the resulting person be me, or would he merely be someone else who is just like me?'

A reductionist would claim: 'This is an empty question. These are not two different possibilities, either of which might be true. They are merely two descriptions of the same course of events. When you know which of your cells will be replaced, you know everything.' Here is a similar example. Suppose that a certain club, after existing for years, ceases to meet. Some years later certain people start up a club with the same name, the same rules, and (perhaps) some of the old members. Someone might ask, 'Did these people start up the very same club, or did they merely start up another club, which was exactly similar?' But most of us would regard this as an empty question. And we would think the same about the question of whether I had the same stereo system if I had replaced about half of its parts.

It is hard to take this view, however, when I think about my own future. On the reductionist view, it would be an empty question in these cases whether the resulting person would be me. Even without an answer to this question, I could know everything. But how can I know everything if I do not even know whether I shall live or die? If we imagine being in my place, most of us would think that this question must have an answer. We might say, 'Any future person must be either, and quite simply, me or someone else. If there will later be someone who is in pain, either I shall feel that pain, or I shan't. One of these must be true.'

Professor Swinburne suggested that, on the reductionist view, the answer in such a case is that the pain would be partly mine. I didn't intend to suggest that. I agree with him that we cannot make sense of this. This is well argued by Bernard Williams in his paper 'The Self and the Future',[30] though in most ways Williams's view is very different from Swinburne's.

On the reductionist view, our continued existence over time just involves various kinds of physical and psychological connection. In the imaginary cases I have just described, the physical connections would hold to different degrees. In other cases, some of them actual, it is the psychological connections which would be matters of degree. As our reactions to such cases shows, most of us are not reductionists. We do not believe that our own continued existence merely involves such connections. It seems to us to be a further fact, of a deep and simple kind: a fact which, in every case, must be either wholly present or wholly absent.

I then tried to show that our beliefs are false. There is no such further fact. I shall not summarize here how I tried to show this – except to remark that the question seems to me only in part one that might be settled by philosophical arguments, since it is also partly a matter of observable fact, or of how we should interpret various kinds of evidence.

If we give up these natural beliefs and become reductionists, this may affect some of our emotions. It is when we think about ourselves that the reductionist view is hardest to believe, and this is where the main effects would come. We have two kinds of concern about our own future. One is direct concern, such as our fear or dread of pain and death. The other is derivative concern: a concern about ourselves which results from having various other concerns. We want, for example, to remain active so that we can achieve certain ambitions, and protect those whom we love. If we became reductionists, this would not affect our derivative concern, but it might affect our direct concern.

Reconsider the Branch-Line Case. I claimed that, since the reductionist view is true, my relation to my Replica is as good as ordinary survival. This claim can be reversed. Ordinary survival is as bad as, or no better than, being destroyed and replicated. What we fear will be missing, after we die, is always missing. Our survival never involves the specially intimate relation in which we are inclined to believe.

If we grasped these truths, we would care less about our own future. We would have for ourselves in the future only the concern that we would have for a mere Replica. Suppose I know that tomorrow I shall be in pain. If I knew that, after my death, a Replica of me would be in pain, I would not fearfully anticipate this pain. And my relation to myself tomorrow is no closer than my relation to my Replica. It is hard to grasp this truth. When I forget the arguments, my belief in the further fact returns. But when I reconvince myself, this for a while stuns my direct concern.

There is a similar effect on my attitude to death. Instead of thinking, 'I shall die,' I should redescribe this fact in reductionist terms. I should think, 'After a certain time, none of the experiences that occur will be connected, in certain ways, to these present experiences.' In this redescription my death seems to disappear.

I turn, finally, to one of the moral conclusions which, if we became reductionists, we might draw. Suppose that, in the Branch-Line Case, I had earlier committed some crime. When I talk to Backup – as my Replica is called – I warn him to escape. But he is caught and convicted. The judge says: 'Given the gravity of Parfit's crime, you deserve a life sentence. Though you are not Parfit, between you and him there are all of the normal psychological connections. You have apparent memories of Parfit's life, and in every other way you resemble him. These connections are enough to make you guilty.' Backup protests: 'This is outrageous. These connections are irrelevant. I did not choose to resemble Parfit, or to have these apparent memories. I cannot deserve to be punished for what Parfit did before I even existed.'

Most of us would side with Backup. We would believe that, in the absence of personal identity, these psychological connections cannot carry with them desert or guilt. But on the reductionist view personal identity merely consists in these connections. Backup is not me only because, in this case, these connections do not have their normal cause: the continued existence of my brain. Is it the absence of this normal cause which makes Backup innocent? Most of us would answer no. We would think him innocent because he is not me.

This reply would show that we are not reductionists. The fact that Backup is not me seems to us to be different from, and more important than, the fact that the psychological connections have an abnormal cause. What we believe to be missing is not the normal cause, but the further fact: the specially intimate relation which we assume to be involved in our own continued existence over time. This is the fact which, on our view, carries with it desert and guilt.

Suppose next that we become reductionists: we decide that there is no such fact. An obvious conclusion follows. If it was only this fact which could carry with it desert and guilt, these have also disappeared. No one ever deserves to be punished for anything they did.

I hope these remarks may at least roughly suggest how, if we change our view about the nature of personal identity, we might also change our view about its significance.

DISCUSSION

ROBIN ATTFIELD. I wish to make a point about method. Gillett has referred to our concepts being stretched beyond recognition so that vertigo sets in when we consider some of these fictional cases. I wonder if the point could be better expressed in terms of coherence. It does seem to me that on a straightforward reading of the initial passage [in D. Parfit, *Reasons and Persons*] teletransportation, the identity of the person before the transition and the replica afterwards are just assumed. Is the idea that these two are identical, coherent? I would have thought that on a great many traditions this coherence would not be granted.

PARFIT. The passage you mention was just a piece of science fiction. In my discussion of this story I didn't assume that I and my Replica would be one and the same person. I did begin by assuming that it made sense to suppose that this might be true. But I argued later that this was not a real possibility, so we may agree.

Can I put a question to Dr Gillett? I imagined that my Replica would be psychologically exactly like me. I imagined this because I assumed that a person's mental states depend entirely on the states of his brain. I admitted that this might not be true. We might discover that the carrier of psychological continuity was not the brain, but something like the soul as Professor Swinburne describes it. But this doesn't seem to be your view. So why do you assume that, if some or all of my brain cells were replaced with exact duplicates, the resulting person would not be psychologically exactly like me?

GILLETT. I suspect that the function of any given cell is intimately connected with its history in which it has come to take on those functional characteristics.

PARFIT. This seems to me unlikely. If mental states do entirely depend on states of the brain, wouldn't they depend only on the *present* states of particular cells? And, to consider my example, we only need to *suppose* that this is true. You also suggested that my example made no sense. I assumed that I might survive if some percentage of my brain cells - say, 5 or 10 per cent - were replaced. Are you claiming that this isn't even coherent?

GILLETT. I am trying to say that if a particular part of the brain is taken away, it leaves you with that much less mental function, which is irreplaceable by physical means, and thus that your claims cannot be unproblematically allowed to apply to the mental life of persons.

PARFIT. In this range of cases I took, it seems to me that I do not have to say more, to defend the claim that we can coherently suppose that there might be some future person of whom it is true that *n* per cent of his brain is my brain, but the remainder is his. But why do I have to show that this is coherent? It seems so obvious. We think there must be a deep difference between my waking up and somebody else waking up who is just like me, but I do not think those are even different possibilities. So I am not begging any question about identity when I say that it is an empty question.

SWINBURNE. Dr Gillett seems to have an extraordinarily narrow conception of the coherent, and (an *ab hominem* point) it is a great deal narrower than Wittgenstein's. In the *The Blue Book* he discusses in a couple of pages the questions of personal identity, and he talks about, suppose we had an oscillating person, who, for example, purports to be me on even days and not on odd ones. He can make sense of this description; what he finds difficult is what we may say about 'Is it me?' or 'Isn't it me?', but he can set up the problem case without any difficulty. You think he cannot even set up the problem case.

GILLETT. It does indeed seem to us that what we are describing is able to be conceived, but my argument is that, in describing it, we make use of certain concepts, many of the presuppositions and conditions for the use of which are not obvious to us, so that when we move beyond the normal conditions of application, we may inadvertently stray from an area where their use is clear and unproblematic into an area in which many of the conceptual connections that we rely on in using them are no longer sustained.

PARFIT. Yes, I concede that. But I fail to see how that applies to simple replication.

GILLETT. Let us take your Branch-Line Case for instance. I meet my Replica. Which one is me? You describe it as if I am meeting my Replica. But you cannot describe it like that because there is no 'I' to identify him.

PARFIT. That is not my view. It is not my view that there are no true answers to questions about identity.

GILLETT. Well, is he looking at me? Or am I looking at me? Or am I looking at myself? Which is correct to say?

PARFIT. You are looking at him, and he is looking at you.

LOCKWOOD. I feel considerable unhappiness with what both of you have said. It seems to me that the character of our experience simply forces upon us the idea that there is a genuine fact of the matter, at any rate in most cases, as to whether I am the same person as a certain person occupying the same or a different body at an earlier time, or not. The unity of consciousness both at one time, and over time, strikes me as an inescapable feature of our mental lives. Gillett seems to be agreeing with this, but insisting, nevertheless, that we need not suppose that there is any 'deep referent' here, some mysterious kind of continuity lurking behind the facts that are immediately and casually observable. According to him, we are just talking about persons, and we know what persons are when we have command of the language in which we ascribe mental states to ourselves and to others. Parfit, on the other hand, thinks that it is part of the common-sense view that there is some genuine unity, some deep continuity, but that here common sense is mistaken.

My own feeling about all this is that philosophers have been led astray by Locke, who embarked on the project of trying to define personal identity in terms of psychological continuity, primarily memory, in Locke's case; but one might include continuities of personality and behaviour, the association between intention and action, and so forth. It seems to me that personal identity defies definition in these terms, and for reasons that are fairly easy to explain. Consider the analogy with the concept of gold (appealed to by J. L. Mackie in his book *Problems from Locke*).[31] People in the seventeenth century had, in one sense, a perfectly good concept of gold. They believed in the existence of a certain kind of stuff such that, if one were presented with a yellowish slab of metal, there was a fact of the matter as to whether it was really gold or not. Moreover, they recognized implicitly that this question could not simply be identified with the question of whether or not it passed certain tests – resistance to certain acids, malleability, and so forth. It remained a possibility for them that something might pass all the tests currently available, and yet not be gold, or even fail to pass some of the tests, and yet be gold all the same, in a different form. And this is because, for them, as for us, what it was for something to *be* gold was for it to have a certain kind of inherent nature, the nature in question being whatever it is, in paradigmatic instances of gold, that underlies and explains its characteristic detectable features: its density, malleability, chemical properties, and so forth. Formerly, however, people were not in a position to say what this underlying nature was; we, on the other hand, are, or think we are. To be gold, we now think, is to be composed of atoms with atomic number 79; for it is this that provides the deep explanation of its colour, chemical properties, electrical conductivity, and so on.

Personal identity, so I believe, has a similar logic. For A to be the same person as B is not, I would argue, merely a matter of A and B standing in certain relations of psychological continuity – continuities of memory, personality, or behaviour. It is for there to hold between A and B whatever underlying continuity provides, in the normal case, the deep explanation for such superficial, casually observable continuities as those of memory, personality, the matching of action to intention, and so on. And what this underlying continuity is cannot be determined simply by conceptual analysis. It is a substantive, scientific, or – some might think – metaphysical question. Some, such as Swinburne, would appeal in this context to the persistence of an immaterial soul. Others, such as myself, would look rather to a continuity of physiological structure within a continuously existing brain. I think, however, that in order for this to account satisfactorily for the character of our experience, there has to be more to matter, or at least the matter of the brain, than meets the physicist's eye.

From this point of view, Gillett is wrong to suggest that there is no 'deep referent'. And I also think that, in many at least of Parfit's puzzle cases, there will, after all, be an answer to the question who is who, roughly along the lines of: I go wherever (the relevant part of) my brain goes. Reppy, for example, is not me, according to theory. Since he does not have my (former) brain, it follows, *a fortiori*, that there does not exist between the present Reppy and the former me a continuity of structure within *the same* continuously existing brain. Reppy's a 'ringer', therefore, just as a fake Rembrandt is still a fake, even if it is a perfect copy of a genuine Rembrandt. That is assuming that what provides the deep explanation of the more superficial psychological continuities is indeed a continuity of structure within a continuously existing brain. As

I said just now, it seems to me a perfectly possible, albeit scientifically implausible, view that what actually provides the deep explanation for these psychological continuities is the persistence of an immaterial soul. In that case, whether Reppy is me depends on whether he has my soul, whether the powers that be have so arranged things that my soul passes into his body, though there is no obvious reason why it should.

PARFIT. On your view, whether some future person will be me depends on whether there will be continuity of structure within the same brain. If that was what we believed, we would think that, in my imagined cases, the question, 'Will he be me?' must always have a definite answer, which must be either a simple yes or a simple no? This is what most of us are inclined to believe. And this couldn't be so if your view was true. Though your view may be true, it isn't the natural view.

LOCKWOOD. I grant you that if I am right in thinking that what constitutes my continued existence over time is a continuity of structure within a continuously existing brain, then there may be imaginable cases in which the question of whether a certain future individual is me does not admit of a definite yes or no answer. Suppose, for example, that someone were to open up my skull, insert a wooden spoon into my brain, and stir. And suppose, further, that by subjecting the brain to a powerful electric field or something, it were possible to persuade the nerve-cells to join up again so that the brain could continue to function, but that the connections were all completely different from before, implying total loss of memory, change of personality, and so on. Then this new individual would not be me, according to my view, for there would not be the requisite continuity of physiological structure. But now suppose the disruption to be significant but less than total: the brain is only partially scrambled before we switch on the electric field to make the cells join up. Then I agree that there might be nothing in the facts to warrant one's saying either that it was definitely me or that it was definitely not me. I am inclined to doubt, however, whether this would be an appropriate thing to say of any actual cases of brain damage: if the degree of disruption was compatible with the restoration or consciousness, then I would think, as a contingent matter, that there would have to be sufficient continuity of physiological structure to justify one's regarding the original person as having survived, however incapacitated or otherwise altered.

STEVEN COLLINS. What diverted me from philosophy to the study of Buddhism was a tremendous sense of frustration with this notion that what we should do in philosophy is consider what we *normally* think. It occurred to me that the planet probably contained all sorts of people who thought quite differently from the way 'we' *normally* do. One of the interests of Buddhism in this particular context is that it involves beliefs which, although not empirically verified (Buddhism does claim that they are verifiable), do not deny science-fiction cases. Buddhism constitutes beliefs and ideals which have been held and aspired to by a very large number of people throughout history and which should be taken seriously. This does not mean they cannot be wrong!

Let me sketch out an argument, starting from a paper by Peter Geach on reincarnation.[32] He suggested that it is perfectly conceivable that somebody might turn out to remember episodes in the life of Julius Caesar, and that this could be checked by historians for accuracy. By every test that historians could apply, his memory might indeed be that of Julius Caesar. But, he argues, this would be more interesting to historians (as a new source of information about Caesar) than to philosophers, for it would not in itself help us to decide the relationship between the rememberer and Julius Caesar. In one perfectly obvious sense of the words, he could say 'I am not Julius Caesar.' Now a Buddhist construal of this case would be as follows: such memories of a former life are perfectly possible: they are presented in the first-person mode, 'I did it.' It is also perfectly obvious that these reported memories of Caesar's life would not form part of the rememberer's life as it is now. Therefore this seems to be a case where the notion of quasi-memory is perfectly appropriate. What would be the relationship between those two lives? What sorts of pattern of concern could Caesar have had for the rememberer and vice versa? The relationship between the two lives would involve, to be sure, a rather unusual pattern of causation. But then there are many connections between beings and things in the universe which have not been anticipated. The connections between these two lives would be a special case of the connections which exist between all sentient beings. We could say that what Caesar did affects the rememberer in a particular way, more than it affects others. Caesar's relationship to him could not be one of simple prudence or self-interest. It would have to be one simply of general concern for the well-being of a person to whom he happened to stand in a peculiar causal relation.

These thought experiments do not have to involve bizarre science-fiction cases, because many Buddhist meditators have led their lives for 2,500 years in terms of the alleged perceptions I have described.

PARFIT. Though I doubt that there are such apparent memories which fit earlier lives, I would agree with much of what you say. There's a striking similarity between some strands in Buddhist thought and the view that I and others hold. Buddha also claimed that most of us have false beliefs about our own nature, and that if we grasped the truth – what he called the 'No Self View' – this would have various good effects.

GILLETT. My position is that we understand the mental lives of persons solely because we identify and re-identify over time (and in different experiences) continuing conscious subjects whom we come to know as persons. These persons have natural limitations and develop and refine their mental faculties over an extended set of experiences. They also exert an integrating reflection and inventiveness within their mental lives to which they stand almost as an artist to his creation. For these reasons, I maintain that a person has an identity as a mental subject which is presupposed by the conceptual repertoire we apply to his mental functions.

6

Persons and Selves

ROM HARRÉ

THE CASE FOR SYNTHETIC UNITY

There has been a marked tendency in recent philosophy to use the word 'person' for the most general category encompassing human beings. Persons are said to have mental powers and to be embodied; they are to be morally protected, as well as held morally responsible for at least some of their doings. It is persons who are said to be aware of the world, persons who act and feel. The self, the still centre of experience, that to which conscious states of all kinds are ascribed, has disappeared from the philosophical scene, the last wraithlike appearance of the ghost of the Cartesian ego. Yet, although the fact of human identity seems to be secured through the use of the concept of 'persons', it is not clear that our sense of self has thereby been accounted for. Persons, human beings as individuals, are recognized in public and collective practices, conversing, praising and blaming, playing rugby and then commenting on the game, and so on. But it seems to me quite plain that the persons recognized are not the unified subjective organizations of memory, perception, agency, and so on.

An argument for holding on to this distinction in some form can be found in the fact that simpler 'minded' beings such as chimpanzees seem to live in a framework which includes the recognition of the fact of personal identity, while at the same time there is evidence to suggest that their sense of identity is weak. Here are rudimentary persons who are probably not rudimentary selves. Contemplating the lives of such creatures, one may wonder what it is like to be a chimp. In one way it must be very like being a human being. One's experience of the physical world is centred on oneself, and specifically on one's head. When a chimp feels pain in a foot, it apprehends it at much the same location as a foot for a human being. Functionally, at least, a chimp must perceive the physical world as a thing among things. But we have no reason to believe that a chimp could formulate such a thought. In short, we have no reason to think that even the most sophisticated chimp has a concept of itself as a subject of affective and activity-oriented attributes. Even the famous experiment in which a chimp was shown its face in a mirror with a spot of paint on its forehead and tried to scrape it off shows only a grasp of indexicality to itself as a public being. It is a self-consciousness of stage fright, which need involve no self-awareness at all, but only a sense of how others may see our public and social being.

The concept of 'person' seems to be embedded in all sorts of communal human practices. We could say that a human being acquires a concept of 'self' in gaining mastery over pushing and pulling, hitting and being hit, in peekaboo game, in praising and blaming the public performances of himself and others, in promising, and so on. But chimps have social practices not unlike some of these. Hence, if human beings have, in addition, a sense of self as an inner unity, what is its nature, and whence does it come? Tradition offers two possible answers. First, it might be that human beings, each and almost everyone of us, make an empirical discovery; 'Eureka! I'm a self.' We might imagine each of us as a kind of infant Husserl,[1] sliding down the epochés to a realization that there must be a centre of the *Eigenheit*, and that it is 'I'! But student philosophers, with a cheerful confidence acquired in disposing of the resemblance theory of primary qualities, move on to dispose of the empirical self. The second answer was invented to deal with Hume's troubles with his elusive self.[2] The 'self' is no longer a kind of thing. Rather, it is a structure, a unity imposed on the flux of sensations by an active, minded being. I think this is right, but in pursuing the question of how it is possible, and making some guesses as to how each of us manages to achieve it, we will stumble on some quite startling results.

Interestingly, Hume seems to have had a synthetic theory before Kant.[3] But it was Kant who thought that a synthesis required an active noumenal being – that is, one who is beyond all possible experience. In other words, syntheses do not just happen; they are brought about. But we can do better than this, for we can do without the noumenal. There are plenty of active beings in the universe with an interest in synthesizing minds. Colloquially, each of us call them 'Mum' and 'Dad'. Hence I propose to update synthesis theory, drawing from the rather similar ideas of Mead[4] and Vygotsky.[5] There is a social source for the inner organization of the conscious contents, emotional fluxes, intentions to act, and so on of human beings, just as remote from personal experience as the noumenal, but not half so mysterious. My argument for this thesis turns on the spelling out and defence of what I call the 'axiom of development'.

This axiom has three clauses. First, people treat babies as persons from the moment of their first appearance. (This use of 'their', readers may be interested to learn, was suppressed by Act of Parliament in the early years of the nineteenth century, an act about as effective as that suppressing wigs.) Second, by copying their every word and gesture as best he can, a baby seems to be treating those around him as persons. Third, among the ways of speaking and acting that a baby imitates is the way in which other people treat him as a person. No empirical discovery of an inner self is even hinted at in this story of public events.

In acquiring these (partially linguistic, partially deictic) practices, a baby also acquires a concept of himself. In teaching infants to talk, point to things, and so on, people-makers provide their infant with a sense of self. That is the developmental axiom; but it needs to be spelled out in some detail if it is to carry conviction as a theory of the unity of mind.

The undefined, inexplicated element in it is the idea of being treated as a person. What is it to be so treated? I want to emphasize three main ways of being treated as a person. First, there is a linguistic way. There are special ways of referring to persons, by proper names, or, more usually with infants, pet names. And there are special things that are said to people about people; characteristically, people are ascribed intentions, wants, emotions, feelings, memories, and the like, even in the cradle. Second, there is psychological symbiosis. Long before there is the faintest hint of a discourse controlled by the infant, mothers, particularly, ascribe very sophisticated cognitive abilities and morale sensibilities to their children. Recent work by developmental psychologists has shown that mothers (and I daresay fathers will also be included in this claim when they have been studied) interact with their offspring in terms of psychological attributes that they assign to the infant. Third, there is the way in which we comment on the quality and worth of other people's ideas, judgements, actions, and so on. This often takes the form of an epistemic commentary, and employs phrases like 'I think he's right,' 'I don't believe he's really ill,' 'I'm sure she'll come,' and so on.

It is worth noting that all these ways of treating infants are characteristic of how we treat favoured domestic animals. But only very few, if any, of the latter ever pick up the trick for themselves. In learning these practices, I will claim, a nascent member of the human community picks up the concept of 'person'. I will argue that it is that concept with serves as a source of a unifying concept of 'self'. Students of Mead will recognize this suggestion as an amplification of Mead's idea of the origin of the self in public practices. Admirers of Vygotsky will recognize that mental organization is imposed on a native endowment that lacks intrinsic order by appropriation from public practice.

THE GENESIS OF THEORIES

It is good practice in scientific circles to draw on a well-understood analogue in formulating a theory for a new, ill-understood domain. In this case, the ill-understood domain is that of the formulation of a concept of 'self'. As an organizing concept, it could perhaps be compared with theoretical concepts in the sciences, some of which seem to facilitate the imposition of order on many disparate phenomena. Thus the concept of natural selection helped Darwin and all generations of biologists since him to bring into an orderly structure of phylogenetic relationships the myriad organic forms available to empirical discovery and investigation. It does seem to make sense to compare the role of the concept of 'self' in our individual psychological economies with that of a theoretical concept in natural science. But can we push the comparison further and use the way in which concepts like natural selection come into being to illuminate a possible origin for the organizing concept of 'self'?

Darwin[6] gives a fairly detailed account of the genesis of his famous concept, though some commentators have argued that there are other sources for it besides those made much of by Darwin. At any rate, even if Darwin's account is merely pedagogy, it is highly illuminating philosophically. He begins by carefully setting out three components of a theory, regarding the breeding of animals and plants. There is the exploitation of domestic variation through selection of animals and plants with advantageous characteristics, from which to breed the next generation. This leads to an accumulation of changes in a direction that satisfies the stock-breeder or seedsman, and thus a new variety or breed is established. Now take this conceptual *structure* into nature. There is natural variation from generation to generation, and natural novelty in the appearance of new species. The analogy suggests that there should be a process, *natural selection*, that acts on natural variation so that favourable (to that environment) changes accumulate, giving rise to natural novelties, new species.

In a similar way, I suggest that each of us forms a concept of 'self' which is analogous to the concept of 'person' that controls the way in which we are treated by others, and the way in which we treat them. This concept of 'self' will have some of the characteristics of the local concept of 'person'; and if that concept varies from culture to culture, so might the concepts of 'self' indigenous to a human population. In the case of Darwin's famous evolutionary theory, most of us believe that there is indeed a process that has actually occurred in the world, a process referred to as natural selection. The theory would have been helpful heuristically, but not quite so important perhaps, if it had turned out that nature was not like that at all, and that there was no such process. There are many cases in the natural sciences in which a concept is so useful and powerful in organizing a field of phenomena that we adopt it regardless of whether anything corresponds to it in reality. For instance, the idea that light travels in straight lines has an obvious analogue in everyday experience of projectiles, and exploitation of the analogy has been of inestimable value in bringing order to the elementary phenomena of light, and is still in use, even though we now know that this image bears little, if any, resemblance to the mysterious 'real nature of light'. The utility of a theoretical concept may be quite impressive, even when we have grave doubts about its referential veracity, so to speak. The same is true, I believe, of the concept of 'self'. We come to believe that we are selves; or, to put it another way, in being initiated into the kinds of practices sketched above, we come to master the use of such a concept. The concept helps us to think about ourselves, to reflect on our thoughts and doings as our own. But there may be no inner entity, no self. Or, to switch to yet another rhetoric, although it may seem as if the term 'myself' is like the term 'gold' for example, and refers to a real essence, an inner core that is the real me, there may be no such core. But given that this sketch more or less adequately picks out the role of concepts of 'self' and their formal relationship to concepts of 'person', just how is this relationship mediated in real life? We shall find a clue in studying how psychological and moral attributes are predicated of people.

TREATING MYSELF AS ONE OF US

Instead of vainly trying to bring off a phenomenological reduction of experience in pursuit of the centre of the *Eigenheit*, we shall study conditions for the possibility of certain kinds of talk, first-person talk. One of the most significant ways in which I treat myself as a person is to talk to and of myself as one. But before discussing this level of sophistication, it is essential to say a word about more humdrum first-person ways of speaking, those that begin with a simple 'I'. Suppose we are out in the family car, and Father, unaccustomed to driving the family, is taking the curves in fairly sporting fashion. He may hear a voice from the back, 'I'm going to be sick!' What are we to make of it?

The least interesting aspect of the utterance just now, it seems to me, is its status as a true or false report of a current experiential state. The illocutionary force seems likely to dominate the conversation. It is a warning, but is it a 'final warning' or merely a notice of trouble ahead? Most important, who said it? 'I' is indexical for persons, and we need to have someone privy to the occasion of its use to tell us to whom it referred. Even if it turns out that for their own amusement the junior passengers have been crying wolf, it is the sincerity or insincerity of their avowels that is likely to be central to further negotiations. There are many occasions on which the performative force – in a request, for example – may so outweigh the issue of veracity that only the former is taken up. To prove this point, Austin[7] cites the act of promising, but there are many other cases – for example, a childish bid for nocturnal attention couched in terms of a request for a drink.

So far, no hypothesis of an inner self has seemed to be called for to understand the philosophical grammar of these utterances. The public person has done quite nicely. But further pursuit of any of the conversations sketched above will tend to raise questions of epistemic warrant and the like. Was this the right thing to say under the circumstances of just that feeling? There is not much room for doubt and renegotiation with nausea, but whether one is sickening for something or just tired may be a matter requiring careful analysis of feeling. Sometimes, therefore, I am required to take up epistemic attitudes to my own first-order utterances. How do I know how to do this? It can scarcely be a native endowment! I suggest that I learn to do this in the way that I learn to do most other things, by imitating someone else who is doing it. And the one to whom they are most likely to be doing it is me. When someone else gives an epistemic commentary on my avowels, I am the other to him. 'I think you are more tired than ill'; 'I don't find your line on that very convincing'; 'Gosh' I didn't know you knew how to do that!'; Fancy you not knowing how to do that!', and so on.

In making this kind of remark, the other is likely to have been reflecting on the kind of warrant that I may have had for my initial remark. Was I in a good position to see which was the winner? Is it likely, given my rubicund flush, that the feeling was nausea? Is it likely, given my reputation for lying about small things, that I really saw Halley's comet with the naked eye? Here we have a cluster of those practices which Wittgenstein[8] calls 'language games'; though not identical, they do resemble one another in one crucial respect. They have a tendency to induce me to reflect on my warrants in much the same way as the other has been reflecting on them. Small wonder then if I begin to play his language games to express the results of my excogitations. But now we have a dangerous situation. The necessity of expressing my assessments of my own avowels has drawn me into the habit of following a certain grammatical model, that in which the other utters a judgement whose first pronoun indexes the judgement to him, and whose second pronoun refers to me, a public person. But when I use the models to whom does the second utterance of 'I' refer? I am quite used to keeping my thoughts and feelings, sensations and opinions, to myself. For me, the distinction between public face and private being is routine. No wonder, then, that I am inclined to slip into following the model all the way, and am likely, therefore, to fall prey to the idea that there is an inner self to which my private thoughts and feelings are annexed. But, paradoxically, it is only because I slip into such a belief that a centred organization of thought, feeling, actions, and memory does emerge in the nascent person who becomes me. It is like perspective; without it, I wouldn't be able to find my way around, but the road isn't really narrower at the horizon than it is at my feet.

This can be illustrated by the kind of qualified performative utterance in which there is an iterated first-person device, usually the pronoun. The statement 'I'm going to be sick,' indexed to the speaker, serves as a fairly strong warning. But if it is prefaced by an indication of epistemic attitude, the performative force can be strengthened or weakened. Thus, 'I'm quite sure I'm going to be sick' and 'I think I'm going to be sick' are respectively stronger and weaker warnings than the simple avowel. But how is the performative force weakened? I suggest that the epistemic qualification portrays the result of reflection on the grounds for the simple unqualified avowel, reflection in which that avowel is treated as if it were uttered by a third person. As such, it is not part of what it is to feel sick when uttered by the commentator. So 'I think he is going to be sick' is a comment on a putative empirical prediction of future behaviour, for which we may well be asked to produce evidence. To comment in this fashion on my own avowels is to take the attitude of another towards them, and to reflect on the strength of the grounds of that other. A declaration of a qualified epistemic attitude weakens the performative force because it expresses a realization of the relative weakness of these grounds. So, whereas the original unqualified utterance can be assessed for sincerity or insincerity, the embedded utterance is assessed for truth or falsity, or for the qualification appropriate to a prediction. In order to reflect on the grounds for my expression of some psychological or somatic condition, I have to pay attention to my state. But to what is this attributed? And here arises the temptation to proceed from the grammatical model which uses a notional subject, to a belief in an inner self. Moreover, it is easy to see how this form of talk could be one of the practices through which a concept of 'self', as the organizing concept of experience, is acquired.

On this view the study of self-consciousness would be the investigation of the conditions necessary for the well-controlled use of a certain form of talk. In this context, self-consciousness is not consciousness of self, but the ability to use certain grammatical forms which are typical of those of talk in which we express epistemic attitudes to both our own declarations and those of others. Metaphysically, the existence of these forms of talk can now be seen to be explicable without recourse to the hypothesis of a real entity corresponding to the embedded pronoun. Parenthetically, it is worth remarking that this line of thought casts doubt on the viability of the idea that memory is the faculty that lies behind the apparent inner unity of self. Only if it is already possible to predicate inner states of the same notional subject could a remembered state be tied into the 'me' sequence. There are no Husserlian marks that distinguish my experiences as mine, so far as I can see. The use of memory to unify the sequence of mental states, feelings, and so on as mine is parasitic on a capacity to predicate states of a notional subject. And that makes the grammatical models that are available in a socio-linguistic community fundamental.

TESTS AND CONSEQUENCES

If the ideas sketched above are right, then one would expect different cultures, with different language games of self-ascription and hence different grammatical models, to produce people with rather different senses of self. Many languages have more refined pronominal systems and demonstratives than English, which is somewhere in the lower third of a world table of expressiveness. In standard English the pronoun system lacks a means of marking social distance. The third-person plural is insensitive both to gender and to the presence or absence from the occasion of utterance of other members of the collective of which the speaker is a member. Social, spatial, and temporal distance between a speaker and others to whom he makes reference is not easily expressible in English, nor is there any sensitivity in the pronoun system to family relationships. We are adept at such makeshifts as 'you lot', 'we here today', and the like. Societies differ in the relative balance between the individual and the collective in certain psychological states and practices. We might do well, therefore, to look for some kind of empirical test of the self theory presented in this paper in comparative anthropology. It won't do simply to cite differences in linguistic practices and grammatical models of the sort described above. The position attributed, albeit wrongly, to Sapir and Whorf, that linguistic forms determine the shape of the mind, is certainly too strong. Grammatical differences are clued to the possibility of differing organizations of experience, but the linguistic evidence must be tied in with ethnographic differences if it is to be convincing. I shall canvass support from three different peoples: the traditional Eskimos, the Japanese, and the Amerindians of Yucatan.

Traditional Eskimos

Eskimo languages are variants of Inuit, an agglutinative language which builds up word-sentences by adding suffixes and affixes to a root in a rigidly fixed order. As far as I can make out – and I am deeply indebted to Colin Irwin of Syracuse University for help with this language – person reference is accomplished with only two suffixes, '–ik' and '–tok', the former indexical of the speaker, the latter referring to any other person or group of persons. One might be inclined to treat these suffixes as demonstrative adjectives, rather than pronouns proper. In making a self-predication of a psychological state, an Eskimo would say the equivalent of 'Hunger here now,' rather than 'I am hungry,' for example. This suggests a much weaker sense of self than is prevalent among speakers of the Indo-European languages of our cultural community. But does ethnographic evidence support this hypothesis? Ethnographers have described Eskimo life in considerable detail, and it is not difficult to find evidence for such a weaker sense of self. Eskimo emotional states appear to be much more socially dependent than ours. Isolated Eskimos, in so far as they can be observed, seem to be stolid, neither cheerful nor depressed. But once they become part of a community (a family, say) they quickly take on the emotional tone of the community, whether they are intimately bound up with its concerns or not. This seems to go for a pretty wide spectrum of emotions. including grief, joy, and guilt. It is said that *all* moral issues are referable only to relationships of the individual within a family group. The active, decision-making unit is not the individual human being, but the family. This is apparent even in Eskimo theory of art. Ethnographers agree that Eskimo sculptors do not regard themselves as actively imposing on passive material a form which pre-existed in thought. Instead they feel themselves to be releasing a being that was already latent in the horn, tusk, or whatever they are carving. (This theory has also held a minor place in Western accounts of the creative process, of course,) Finally, I report an astonishing practice, of which I have been unable to obtain independent confirmation, however, It is said that there is a form of Eskimo singing in which one person shouts into the mouth of another, who then shapes the sound into a melody. Adding together the evidence of empathetic emotions, a group morality, and a generally passive attitude to action, we have some support for the idea that the paucity of grammatical models for self-reflective talk is part of a cultural complex in which self-reflection and individual self-attention are minimal.

The Japanese

But there are other axes along which alien and exotic selves might differ from ours. In elementary teach-youself-Japanese textbooks, Japanese ways of referring to persons are translated into the usual repertoire of English pronouns. But careful study suggests that this is thoroughly misleading. The first-person expression 'watashi' does seem to be a fairly good equivalent of the English 'I'. However, there are at least *nine* – and some linguists would say more – variants of it, marking levels of formality in speech ('watakushi' rather than 'watashi'), gender differences ('atashi' for women), and even a kind of dialect vulgarity ('boku' used by men). The Emperor has his own special pronoun for official pronouncements. But there any close resemblance ends. Second-person reference is usually achieved through a system of honorific suffixes. We all know '–san', but it is only one in a chain of five, which run from very polite, '–sama', through declining levels of respect, '–san', '–kun', to the diminutive, '–tyan'. In an excellent paper on Japanese self-referential expressions, Jane Bachnik points out that, whereas in English, 'I' has one anchor point, namely the speaker, Japanese self-referential terms require two, because they are sensitive to the social distance between speaker and addressee. This appears both in the quasi-pronouns for first-person reference and in the system of honorifics for second-person reference. Finally, the translation of third-person referential devices as 'he', 'she', and so on is also misleading. Such reference not only distinguishes in-group from out-group (as indeed do first- and second-person systems, a complication, that I have passed over), but is achieved by the use of demonstrative adjectives, roughly 'this person' or 'that person' or persons. We are presented with a system which exhibits an extraordinary sensitivity to social relationships and social categories.

In knowing all this – and the above is a mere outline of a system of daunting complexity – what sort of sense of self would we expect a Japanese person to acquire? It seems obvious that his attention must always be on his relationships to others. His place in the collectivity matters, for without sensitivity to it, he can hardly 'talk "proper" '! So he is surely driven to thinking of himself not so much in relation to his own thoughts and feelings, but in relation to other people. The Japanese sense of self must be 'open-ended' or 'diffuse', to use two metaphors from anthropological writing about Japanese psychology. But what of the ethnography?

Parallel to this aspect of Japanese psychology is a complex system of social relationships, marked by steep grades of respect and condescension and a formal rigidity in their expression. Morsbach and Tyler[9] have written about the gift culture of Japan, in which exact values, both monetary and symbolic, mark the various relationships in which one can stand to others. A steady flow of gifts floods up and down the system, ritually expressing, and so maintaining, its structure. Once again, it is obvious that attention must be paid to all the minutiae of these relationships and to the calculation of the appropriate value of a present. This practice seems to mark pretty much the same aspect of Japanese relationships as does the elaboration of the language of personal reference.

The point at which self-understanding and agency intersect is the moral order of a society. Our moral order is based on ideas of individual moral choice and individual intentional action. Our 'moral' emotions – guilt, for example – suffuse the whole of our mental life, spreading from some cankerous centre, the memory of an action of mine, the intention for which was the last stage in an individual train of deliberation. According to students of Japanese life, such as Ruth Benedict[10] and Ivan Morris,[11] the Japanese moral order, like all other Japanese self-referential practices, is bipolar. Moral issues can never be isolated as the personal problems and triumphs of a single individual. They are always conceived of as relational, as defined by two poles, the Japanese 'self' and some other person, with whom the individual has definite, and usually asymmetrical, social relations. The moral life of a Japanese person is compartmentalized; hence there are successes and failings relative to the world of work, relative to the obligations and relationships within the family, relative to the state and the Emperor, and so on. Ruth Benedict suggests that there are five main systems of responsibilities, obligations, moral emotions, and so on, each defined relative to a distinct set of others. In his moral life, a Japanese who is clearly an individual when considered as a person, must be multiple, or a set of selves. The shame that diffuses that part of the psyche which has to do with others in the world of work cannot diffuse into the system within which a Japanese manages his home life. Obviously the Japanese are not exotic beings, as Martians might be, and there is, in this compartmentalization something we can recognize to a lesser degree in our own moral life, but something that plays a far larger role in the life of the Japanese.

Taken together, the language and the social practices of which it is an essential component facilitate a form of life in which the 'self' is ontologically different from the centre of our personal being. It is relational, not atomistic.

The Amerindians of the Yucatan

For my final example I turn to the Amerindians of the Yucatan. I am indebted to Bill Hanks for information about these people; his painstaking studies of their self-referential and deictic language games have been exemplary in their patient, comprehensive care. The Amerindians of the Yucatan have a personal reference system, approximately a system of pronouns, which, like that in English, is insensitive to social status. Indeed, it is a remarkably simple system. But the language of these people is elaborated along another grammatical dimension so as to be extraordinarily sensitive to spatial and temporal locations of persons, things, and events relative to the speaker. There are more than twenty distinct demonstratives for place and moment, compared with the six with which we make do in English. For instance, 'now today' and 'now this moment' are lexically distinct in Yucatan. Expressions of location in Yucatan mark distinctions for which we have no resources – for instance, tactual, visual, and audible distance. I think we can say that these people are embodied as distinctive individuals more precisely and finely than we are, find that they pay greater attention to the spatial and temporal environment than we do. I have no detailed ethnography to draw on, but it is worth recalling that these people live in a jungle so dense that even the great stone monuments of the Maya were swallowed up and lost for generations. Is it too fanciful to think of the Amerindian sense of self as more closely connected with awareness of physical time and place than ours or, for that matter, that of the Japanese? For the latter, the sense of self is tied into a social environment as fraught with danger as the jungles of the Yucatan peninsula may be for their indigenous peoples.

SUMMARY

I have tried to establish a working distinction between the concept of a person, the publicly recognized human individual who is the focus of the overt practices of social life, and the sense that a person has of his own being. Most important for selfhood are ways of talking about persons. By imitating the way people talk about us, as public persons, we acquire a knack for talking about ourselves. In picking this up, we are enabled to comment on our own speech acts and other public doings, and particularly on expressions of feeling and other avowels. But in contemplating our own states, we need at least a notional peg on which to hang them, and since the states which often matter most are subjective, the public person who may have good manners or who may be Machiavellian enough to keep such things to himself, won't do as such a subject of predication. Hence a second self-referential expression appears on the grammatical scene, offering a model for metaphysical elaboration of an ontology of persons which conjures up an inner being, a noumenal source of inner order. But a more economical theory would ascribe the source of that order not to the noumenal realm but to the people-makers of the culture, the parents in whose ocean of talk we all begin our public lives, as junior members of symbiotic dyads. Support for this way of looking at things can be found in anthropology; as we have seen, it is not hard to find examples of cultures whose distinctive language games seem to be closely interwoven with other practices of their societies, in such a way as to seem to cry out for the hypothesis that the sense of self is also different.

DISCUSSION

BASIL MITCHELL. What happens, for example, when an Eskimo learns English? Because it would seem to follow from what you said that the Eskimo, to the extent that he or she can speak English, automatically forms a barrier around himself. For in learning English, he also comes to think of himself as a self. Can something which is so significant as whether or not one has a self happen quite so simply?

HARRÉ. It is uncertain whether in learning English an Eskimo does acquire the same kind of mental state as we possess. There is a lot of evidence that bilingualism never involves an equal relationship: the second language is glossed in terms of structures which we acquired in learning the first language. I have been told by Colin Irving, whose wife is a bilingual Eskimo (Canadian English is her second language), brought up as an Eskimo, that, according to her, Eskimos have considerable difficulties in understanding ordinary Canadian moral stances – what we would call individual moral responsibility – because they tend to think of moral problems in terms of groups. I am told that the Eskimo are keen on blood feuds. They think that the family is the object of moral censure if one member of it misbehaves.

The warden of an autistic children's home near Oxford said at a meeting recently that autistic children have a similar difficulty in managing the idea of individual moral responsibility. They also, as is well known, have great difficulty in handling the complexities of pronouns. But once they have learnt the pronoun system, there is a dramatic change in their behaviour. That is, their sense of moral responsibility seems to go hand in hand with their capacity to handle this system which involves the understanding of the self as a distinct being.

ROGER TRIGG. Are you saying that our concept of self involves acquiring language, and that one cannot have a concept of self without acquiring it?

HARRÉ. No, I was very careful to say that there were many collective practices which were involved in acquiring the concept of 'self'. Language is one of the easier to examine, because we can write down speech and study its evolving structure. But it arises also from moral and material practices. Jerome Bruner argues that the acquisition of this kind of language skill is closely related to the development of the peekaboo game, which takes about 18 months to work its way through its whole cycle. He shows that the game is widespread among cultures with complex languages, and that it is one of the ways in which an infant begins to see itself as a possible object in the eyes of another. This game changes its character and moves through a whole series of stages, and runs parallel with the capacity to make these kinds of self-referential moves. It has, in the language of developmental psycholinguistics, didactic functions. Bruner, of course, is very interested in how this is related to the growth of particular linguistic capacities.

WILLIAM FULFORD. Do you see the Eskimo as not having a concept of self? Or has the Eskimo a concept of self only in the collective, consisting of several bodies, whereas my concept of self is made up partly of my hand, my foot, and my memories and all the rest of it. Do they have a concept of self? Or is it embodied differently?

HARRÉ. For us, the public person and the inner self are differentiated, We are familiar with things like hypocrisy, lying, tact, and so on; and it is in this *public* realm that the distinction is regularly made. So that it becomes a philosophical problem for people like Derek Parfit and myself to try to explain how it is that there *appears* to be an inner unity. Now the crux of the argument from cultural diversity would be to say that a relation between public person and inner self is not established, nor are they rigidly differentiated, among the Eskimos. So for the Eskimo to lie is rare and problematic. The idea of an individual being morally responsible just makes them laugh: the Eskimo does not think that stealing can be done by an individual. Groups of people can steal from other groups, but individuals logically cannot steal, since both taking and owning are defined collectively. So the person – self distinction is extremely weak. Their morality is to be understood with the concept of 'person'. That is, an Eskimo's moral being, his moral qualities, are the qualities of the family to which he belongs. There is a curious problem for Western law in applying the concept of 'murder' in Eskimo society, since having a socially given murderous *name* is a defence.

GUY SCOTT. Are there any biological constants between human beings? In particular, is morality, or moral sense, as much a biological constant as having two legs, for instance?

HARRÉ. I do think there are biological constants, and that they are reflected in first-order talk. I think they are very closely related to perception, which is really a subject for physiologists. Psychologists get into this at their peril. The biological organism experiences the world as a structured entity, as both the perceiver and the centre of a spatio-temporal framework, which has many culturally distinct versions. This is the kind of centring upon which the use of first-order predicates as applied to or avowed by individual human beings is based. So we should expect any creatures of a certain level of biological organization to be capable of indexical speech of the first order. Once you give a chimpanzee the capacity to be a predicating creature of first order, that will do it.

MICHAEL RUSE. Are we to expect to see, say, chimpanzees and humans showing what looks like moral behaviour from the outside, even when they do not have the categorical imperative?

HARRÉ. I do not think it is gross anthropomorphism to see the behaviour of adult chimpanzees to juniors, even older siblings to younger siblings, in terms of moral concepts. I am quite happy to ascribe certain moral attributes to Washoe (the chimpanzee who knows a type of sign language), but I would be very uneasy to go on doing it indiscriminately. The second level of linguistic capacity, the ability to comment on the quality of first-order speech acts (or gesture acts), is something which is distinctively human. It involves taking epistemic attitudes to ourselves on the basis of the way other people take them to us. I am sure that George Herbert Mead, Vygotsky, and others are right in saying that this is the point at which something distinctive and human enters.

SCOTT. My worry is that there is difference between a 'shaping force' and an 'explaining' or 'supplying force', terms which tend to be confused in our culture a lot. As a farmer, I used to say 'I grow maize'; but actually, maize grows itself. I shape by supplying the conditions to realize its potential. Similarly, the language, the environmental interaction, and so on shape the concept of self, or allow it to develop along certain channels. However, what it is that is growing and what it is that has the capacity to be shaped in this way remains entirely an unanswered question.

HARRÉ. What I am supposing is certainly the shaping point of view; I am not holding an entity theory. But what is being shaped? I like Vygotsky's idea that nature provides us with a complex physiological mechanism which produces fragments of cognitive and sensory bits and pieces. The question is, how do these get organized? For Vygotsky, the flux is organized by virtue of social relationships into which this creature enters. It is not organized by some progressive natural maturation. So we would expect on those very anti-Piagetian grounds that different forms of cultural practice would always produce subtle differences, and sometimes rather gross differences, in the modes of self-organization. The basic unity is the socially reorganized person who has those various capacities. The question for our understanding of the self, then, is how that structure is organized? My claim is that cultural practices will lead to different forms of organization. Our current form of consciousness is one in which, with the linguistic means available, we are capable, so to say, of distancing ourselves from our own thoughts and feelings. That is what I call taking up an epistemic attitude to myself as a third person. It seems to me that there are other cultures very different from our own. It may be that we perform the act of objectifying our thoughts and feelings in a different way from any way an Eskimo *could*. He or she may need another person, may not have the kind of homunculus to which we can, surprisingly, attribute these things. It may be that an Eskimo has *actually* to get another person's point of view.

SWINBURNE. I admire the story of how we get the concept of self, and no doubt there is a lot in it. But you might have given a rather similar story of how we get the concept of the atom. Indeed, it is a fine story, but we would not have been tempted to suppose that this process in any sense created the atom itself; it just created our concept of it. Likewise I take it that you are not attempting to persuade us that all this interaction with others in any sense *creates* the self?

I think that you, Harré, think in your off-guard moments that in fact the self is empirically given, because I noticed a very interesting casual phrase you used. You talked of Kant's 'transcendental unity of apperception', something we all experience, and that is undoubtedly so, despite Hume, despite Ryle and others. We are all aware of ourselves as common subjects of diverse experience. That is to say, that at any given moment I am having all sorts of different experiences – auditory, visual, and so on – of the world; I am also performing various actions. Among the most primitive data of experience is the fact that I am aware of a common subject of these. That is to say, what I am aware of is not merely that X is moving his hand and Y is having a sensation and Z is hearing a noise. I am aware that one (whatever word can we use? person? subject? soul? – call it whatever you like) is doing the action and is aware of what is happening. Any failure to recognize that is a failure to do justice to the phenomena of experience of which all science ought to take account. Hume thought that by looking into his mind, he ought to be able to find the self, or soul, if it existed; but he reported that he could not do so. I wonder what he was looking for. What he ought to have been looking for and to have found is that his data were not just blue visual fields, say, but himself as aware of blue visual fields or something aware of blue visual fields, the same something that performs actions. Obvious words for that something are 'person' or 'self'.

HARRÉ. When I speak about the 'transcendental unity of apperception', I have in mind a synthetic unity. Kant himself thinks that the transcendental unity of apperception is not an entity, but a synthetic unity; that is, that it is something which nowadays you would call a 'structure'. I do not believe that I have a sense of self in the sense of a referential relationship to an entity that has X, Y, and Z properties. I am inclined to think that what I do is discern the organization among properties. It is quite another thing to say that what I am discerning is a being which has those properties. I think that what Mach said about the physical world is very deep, even if perhaps ultimately mistaken. But that point of view is right about the mental world. There we do have co-locations of properties that hang together structurally, which we then take to be the properties of adult beings. What you are referring to when you say, 'Oh yes, I have this sense of self' is the sense of being organized as a certain kind of structure which is imposed upon our psychological attributes, and then expressed in them. It is quite another thing to postulate an entity and say that it has certain properties.

SWINBURNE. You have to have some sense of an entity. Nobody is asking you to have a sense of the entity without any properties at all. You can imagine that instead of sitting there having *these* visual sensations, you are sitting somewhere else having *those* visual sensations. You *have* got that concept.

HARRÉ. But that is still acceptable as an organizational analysis.

SWINBURNE. What do you mean by 'organizational analysis'? I take it that what you are suggesting is that what we are aware of is certain experiences as co-experienced?

HARRÉ. Yes.

SWINBURNE. Well, what do you mean by 'co-experience'? And how is anybody ever going to spell *that* out except as 'had by the same person'? Why are you reluctant to spell it out in that way? Experiences are things which do not float loose, as it were. An unexperienced visual image is not a visual image. To describe what an experience is like is to describe some characteristic or feeling or action. But that is not enough to describe what is going on, because these are just properties, like being brown or square or round. They are had *by* something. One can conceive of them being instantiated separately or instantiated together; but to say *that* is to conceive of them as belonging to something. Properties are universals which are exemplified in particular instances; and when they are exemplified in particular instances, what that means is that they characterize a particular thing. What makes you resist that is your prior notion of the 'entity', to use your word, as something you must spot outside yourself. That already begs all the questions – namely, that the only entities are physical entities which have spatial locations, and that the only grounds for believing in their existence is that one perceives them, and so on. If you did not have that prior constraint on your notion of entity, and did not have a philosophical overview you wanted to impose on the data, how could anybody refuse to describe the data as somebody having an experience?

HARRÉ. I am perfectly happy for you to say that somebody is having an experience. Then the entity which we are talking about is the Strawsonian person. The next question is, what account is to be given of the unity of subjective experience? Is it to be given a subject–predicate account on the traditional model of how it is we explain things hanging together? No. I can given an account of the sense of self which requires only that unification is by synthesis, not by the co-occurrence of attributes *of* some continuous substance. It does not matter whether the subject is observable or not. It is a question of whether you need two things, two substances, or one. I am quite happy with one substance and two kinds of organization. I have to see an argument which says that all co-location must be the result of common properties of a common substance. I do not see that there need be that common substance at all.

7

The 'Person' in Law

RICHARD TUR

I should confess at the outset that, as a lawyer, I may have rather uninteresting
conclusions to draw with respect to the concept of the person. The law may
well have to admit itself defeated by the ethical issues raised by certain aspects
of personality. In particular, it may be that the law requires to be informed
by ethical considerations about the person, rather than that the law itself
provides a clear and non-contentious concept of the person.

ROMAN LAW

In any event, I start some distance away, both historically and geographically,
with a well-known passage from the *Institutes* of Gaius. Gaius says that 'the
whole of the law observed by us relates either to persons or to things or to
actions'.[1] Thus we have the idea that private law is divisible into three main
parts: the law of persons, the law of property, and the law of obligations. It
is a matter of serious theoretical debate among legal philosophers, legal
theorists, and lawyers, however, as to whether one can subdivide the law of
any legal system into these three categories without remainder and without
overlap. Clearly there is overlap in the sense that it is persons who have
obligations in relation to property, for example. But let us persist a little with
Roman law, because that will allow us to draw an important conclusion about
the nature of legal personality.

In Roman law there was certainly a considerable corpus of rules – principles
if you like, and certainly practices – relating to persons. Paul, in the *Digest*, tells
us that the Romans had three treasures: liberty, citizenship, and the family.[2]

Now, whatever else might or might not fall under the law of persons, few would dispute the inclusion of family law. Corresponding to the three treasures are three degrees of status: The *status libertatis* (all men are free or slave), the *status civitatis* (all free men are citizens or aliens), and the *status familiae* (all citizens are either *paterfamilias* or *filiusfamilias*). Related to these three degrees of status is the concept of *capitis deminutio* – that is, loss or deterioration of status. Predictably and logically – and the Romans were usually predictable and logical – there were three degrees of *capitis deminutio*: *minima*, *media*, and *maxima*, depending on whether one, two, or three lives were lost.

The thing to look at, however, is the effect of diminution in status, which was that of a new person taking the place of the old person. Thus, with regard to a life interest such as *usufruct*, the right to use the fruits on a farm lasted for a lifetime; but if a person suffered *capitis deminutio*, his life effectively stopped, and therefore his life interest was terminated. A celebrated example in the Twelve Tables[3] relates to what is to be done in the case of manifest theft – that is, when the thief is caught red-handed. If he is a freeman, he is to be flogged and enslaved – thus, he loses all three treasures. If he is a slave, however, he is to be flogged and flung from the Tarpian Rock – in a word, put to death. Now at first glance, we might see this as a manifestation of primitivity that a society would have a set of decent rules for its citizens and a set of less decent rules for its slaves. But if we pause, we will see a certain logical consistency. In his three treasures, Paul did not include what we might regard as a fourth treasure, namely physical life itself, because everyone has that, and Paul was looking only at what distinguished Romans from others. What happens in the case of theft is that the freeman loses one life, a legal life, whereas the slave, not having a legal life to lose, loses the only life he does have, namely his physical life.

But apart from the *paterfamilias*, who was the hero of the Roman law story, all Romans possessed partial, rather than full, legal life. And what is interesting is that Romans could have a series of different legal lives, through the loss or acquisition of particular statuses. Even a slave, who started off theoretically as a thing, and therefore subject to the law of property, could acquire freedom, and thereby become subject to the law of persons.

When I ask my students, 'What did the Romans have in common with cats?', the answer I seek, but very rarely get, is that both have many lives. Now, if the underlying idea of personality is the word 'persona', meaning 'mask' or 'role', then Romans could be said to play several roles in legal dramas, simply by changing their status. It follows, of course – and this is significant – that there was in Roman law no one-to-one relationship between the physical being and that physical being's legal life or lives. Thus, while it is often thought that the legal life of an individual human being is in some sense natural, and that the legal life of other things, such as corporations, is in some way artificial, even the legal life of a human being is artificial in the sense that it need not – and in the case of the Romans, did not – stand in a one-to-one relationship with his physical life. This may be important in some kinds of debates, because many people insist that the legal person comes into being at birth and ceases to exist at death. But in Roman law, human beings had legal lives that started and stopped during their natural lifetimes.

VARIETIES OF LEGAL RULES

Whatever else the law is concerned with, it is concerned with human behaviour. To simplify things – which is to run the risk of distortion, of course – I am going to identify three kinds of legal rule. The first I will call administrative. Suppose some event – an outbreak of foot-and-mouth disease, for example – occurs. Then a legal official ought to do something – in this case, let us say, order the cattle to be slaughtered and their carcasses burnt. Notice here that there is only one piece of human conduct, namely that of the legal official. In the second kind of rule, which I will call criminal, an individual does something – that is, we have an act, rather than an event. Two bits of conduct are thus involved, that of the criminal – his alleged criminal conduct – and that of the legal official involved in the case. In the third kind of rule, which I will call civil, it is even more complex, since there are three bits of conduct to consider. For example, A assaults B; B then does something – takes action in the court, say – and then the legal official must also take some action. Crucial in this case is the power of the victim to seek a legal remedy.

The business and pleasure of law is – and in my view must be – carried out solely by human beings. But these human beings, when acting as legal officials, are living different lives from their individual physical lives. Their acts are attributable not to them, but to the law. The law is itself personified, as an agent capable of acting. Now with regard to philosophical theories of the state or the law, there are those who advance some sort of realist notion of the personality of the state – the state as some kind of superman or super-being. I have very little use for this kind of metaphysical edifice; when I talk about the state or the law doing this or that, I am speaking metaphorically, and a justification for the metaphor is that the law is in some sense a unified and purportedly coherent attempt to regulate or determine what ought ot be.

With regard to the different types of rule outlined above, I want to make a further point. In the second type, the person who commits an assault is clearly an addressee of the law; but the person who suffers the assault is simply an object of the law, and not yet a legal subject. Thus, in a society which rules,

'Thou shalt not assault other people, and if you do, you shall be punished,' other people are the equivalent of birds or their eggs or their nests in the Protection of Birds Act of 1954. They are like slaves under Roman law, entities with no legal rights, no power to make legal things happen through the exercise of will or judgement. In the course of Roman history, however, a law was passed which said that if a slave who had been cruelly treated by his master was able to escape to the shelter of a statue of the emperor, the magistrates would then examine his case. This was a very primitive action that a slave could take in order to secure the possibility of legal consequences.

In the third type of rule we see what perhaps is crucial, namely, what the slave acquired – the capacity to take, or at least attempt to take, effective legal action. Now one possible definition of full legal personality – and I stress the word 'full' for reasons which will become evident as we proceed – requires that a person be able to initiate actions in the courts, 'sue or be sued' as it is frequently put. But if you take this high threshold for legal personality, as some writers do, saying that full legal personality means not only the ability to bear rights and suffer duties, to enter into contracts, and to own property, but also includes the right or power to sue and the liability of being sued, then legal personality is not of any relevance to practical problems such as those involving girls under 16 seeking abortion or contraceptives. Nor does it help us in dealing with situations pertaining to even earlier phases of human life, either before or soon after birth, because the concept is relevant only to the full range of capacities of an individual within the legal system. And there is a clear view that that is what legal personality is: 'In law a person is any entity recognized as having existence in law capable of suing or being sued.'[4] But so high a threshold for legal personality will not take us very far towards solutions to the practical problems that exercise us.

ANIMALS AND INANIMATE OBJECTS

There is, however, the risk that I sold you a pup when I said that law is concerned only with human behaviour. For, in the Oration against Aristocrates, we find the following:

> There is a fourth tribunal, that of the Prytaneum. Its function is that if a man is struck by a stone or a piece of wood or iron or anything of that sort falling upon him, and if someone without knowing who threw it, knows and possesses the implement of homicide, he takes proceedings against that implement in that court.

There are similar examples in Plato's *Laws* and in the works of Aristotle. In the Middle Ages, it was still possible to bring a lawsuit against an animal – for instance, a dog or a bull which had killed a man, or locusts which had eaten the crops. And in due process of law, the court would condemn the accused animal to death, whereupon the animal would be executed in exactly the same way as a human being.[5] In Germany during the Middle Ages, a cock was tried for 'contumacious crowing', and in 1508 in Provence, caterpillars were condemned for ravaging the fields.[6]

We have, then, examples of cases in which animals and inanimate objects can apparently be sued, or at least tried, and can be condemned to something akin to the death penalty. It is rather more difficult to imagine actions sounding in tort being brought against a spear or locusts whereby damages could be awarded for the loss suffered. Primitive legal systems, and even systems of some sophistication, do not always draw clear distinctions between crime and tort.[7] In any event, these examples can be explained away fairly easily. The law is of course concerned with *human* conduct; it is just that primitive societies had a very broad notion of human conduct. We are dealing here with animism, the belief that there are spirits, or souls, behind everything – for example, a dryad behind a tree or a nyad behind a river. From such a perspective, it is not events that are occurring, but acts; and acts presuppose agents.

Here I turn to a book that has made a lasting impression on me since my undergraduate days. It is by Frankfort *et al.*, and is entitled *Before Philosophy*. It is in many ways a quite magical book, but there is one passage in particular that intrigues me enormously.[8] The question there under consideration is, When a river fails to rise, what should be done to persuade it to rise? Note the use of the word 'persuade'. It is not a case of doing something that will cause rain to fall, but rather of cajoling the river itself, by going and talking to it. It is not a technological, but a human, matter. We treat the river as if it were a person, a human being like ourselves. We therefore in our initial, least confident phase offer the river a gift. We know from our everyday experience with each other that if we give someone a gift, it disposes the recipient favourably towards us. The question which then arises is, What would a river like? But that is very easy to answer: a river likes precisely what human beings like, because it is an 'I' or a 'thou', just like us. So one gives it whatever is valued in the society, which for primitive peoples usually turns out to be goats, camels, and virgins. But as time goes by, goats, camels, and virgins tend to be depleted through repeated giving. And inevitably the river rises ultimately. If it fails to rise the first time, it simply means that you didn't give it a big enough gift, or that you didn't say the right words. Later, however, as confidence grows, you enter into a contract with the river. Indeed, added to the sacrifices which were thrown into the river would be a document in the form of either an order or a contract stating the obligations of the river, the Nile, say. This strikes me as amazing. I understand that if you can make gifts to someone, even a river, you can certainly enter into contracts with it and issue decrees to it. But notice that what we are calling primitive thought is thought that exists in a society sufficiently advanced to have written documents *and* the legal institutions of contract, or legislation. In this second phase, a contract would be issued, stating that if the river rose, it would be given x goats and y of the other things the society deemed valuable. Of course, you were under no obligation if the river didn't rise. In the final phase, however, the river was commanded to rise upon the solemn authority of the law. What I want to stress is that this animistic notion of human conduct exists in a society with relatively modern legal institutions. Indeed, even today, we reveal animistic tendencies, as when we kick our cars or thump our television sets; moreover, sometimes such actions seem to work!

It is clear, of course, that we do not always need to invoke animism to explain instances of non-human legal personality. For legal personality can be given to just about anything. As recently as 1925, the Privy Council solemnly declared an Indian idol to have legal personality.[9] An idol itself cannot act; it must do its business through its guardians. Nevertheless, it was the idol to which acts were attributed, not its guardians. As with the idol, so with a corporation in my view. A corporation has no soul to be damned or body to be kicked; yet it has legal personality. Its acts must be carried out by individual human beings; but this does not prevent those acts from being attributed to it, rather than the individuals concerned.

LEGAL PERSONALITY

If legal personality is the legal capacity to bear rights and duties, then it is itself an artificial creation of the law, and anything or anyone can be a legal person. It all depends on the particular, concrete rules of particular legal systems. The first thing a jurisprudence student coming to analyses of legal concepts is told with respect to legal personality is that the philosophical notion of a person as an actual, or perhaps potential, rational individual is to be utterly disregarded, since it can only be misleading. For the law of any jurisdiction you care to choose will have a myriad of specific rules such that the concept of legal personality stands in no comfortable one-to-one relationship with anything remotely approaching rational individual human beings, either actual or potential.

In a sense, then, the concept of legal personality is wholly formal. It is an empty slot that can be filled by anything that can have rights or duties. It is possible, of course, to take the law of a society and to seek to distil from it what might be called the tacit major premiss or principle behind the law. It might thus be possible to build up an extralegal criterion or a cluster of extralegal criteria of legal personality. Thus, we might ask what all things termed legal persons in English law have in common. One possible answer might be the physical capacity for action. But this could be disproved fairly easily by the examples of the idol or the corporation, which cannot act except through particular human beings. And of course it is quite clear from the history of legal systems that the physical capacity to act is not confined to legal persons. Outlaws, slaves, those regarded as civilly dead, and therefore in some sense beyond the law, are clear examples of beings with the capacity for action but without legal personality. Thus the capacity for physical action cannot be said to stand in one-to-one relationship with legal personality. Turning to the details of English law, one finds as many – maybe even more – statuses or degrees of legal personality as in Roman law.

So my second conclusion is that legal personality is a matter of degree. The law will ascribe legal personality to two entities even where they bear different clusters of rights and duties. So, legal personality is a cluster concept, where in some cases one cluster of rights and duties is present, and in other cases a different cluster of rights and duties is present, perhaps overlapping somewhat with the first. A third case might be different again, with less of an overlap; but it is conceivable that two entities, both of which are legal persons, might have no rights and duties in common at all.

It is also interesting to note that even if something is called a legal person, normal consequences are not guaranteed. The legislature may treat the concept of legal personality as a general point of reference, so that if you want to stop contracts involving womb-leasing, for example, you might pass a law forbidding any person to do it. And that law would appear to apply to all human beings with legal personality, corporations, and so forth. But it may not work. For example, the Representation of the Peoples Act of 1868 said that every person whose name was on the register of the general council of specified universities was entitled to vote. The Universities Elections Amendment (Scotland) act of 1881 then provided that the registrar of such a university was under a duty to issue voting papers to any person on the general register. The Universities (Scotland) Act of 1889 then empowered universities to admit women, the first of whom were admitted to St Andrews and to Edinburgh University in 1892. In the course of time, some of these people, unbelievably as it may have seemed to those who had argued against higher education for women, obtained degrees and had their names added to the general register. These women then claimed the right to vote, or at least insisted that the registrar send them voting papers. But the House of Lords in 1909, in *Nairn* v. *University Courts of St Andrews and Edinburgh*,[10] said that this was nonsense, that 'any person' meant 'any man', and that it was contrary to the fundamental principles of the Constitution that women should vote. Now I cite this example to show that even though the word 'person' might be thought to have a clear meaning, lawyers are able, before your very eyes, to turn one thing into another! A further illustration involves Section 11A of the Abortion Act of 1967, according to which it is not an offence for a doctor to perform certain procedures in the case of a 'woman'. But does the phrase 'a woman' include a girl capable, on a physical level at least, of undergoing the same procedures?

The authority of Gaius notwithstanding, the law of persons is not a clearly delineated area. In the undergraduate course of study called Jurisprudence at Oxford, there is no such subject as the law of persons. Moreover, if such a subject were devised, it would involve pulling together bits and pieces from other subjects, such as the law of crime, the law of contract, and the law of tort. Even then, it would soon come down to a recital of the general rules of status and the capacity to enter into legal relationships or to be subject to legal liabilities. There is no general law of persons, but rather, a series of rules concerning relationships and liabilities.

From time to time, specialists in Roman law attempt to compare Roman law with English law, the better to introduce students to the latter, so they tell us. The most recent such effort is Peter Stein's *Legal Institutions*,[11] in which a chapter on the Roman law of persons is immediately followed by a chapter on the modern law of persons. But in my view, such attempts lack conviction, since they really do not get us into the core of our legal system or give us a coherent conception of personality upon which the law is based. We do not even have – or so it seems to me – any clear idea of when a legal person comes into being or when he ceases to exist. Nor does legal personality come into existence all at once, in one great leap. What happens is that as a person moves from conception to birth to infancy and grows up, he acquires legal personality by degrees, by acquiring rights, powers, and duties, which gather cumulatively. Nor should we regard physical death as marking the termination of legal life, if for no other reason than the existence of a legal will, through which the physically dead person seeks to control the disposition of his property.

Criminal Law

If we cannot say when legal personality begins or ends in a general way, what we must do is to look at particular situations and see what conclusions we can draw from them. First, then, let us look at crime. In English law generally, one is either an infant or an adult, and anyone who is not yet 18 is an infant (although in modern usage we tend to find the word 'minor'). However, English criminal law does not say that you have to be an adult before you can be liable for the commission of a crime. 'A child knows right from wrong long before he knows how to make a prudent speculation or a wise will.'[12] Accordingly, criminal liability is divided into three age-groups. In the first, up to 10, children are presumed to be incapable of committing crimes. (In the legal systems of other countries, the age may be different.) As an undergraduate, I remember hearing the following story from my criminal law lecturer. A little boy in Glasgow, 7 years old apparently, at a time when the age of criminal responsibility in Scotland was 8, under the eagle eye of a large Glasgow policeman, picked up a brick and threw it gaily through a shop window, whereupon the policeman purported to arrest the boy, and the boy, obviously a budding criminal lawyer, said, 'You can't arrest me; I haven't got *mens rea!*' Such a total bar on liability, however, can produce odd results. In *Walker* v. *Lunt*,[13] a 7-year-old child 'stole' a tricycle. His parents, knowing that the child had taken the tricycle improperly, nevertheless received it. They were charged with handling stolen goods, but were acquitted because, since the child was under 10, technically speaking, he could not steal, which led to the bizarre conclusion that the tricycle was not stolen.

The second age-group runs from over 10 to under 14. Here there is a curious rule, for the person may or may not be liable, depending on whether or not he has 'mischievous discretion' – that is, whether the child knew that what he was doing was wrong. But of course, some 14 year-olds are pretty intelligent, some not so intelligent, and moral development is inevitably a matter of degree. In the third age-group, the over-14s, the child is as liable 'as if he were forty.'[14]

So you have three different statuses, and in the middle status an either/or. I should also add that it is very unusual for children in the middle age-group to be found guilty of crime and punished through criminal procedures; the usual recourse is to opt for some kind of care proceedings, so that even though the youngster knew he was doing wrong, he is not punished so much as treated paternalistically.

Contract

In the area of contract, anyone younger than 18 is of course an infant. In this case, one might expect a simple rule to the effect that one cannot enter into valid contracts unless one is at least 18. Nothing so silly, of course, could possibly be the case. Another possibility would be to say that a person under 18 can enter into contracts only if some adult acts on his behalf. But this doesn't happen in English law either. Rather, contracts are divided into different kinds.

Some are binding; some are binding but can be repudiated by the infant; some are not binding at all; and others may be absolutely void. The sorts of contracts that are binding are those involving what in Scots law are called 'necessities', but which English lawyers call 'necessaries'. A 'necessary' is precisely what the word implies, and in Oxford nearly a hundred years ago, a jury held that champagne and wild duck were necessaries for infant undergraduates!

Tort

With regard to the law of tort, the extent of liability for causing the death of, or injury to, another human being is pretty straightforward and well established. But now suppose that the injured party is an as yet unborn child. The question here, of course, is whether a foetus has sufficient legal personality to bring an action. No English court has ever ruled regarding whether at common law a child injured while still in its mother's womb could maintain an action for damages. The general view of the textbook writers is that if, after birth, negligence could be established, such an action would probably succeed. Indeed, that is the rule found in many other jurisdictions, and one would have thought that it would not have been too difficult for the common law to have arrived at this position by way of a fiction that the pre-natal injury occurred just after birth, and therefore that the child, not the foetus, brings the action. But the Congenital Disabilities Civil Liability Act of 1976 replaces all common law remedies. To be covered by this act, a child must be born alive, but with some deformity, disease, or abnormality, or some disposition to physical or mental defect in the future. The aim here is to limit compensation to losses that can be turned into a pecuniary sum.

An interesting case, called *Williams* v. *State of New York*,[15] is that of an illegitimate child born to a mentally defective mother who was sexually assaulted while a patient in a mental institution. The basis for the action was the negligence of the institution in running affairs in such a way that this could happen, and the question that arose was whether damages could be awarded to the child as compensation for the stigma of illegitimacy. The court dismissed the claim because it found it impossible to decide whether non-existence was preferable to existence as an illegitimate child. In *McKay* v. *Essex Area Health Authority*,[16] a claim for damages was made by a child who was born deformed as a result of her mother's infection with German measles. The child alleged that, but for the negligence of the doctor, the mother would have had an abortion under the Abortion Act of 1967. The basis of this claim was that the doctor was negligent in allowing the child to be born at all. The Court of Appeal, however, held that the doctor was under no legal duty to the foetus to terminate its life, and that any such duty would run counter to the principle of the sanctity of human life. Furthermore, the court held that, in any event, it could not evaluate non-existence for the purposes of awarding damages to one whose claim assumed that it was better not to be born at all than to be born deformed.

Problematic Cases

We can now begin to see how difficult it is for any a priori conceptions of personality to deal with such problems; for, if we proceed a little bit further, we see that in these cases the courts would have had to say that it were better for these children not to have been born at all. Consider the possibility of someone being born as a result of an incompetently performed vasectomy, for example, suing for the fact that he was born at all. It is certainly the case that one can get a substantial sum in damages if the vasectomy turns out to be one of the small number in which the effect seems to reverse itself afterwards. And relatively recently in England, an action was brought by a man to whom that happened, and he was awarded damages.[17] There was no question at that stage of whether the child to be born could itself claim damages, in an action for wrongful life, which is a very tricky concept indeed.

Then there is the area of pre-conception negligence. Suppose that I am conducting some scientific experiments, and that a certain amount of radioactive material is involved; then suppose that a woman walking past in the street is affected by the radioactivity in such a way as to impair the functioning of her reproductive organs. Months later she conceives, and months later again, a defective child is born. Should that child be allowed to claim damages from me for messing around with radioactive material, thereby causing this child to be born defective? Moreover, if you maintain that there is a strong case for allowing the child so to claim, what in fact are you saying? Are you saying that the child deserves compensation for having been born, or that he deserves compensation for having been born defective? English law will tend to the second conclusion, I think, for it will assume a right to be born normal. But this whole area raises enormous difficulties. I have enough trouble with discourse about the rights of birds and animals, of leaves on trees,[18] and of foetuses; but I have even more trouble with the idea of that which has not yet been conceived having rights, even if, by virtue of the fiction in the 1976 act, the damage is not assessed until the child is born.

The sorts of cases we get into take us further and further away from traditional conceptions of legal personality, and into deeper and deeper ethical and practical problems. In *Paton* v. *British Pregnancy Advisory Service Trustees*,[19] back in 1978, a husband tried to stop his wife from having an abortion; but the court ruled that he had no interest in the matter, and that it was between the woman and her doctors. According to a recent newspaper report,[20] a court in England held that if a doctor decides to perform an abortion on a 15-year-old girl and has complied with all the statutory requirements, then any objections by the girl's mother are no grounds for not proceeding. Thus the court would not grant an injunction against the abortion. This outcome stands in sharp contra-distinction to *Gillick* v. *West Norfolk & Wisbech Area Health Authority*[21] in which the Court of Appeal held that girls under 16 should not be given contracep-tive pills by doctors without parental consent. It would seem to follow, therefore, that the law is now in the bizarre position of maintaining that it is inappropriate for a doctor to give a girl under 16 contraceptive advice of any kind, but that if she becomes pregnant, as a result perhaps of not having had that advice, he may then, even against her mother's wishes, proceed with an abortion. Now I take it that most people would agree that whatever the comparative merits of abortion and contraception, abortion is the riskier and less desirable activity.

The decision of the Court of Appeal in *Gillick* has been overturned by the House of Lords. In rejecting the traditional, all-or-nothing approach of the Court of Appeal, Lord Scarman subjected parental rights to the qualification that they exist only as long as they are needed for the protection of the person and the property of the child. Consequently, when a doctor is satisfied that the patient has sufficient maturity to understand what is involved, the crucial decision is to be taken by the patient. Lord Fraser, however, although he agreed that a parent does not have an absolute veto, would place the ultimate responsi-bility for the decision on the doctor.

That the Court of Appeal and the House of Lords took different views on the question and that, as between two of those voting with the majority in the House of Lords, there are differences at least of emphasis reflects the difficulty one has in even describing the law, when it will not stand still. *In Re B*[22] also focused on the issue of consent, the consent of parents which is usually required for medical treatment of their children. It involved a mongoloid child who would die in a relatively short time unless an operation were performed to remove some kind of blockage; but the parents failed to reach a decision, thereby effectively withholding consent. The predicament of the parents was, of course, a difficult one, and I do not mean to criticize them; but the Area Health Authority simply made this child a ward of the court, obtained the necessary consent, and went ahead with the operation.

CONCLUSION

In all this, we are a long way from anything embodied in the conception of legal personality. Indeed, when the word 'person' is used by a lawyer, it reflects conclusion, not a premiss. Nor can the concept of legal personality provide us with a premiss by determining what ought and what ought not to have rights. I said earlier that legal personality is a cluster concept, that it can spread; and I have just said that it is more a conclusion than a premiss. Let me illustrate this last point with reference to *Miller*,[23] a case that was heard by the House of Lords a couple of years ago. A drunken tramp fell asleep with a lit cigarette; when he woke up, he saw that the building in which he had been sleeping all night was on fire, so, quite sensibly, he left. The question is, is he guilty of arson, arson by omission? The House of Lords held that he was. Now there are two theories regarding criminal liability in cases of omission: one is called 'the continuing act theory', the other 'the duty theory'. The former is illustrated by the case of *Fagan*.[24] A policeman signalled to a motorist to stop; the motorist obeyed, with the front wheel of his car parked firmly on the policeman's foot, as it happened; the policeman then asked him to remove the car, and the motorist none too politiely refused. The motorist was then charged with assault, assault by omission, a charge justified by the continuing act theory. In such a case, the state of affairs prohibited by the law is continuing, and at some point or other, knowledge or recklessness (as in *Miller*) impinges and one has the coincidence of mind and body, *mens rea* and *actus reus*. But the better theory is the duty theory, which says that a person who by a particular act or behaviour puts someone else in danger has the duty of undoing the damage as soon as he becomes aware of it – which makes perfectly good sense. But what does the word 'duty' mean? It cannot mean legal duty, because if it does, the argument is circular. However, textbook writers use the duty theory to explain liability without acknowledging that duty must be in some sense pre-legal or extralegal. But once you admit that, you run the risk of justifying all sorts of Good Samaritan laws, whereas there is no such obligation in our law at the moment.

Now my point about legal personality is that it is rather like duty in this example. If it is something entirely internal to the law, it is not much use for solving practical problems. Of course, once you have reached a solution to your practical problems, you can get a lawyer to use his concepts to produce the result you want – if you are sufficiently clear about what you want in the particular circumstances. But we have now gone beyond the law for guidance in making decisions about what ought to happen. But it may be that there is no one extralegal position – I hesitate to say 'theory' because I worry about too strict a computational model of morality – that can provide us with ready-made answers to such novel questions as are raised by the cases discussed. Indeed, it is not merely that there is no adequate way of calculating damages for wrongful life, but also, I suspect, that some uncertainty as to what is morally right stands between the law and a clear and coherent set of solutions. Whatever decisions we do make can, of course, be implemented and enforced by the law, by its various mechanisms and concepts, among them the concept of legal personality. It is just that legal concepts in general cannot by themselves provide us with an adequate basis for decision making in the more problematic areas at which we have been looking; and legal personality in particular does not provide us with a definition of a person from which to derive solutions to practical problems.

8

Is Medicine a Branch of Ethics?*

WILLIAM FULFORD

On the topic of this meeting – concepts of the person and their ethical implications – some nice paradoxes have been thrown up by medicine in recent years.

In this paper, I will be arguing from these paradoxes for a change in the way in which we understand the nature of medicine, and from there back to certain conclusions about how the paradoxes themselves might be resolved.

THE PARADOXES

Historically, medicine has always been a somewhat loose-knit, opportunistic, and pragmatic subject, hybridizing with whatever beliefs are extant, and adapting them to meet the needs of the patients with whom it is concerned. Yet – and this is our first paradox – its most recent, and surely its most successful hybridization, with science, has been achieved in some respects actually at the expense of the patient, or at any rate at the expense of the patient as a person. For it has been achieved by concentrating on those mainly bodily aspects of patients, in connection with which they may be thought of not as persons but as machines.

This in itself, of course, is not to be deplored. As I have said, the hybrid medicine–science has been a most successful hybrid. No one can doubt that. But – and here is our second paradox – even as the successes of medical science have multiplied, so, apparently, has consumer dissatisfaction. Patients now,

* A more formal and extended treatment of the ideas presented in this paper will be found in the introduction to the author's *Moral Theory and Medical Practice*, to be published in 1987 by Cambridge University Press.

though healthier, though living longer, though more pain free, are less, rather than more, satisfied with their doctors. There are more, rather than fewer complaints to the General Medical Council. There is more, rather than less, pressure for external monitoring of the profession. It seems that the more doctors *can* do to help, the less satisfied are their patients with what they *do* do to help. Patients just don't seem to trust their doctors as they did when doctors were (professionally speaking) untrustworthy! And here is our third paradox: that even as medical-scientific successes have multiplied, so also have medical-ethical problems. There is indeed a clear correlation here – and no doubt a causal connection as well – between, on the one hand, the progress which doctors have made scientifically in dealing with empirical clinical problems, and, on the other hand, the emergence of non-empirical clinical problems – medical-ethical problems as such, but also medico-legal and political problems, often of a largely ethical nature.

These paradoxes – and they are of course not logical paradoxes, but more in the way of 'Catch 22' dilemmas – are nowhere more evident than in psychological medicine. Here, above all perhaps, it really is necessary that the patient should be treated as a person. In physical medicine, with its ever increasing burden of empirical information about the functioning of the body, there is some, albeit dubious, justification for treating the patient as a machine: or if not *as* a machine, at least for treating the patient-as-a-person as being secondary in importance to the patient-as-a-(bodily)-machine; for treating the patient-as-a-person as a kind of fringe benefit, a professional optional extra. But in psychological medicine, dealing as it does with the mind, the patient-as-a-person is somehow more directly, less inescapably, at the focus of clinical attention (indeed, in psychoanalysis, I suppose, the patient-as-a-person actually *is* the focus of clinical attention). Yet here too, it has been mainly by way of the 'appliance of science', pharmacological science, behavioural science, and the like, that progress has been made. So that in psychological medicine too, we have seen the patient-as-a-person if not actually displaced by the patient-as-a-machine, at least dislodged. We have seen, hand in hand with scientific progress, less, rather than more, satisfaction with, and less, rather than more, trust of, doctors. And as progress has been made in dealing with the empirical problems of clinical practice, so non-empirical problems – ethical, medico-legal, and political – have become more and more common, more and more intractable.

THE CONVENTIONAL SCIENCE-BASED VIEW OF MEDICINE

So evident have these catch-22 paradoxes been in psychological medicine, that there was a time – mainly in the 1960s and early 1970s – when the very nature of psychological medicine *as* medicine was seriously contested. I have in mind here the anti-psychiatry movement of that period: authors such as Thomas Szasz and R. D. Laing, and their platform that the very concept of 'mental illness' is a myth. There has never been a serious anti-*physical* medicine movement as radical as this. And it is important to be aware of the fact that, although the old clear-cut, black and white, opposition between anti-psychiatry and psychiatry has largely disappeared, the essential issues, and the debate, continue. In the sixties Szasz and Laing, as anti-establishment figures, were set up in the debate about mental illness against such establishment figures as Professor Sir Martin Roth and Professor R. E. Kendell. But now it is as much among the establishment as the anti-establishment that doubts and fears and distrust of psychiatry are to be found. Not amounting to an outright rejection of the concept of 'mental illness', it is true, but certainly to voicing doubts about the wisdom of deploying the concept as widely as it has been deployed, to fears about the consequences of so deploying it, and to distrust, not least, of the capacities of psychiatrists to deploy it well. Witness here, in the Peter Sutcliffe trial, the rejection by the judge, Mr Justice Boreham, of both prosecution and defence psychiatric opinions that the accused was mentally ill. This was an extreme case, no doubt. But it was also the extreme tip of the iceberg of modern anti-psychiatric sentiment. Mental illness, Mr Justice Boreham was in effect saying, may not be, as Szasz thought, a myth. But we certainly do not have a sufficiently clear idea of just what it is to leave it to psychiatrists alone to decide where and when, and whether for good or ill, it is to be deployed.

Now the issues in the debate about mental illness lead directly to the change in our understanding of the nature of medicine for which I am going to argue. And we can see these issues most clearly, I think, in what I called a moment ago the 'old clear-cut, black and white' version of that debate. Consider, on the anti-psychiatry side, Thomas Szasz;[1] and compare his views with the pro-psychiatry views of R. E. Kendell.[2] Szasz argues essentially thus. 'Illness', he says, means a 'disturbance of bodily function'; it is all to do with hearts, lungs, livers, limbs, and the like; and the criteria by which we decide whether someone is ill are factual criteria – solid, objective, and scientific. But where are the corresponding criteria for calling someone mentally ill? There aren't any, he says. For the criteria for mental illness are not factual at all, but evaluative; they are not solid, objective, scientific criteria, but intangible, subjective, ethical criteria. To call someone mentally ill is not, as with physical illness, to state a biological fact, but to express a value-judgement. So mental illness is not, after all, illness at all. Kendell's reply to this, on the other hand, is equally decisive. It is true, he agrees, that 'illness' means a disturbance of function, but not just of bodily function. And here, like Szasz, he draws on examples of bodily illness, but to show that 'illness' means 'any mode of functioning which leads to reduced fertility and/or life expectancy'. Thus he is able to conclude against Szasz, not only that certain disturbances of mental functioning – such as depression, and, Szasz's main bugbear, schizophrenia – really are illnesses, but that, leading as they do to reduced fertility and/or life expectancy, they are illnesses by the same criteria, the same *factual* criteria indeed, as bodily illnesses.

Clearly, both Szasz and Kendell oversimplified matters. But this is not what I want to go into here. What is important for us here – important in leading us towards a change in our understanding of the nature of medicine – is what their positions have in common.

These similarities have not been widely recognized in the literature. Yet there are a number of them. And the one I want to concentrate on is this: that both authors, although acknowledging, as a matter of observation, that the concept of 'mental illness' is more value-laden than that of 'physical illness', proceed on the assumption that this is a mark of degeneracy or defectiveness. So that both authors adopt, *vis-à-vis* the evaluative connotations of the concept of 'mental illness', a strategy of exclusion or proscription. Szasz is perhaps the more transparent here. He says that to call someone mentally ill is to express a value-judgement, and it is for this reason that he claims that mental illness is not really illness at all. Only physical illness, defined by reference to his supposedly factual criteria of bodily functioning, is really illness, properly understood. But Kendell's argument too, if less transparently a strategy of exclusion, amounts to the same thing. He too, although arguing *for* the concept of 'mental illness', does so in effect by seeking to cleanse or purify it of its evaluative connotations; by seeking to distil from it, as it were, a 'factual fraction', a pure empirical fraction defined just as (he supposes) 'physical illness' is defined, by reference to firmly biological-scientific norms.

Of course, in singling out and bringing to the surface this similarity between the forms of argument adopted by Szasz and Kendell, I have presented something of a caricature of their views. Though let me say straight away that I do not think I have actually misrepresented them. Both authors really do argue by pushing towards purely factual-scientific definitions of the medical concepts, even if neither is as blunt-edged as I have made him appear. The caricaturing of their views, however, is necessary to counteract the effects of a pervasive and deep-seated illusion about the nature of medicine, an illusion which, so long it has remained unrecognized as such, has dominated the debate about mental illness, leading to the similarities between the forms of argument adopted by the two sides in this debate, and, I believe to many of the continuing doubts, fears, and dissatisfactions regarding the concept.

So what is this illusion? It is, in a word, that medicine is a science. Not, note, that science is an important part of medicine (which of course it is); but that medicine is, properly speaking, or at any rate as a technical specialist discipline, nothing more than a science. The source of this illusion is obvious enough; the enormous success of what I called earlier the hybrid medicine–science in dealing with the many empirical problems that form so large and important a part of the concerns of clinical practice. And the illusion is fostered by the necessity that medical students, in their clinical training, do little else but science. So it is really not at all surprising that we should find this illusion at the heart of the debate about mental illness, as it was – in the 'old, clear-cut, black and white' days – and as it continues.

Yet the very existence of non-empirical clinical problems in medicine – all those ethical, medico-legal, and political problems which, under our third catch-22 paradox, have become more pronounced in recent years – shows that this view of medicine, as nothing more than a science, is a distorted view, an illusion. And once we begin to see it like this, as an illusion, we begin to see also just how misconceived are science-based strategies of the Szasz/Kendell type in the debate about mental illness. For what this debate is about is really just these non-empirical problems. It is, as I said earlier, especially in psychological medicine that non-empirical problems have become so pronounced in recent years; this is all part of what is involved in the notion that the concept of mental illness has more marked evaluative connotations than that of physical illness; and this, in turn, is why the debate is about mental illness, not physical illness. But the success of science in medicine has been with *empirical* clinical problems. And it is thus, on the face of it, most unlikely, and certainly should not just be assumed, that the *non*-empirical problems associated with mental illness, can be resolved by more of the same, by pushing medicine even further towards being nothing but a science. Indeed, this science-based strategy is surely just the reverse of any strategy which would be likely to succeed in resolving the non-empirical problems of clinical practice. For it is a repeat, a recapitulation, in argument, of the historical process by which, as I outlined at the start of this paper, these non-empirical problems have come to the fore in medicine in recent years. Our third paradox, as you will recall, consisted in just this, that even as medicine has become ever more successful in dealing scientifically with empirical clinical problems, so non-empirical clinical problems have become ever more pronounced.

AN ALTERNATIVE, ETHICS-BASED VIEW OF MEDICINE

If this is so, it follows that we should be looking for a strategy for dealing with these non-empirical clinical problems which is, in some sense, the reverse of a science-based strategy. And if it is not immediately clear just what such a strategy would look like, it is at any rate clear what the first step must be towards finding out. For if science-based strategies are a product of the illusion that medicine is just a science, the first step towards developing an alternative strategy, must be to correct this illusion, to come to see medicine not as a science, but as something more than a science.

Now, it might be thought that this is a fair amount of fuss about not very much, and that if this is what our required change of view comes down to, it is neither original nor even contentious. Surely, it may be said, even the most hard-nosed doctors would admit that there is more to good doctoring than science alone? Would they not actually take pride in their diagnostic 'instincts'? and in their therapeutic skills combining art as much as science? And as for the not so hard-nosed, are they not at least open-minded about the so-called alternative medicines? Moreover, it can hardly be said that ethics as such is ignored; we have 'ethics committees' nowadays, and a new journal of medical ethics seems to come along almost annually. And as to the concepts of 'illness' and 'disease' (let alone the concept of 'mental illness'), these are well recognized, at least by medical sociology and social science, even if not by mainstream medicine, to be heavily value-laden.

But my reply to this is that none of it is radical enough. In a sense, yes, the idea that medicine is not just a science is an idea whose time has come. But it is an idea which is still very much – and my point is that it is still *too* much – at the margins of the subject. The 'art' and 'instinct' in diagnosis and treatment are (rightly enough) subordinate to, and in most branches of medicine increasingly subordinate to, developments in science and technology. Similarly, any vogue among doctors for alternative medicines is (again, rightly enough) because, and only to the extent that, in certain areas they are proving their worth as judged by straightforwardly empirical scientific criteria. But, by the same token, anything in medicine which is not, in principle at least, subject to empirical-scientific appraisal is kept firmly at the periphery of the subject – and this is nowhere more clearly so than in the case of medical ethics. Ethics committees we may have, but not instruction in medical ethics. The United States, it is true, has its 'medical humanities'; but in this country, this area is left mainly to the odd enthusiast, as something to be pursued in his spare time. And who do we find running one of our very few available courses in medical ethics, but a lawyer – Ian Kennedy, no less!

The current version of the conventional view of medicine is thus one which is still dominated by the science-based illusion. According to this view, medicine may not be just a science; but it is still at heart a science, albeit with non-scientific and especially ethical fringes.

This view of medicine has been well articulated by Christopher Boorse.[3] With respect to the involvement of medicine in what he calls 'ethical issues' – criminal responsibility, sexual deviation, feminism, and so on – he claims that medicine has been gravely compromised by a failure to distinguish between the concept of 'illness' and that of 'disease'. 'Illness', he argues is indeed an evaluative concept. And there is no problem about that – for it is a concept the proper deployment of which is in the practice, rather than the theory, of medicine. But, he continues, the theoretical basis of medicine is fundamentally scientific. Behind the contingencies, the decisions, the plain value-judgements, of everyday clinical practice, there lies a body of theoretical knowledge, which, he says, 'is continuous with theory in biology and the other basic sciences'. And the concept which is properly deployed here, at the heart of medicine as a specialist discipline, is not that of 'illness', but of 'disease' – and 'disease' defined not evaluatively but value-free, by reference to well-established factual-scientific functional norms.

In Boorse's argument then, we find not only a continuing science-based illusion, but also a science-based strategy which is essentially the same as that which, earlier in this paper, we found employed by Szasz and by Kendell. Boorse's is the more highly developed version of this strategy, it is true. He seeks to accommodate, rather than exclude, the non-empirical parts of medicine. But even so, he is able to accommodate them only at the periphery of the subject. Which is, of course, the philosophical counterpart of the peripheral accommodation of ethics in medicine. So, although Boorse's strategy is a more beefed-up science-based strategy, it remains a strategy which, like those of Szasz and Kendell before it, merely recapitulates the process by which the ethical issues to which it is addressed arose in medicine in the first place. And what is needed, therefore, is a more beefed-up reverse strategy. And the first step towards such a strategy is a more beefed-up version of the reverse view of medicine that I mentioned a few minutes ago. What is needed, that is to say, is to see that not only is medicine not just a science, but that even at heart it is not just a science, that at heart it is . . . well, what? . . . a branch of ethics perhaps.

FURTHER DEVELOPMENT OF THE ETHICS-BASED VIEW

With this beefed-up reverse view of medicine, however, it may seem that, having perhaps erred previously on the side of caution, I have now gone over the top. Medicine as a branch of ethics, indeed! Surely, it will perhaps be said, here is some kind of ethics-based illusion. Useful, maybe, as a counter to the science-based illusion, but an illusion all the same.

But if it is an illusion, it is not obviously so. And one way to see that it is not, is to put Boorse's science-based view of medicine a little more firmly to the philosophical test. Thus, Boorse's strategy, taken in its broadest outlines, is based on the idea that whatever ethical issues are prowling at the margins of medicine, there is at its centre a body of empirical-scientific knowledge by which medical theory proper – and hence medicine itself as a technical, specialist discipline – is actually defined. What Boorse in effect says is that if you mark out this body of knowledge, then you have marked off those factual questions with which medicine (as a technical, specialist discipline) is properly concerned from the ethical questions with which it is not. And he seeks to achieve this marking out by distinguishing what he believes to be the strictly factual or descriptive uses of medical terms in technical contexts from what he willingly concedes are their mixed evaluative and descriptive uses in non-technical, or lay, contexts. Reserving the term 'disease' for the former (technical) use, he is thus able to argue that to say that someone has a disease is not to express a value-judgement at all, but just to assert certain matters of fact. It is to describe their condition, not to evaluate it. Here, of course, as Boorse recognizes, matters become more complicated. For the descriptions by virtue of which someone may be said to 'have a disease' are very diverse. But at least, so Boorse thinks, it has something to do with the way in which they, or their bodies and minds, are functioning, and more specifically with the idea that they are 'not functioning properly'. And this idea, so Boorse believes, need not be – as it perhaps appears to be – an evaluative one. For, as it is used in the biological-scientific context of medical theory, it is a purely descriptive idea, determined by such (sufficient though not necessary) descriptive criteria as (shades here of Kendell) 'reduced life and/or reproductive expectations'. And with criteria such as these, Boorse concludes, we thus have an unassailable hard core of fact upon which medical theory – empirical-scientific medical theory – can be constructed.

Now, set out in this way, Boorse's theory rings, for me at any rate, certain philosophical bells. Specifically, it rings certain moral philosophical bells. For, set out like this, is it not strongly reminiscent of – indeed, is it not understandable as a species of – moral descriptivism? The main element necessary for moral descriptivism is there at any rate: the existence of certain terms – in this case 'illness' and 'disease' – which, though etymologically value-terms, and often used with clear evaluative connotations, are none the less also sometimes used with clear descriptive connotations. And Boorse, indeed, though initially defining 'disease' descriptively, tends, in his actual use of the term, to substitute expressions with clear evaluative force. For example, having first defined 'disease' as a 'deviation' from the (statistical) norm, he then goes on to talk of it as a 'deficiency in functional efficiency', the descriptive 'statistical deviation' thus giving way to the evaluative 'deficient functional efficiency'. Thus his thesis is perhaps better understood not (as it is presented) as being that 'disease' as used in technical contexts in medicine is value-free, but rather as the explicitly descriptivist thesis that the value-judgement expressed by 'disease', as it is used in technical contexts in medicine, is one which is entailed – logically or strictly entailed – by certain descriptions. His thesis, that is to say, is better understood not as the claim that 'disease', in technical usage, describes the mode of functioning of an organism as leading, *inter alia*, to reduced life and/or reproductive expectations; but rather as the thesis that describing the mode of functioning of an organism in this way entails – and entails because of what the term actually means – the value-judgement which is expressed by 'disease'.

From a description, therefore, according to Boorse's theory (as I have now re-interpreted it), there comes an evaluation. Just as from an 'is', according to descriptivist ethical theory, there may sometimes come an 'ought'. But there is nothing of all this in Boorse's presentation of his views. And indeed, consistently so. For, as we should expect if he is working, as I have claimed, under the science-based illusion, most of what he says is influenced more by the philosophy of science than by moral philosophy. Hare gets only a footnote. But Boorse's use even of the philosophy of science is curiously selective; on the key question for example, for his own theory – whether function statements themselves are value-free – we again get only a footnote. And in this footnote we are told merely (and without specific references) that 'philosophers of science have made too much progress in giving biological function statements a descriptive analysis' for the view that they are value-laden to be at all convincing. So that even here, in Boorse's – if I may say so – skewed use of the philosophy of science, the influence of the science-based illusion is detectable. Indeed, in his uncharacteristically uncritical reliance at this key point in his arguments, on an authority at once so powerful and yet so ill-defined, there is something perhaps even of the *de*lusion.

What, then, of the alternative view – my ethics-based view? Well, for a start, given that the terms 'illness' and 'disease' are (as Boorse himself emphasizes) mixed evaluative and descriptive terms, it is at least as reasonable to analyze them from the point of view of moral philosophy as from the point of view of the philosophy of science. Why not, after all, interrogate these terms as value-terms rather than as factual terms? And indeed, once we have stopped thinking of medicine as being at heart a science – or have at least stood back from this idea so that we can hold it up for examination, rather than just taking it for granted – then it becomes clear that the issues with which Boorse is concerned are no more and no less than the issues with which moral philosophers have been concerned in that most central of moral philosophical debates, the 'is-ought' debate. Or, to make the point a little more circumspectly, it becomes clear that the issues with which Boorse is concerned can at least reasonably be construed in this way. And the advantage of so construing them is that they can then be reflected on in the light of several generations of careful philosophical inspection. For everything that has been said in the is-ought debate, as far back as David Hume and beyond, can then be said of the terms 'illness' and 'disease' construed *as* value terms.

But I am not going to try to say all that in this paper! Though you will have gathered from what I have said already, that I believe that if we were to comb through the is-ought debate literature with the terms 'illness' and 'disease' in mind, we would come not to a descriptivist conclusion with Boorse, but to a non-descriptivist conclusion. We would come, that is to say, to the conclusion that even in technical contexts in medicine, a medical 'ought' (so to speak) is not to be had from a biological-descriptive 'is'; that the term 'disease', no less than the term 'illness', as it is used in technical contexts in medicine, is indeed a value-term; and that, notwithstanding its mainly descriptive connotations in such contexts, the value-judgement which is expressed by it is one which is not logically entailed – though it is of course very strongly psychologically entailed (if I may put it that way) – by descriptions even of the kind suggested by Boorse. And from all this would emerge the ethics-based view of medicine which I suggested, bold-faced, a few minutes ago. If the very scope of medicine is defined by terms which are essentially, and irreducibly, value-terms, then medicine is indeed, to this extent, a branch of ethics. For built right into the conceptual heart of the subject – whatever the extent of its empirical-scientific development – is an evaluative logical element.

SOME CONSEQUENCES OF THE ETHICS-BASED VIEW

What I want to do now is to look at some of the consequences of this ethics-based view of medicine. For it is through these consequences that we will get back to our three catch-22 paradoxes, and so to the concept of 'the person'.

First of all, what about medicine as a science? Is it all over? Must we conclude with Boorse that if the concepts not only of 'illness' but also of 'disease' are evaluative concepts, then, indeed, 'a value-free science of health is impossible'? Well, my experience here accords with that of Brian Farrell,[4] namely, that this is a conclusion not likely to win friends or influence people in medicine. And in a sense this is fair enough. Medicine, as I noted at the outset, is essentially an opportunistic and pragmatic subject. So the reaction of its practitioners to anything (like my non-descriptivist conclusion) by which its so successful hybridization with science appears to be undermined, will quite properly be hostile. But there is, in fact, no real conflict of interest here. For the success of the medicine–science hybrid has been with empirical clinical problems; whereas the clinical problems with which we are concerned here – those involved in our catch-22 paradoxes – are non-empirical, predominantly ethical, problems. Indeed, the success of the medicine–science hybrid, far from being undermined by a non-descriptivist interpretation of the medical concepts, should be advanced and promoted by it. For such an interpretation will tend to disentangle the factual from the evaluative components of the meanings of these concepts. And it will thus open up the possibility of marking out more clearly than before the precise nature and extent of the contribution of science to medicine. Which is surely no bad thing: to get clear just what are and what are not empirical questions in medicine; and to get clear just what are and what are not the empirical components of medical questions. The value-judgements expressed by the medical concepts may direct the course of medical science. But there is nothing in a non-descriptivist interpretation of these concepts that would obstruct that course or impede its progress. On the contrary.

So there is nothing to worry about here. Medical science survives intact, and perhaps clarified. And when we turn to the other side of the coin, to medicine as an ethical discipline, we find rather more substantial advantages offered by non-descriptivism.

In the first place, the general posture of non-descriptivism towards non-empirical problems in medicine is likely to be more positive than that of descriptivism. The reason for this goes right back to the essential difference between non-descriptivist and descriptivist interpretations of value-terms. The descriptivist interpretation is essentially reductionist: in deriving evaluations from descriptions, the descriptivist effectively reduces evaluation to description, and the net result of this as far as medical ethics is concerned is to suggest that the ethical questions with which it is occupied are, at the end of the day, not really, as they appear, evaluative questions, but questions of fact. Get to the facts, descriptivism seems to suggest, and the evaluations will follow. So it all comes back to science after all. Which tends to be something of a 'cop-out'! Descriptivism certainly need not be as dismissive as this. Even within descriptivism, it is necessary to ask – and this is indeed in part a conceptual question – just what facts are relevant to a given value-judgement. All the same, the tendency will often be to assume that the substantive issues are empirical.

For the non-descriptivist, on the other hand, there is no such tendency. He has no option but to 'cop in'. Maintaining, as he does, the logical gap between evaluation and description, his attitude to evaluative questions in medicine has to be, as it were, full square. He will recognize, of course, that questions of fact are always relevant to questions of value. But in recognizing also that questions of value are not reducible, even in principle, to questions of fact, he must face questions of value on their own terms, *as* questions of value. And in recognizing that there is an irreducible evaluative element built into the very meanings of the terms by which medicine is defined, he must face questions of medical value – medical-ethical questions – as questions as firmly at the centre of medical theory as questions of fact. Non-descriptivism thus leaves no scope for displacing medical-ethical questions to the periphery of medical theory, let alone for excluding them from it altogether.

It is because of the more 'full square' posture required of non-descriptivism – and here we come to a second advantage of non-descriptivism – that when we get round to attempting actually to deal with evaluative questions in medicine, we find rather more in the way of ready-made, 'off the shelf', ethical theory available from non-descriptivism than from descriptivism.

Let me give just one example of this, drawn from the psychiatry/anti-psychiatry debate. As we saw earlier, much of that debate has been inspired by the more evaluative connotations of the concept of 'mental illness', as compared with that of 'physical illness'. It was precisely because 'mental illness' has these more evaluative connotations that it was denied the status of illness by Szasz; while Kendell's defence of it amounted to an attempt to clean it up, to show that, its evaluative connotations notwithstanding, it could be cleaned up to be a factual concept just like the (as he supposed) factual concept of 'physical illness'. And indeed, in what I have called the continuing debate about mental illness – the continuing doubts, dissatisfactions, and anxieties about it – its more evaluative connotations have continued to be important. For it is precisely because saying that someone is mentally ill has a more evaluative ring than saying that he or she is physically ill, that these doubts, dissatisfactions, and anxieties have continued to be expressed.

However, once the evaluative nettle is grasped, once it is recognized and accepted that 'mental illness' and 'physical illness' really are both value-terms, then the difference between them in the relative strengths of their evaluative connotations can be understood quite differently, not so much as something peculiar to mental illness and physical illness as such, let alone as something prejudicial to mental illness, but rather as something which reflects a well-recognized property that these terms – used *as* value-terms – have in common with value-terms in general. For as Hare and others have pointed out,[5] value-terms in general – and not least the paradigmatic value term 'good' – show marked variations in the strength of their evaluative connotations.

Yet – and this is the nub – for the most part, so far as I am aware, it is only non-descriptivists (like Hare) who have given much in the way of detailed thought to why this should be so. Hence, if we are concerned to explain the more evaluative connotations of 'mental illness' compared with 'physical illness', then, in the true opportunistic-pragmatic spirit of medicine, it is to non-descriptivist ethical theory, rather than descriptivist ethical theory, that we should turn. And in this instance, indeed, it so happens that non-descriptivist ethical theory suits our particular medical needs rather well. For the general theory – the general non-descriptivist ethical theory – is that variations in the strength of the evaluative connotations of a value-term follow variations in the extent to which the criteria for the value-judgement expressed by that value-term are settled: the more settled the criteria, the less marked are the evaluative connotations – essentially because, if the criteria are settled, it is mainly questions of fact, questions about whether the criteria are or are not satisfied, which are raised by the use of the value-term as such. And applying this to the medical case, we can see, in a general way at least, that the criteria by which typical symptoms of physical illness, such as pain, are evaluated, are on the whole more settled than the criteria by which typical symptoms of mental illness, such as anxiety, are evaluated; so that we should indeed expect the term 'mental illness' to have more marked evaluative connotations than the term 'physical illness'.

With this conclusion goes a third advantage of non-descriptivist ethical theory – that, as between mental illness and physical illness, it is a neutral theory. Descriptivism, with its reductionist tendency, has the effect of reinforcing the science-based illusion. As long as medicine is thought, properly and at heart to be a science, those uses of medical terms which are value-laden will inevitably be thought of pejoratively; as degenerate, or as defective, or at any rate as primitive, uses. But once medical terms generally are recognized to be value-terms, and once medicine itself is thus recognized to be, properly and at heart, an ethical discipline, this pejorative way of thinking about the value-laden uses of its terms ceases to be possible. With non-descriptivist ethical theory, we thus see that 'mental illness' in *being* value-laden is at least as sound logically as is 'physical illness' in *not* being so laden. For in this respect, both reflect the properties of the phenomena – anxiety and anxiety-like phenomena, and pain and painlike phenomena – by which they are respectively constituted. Furthermore, they reflect the properties of these phenomena equally faithfully. So that with non-descriptivist ethical theory, the logical respectability of mental illness compared with physical illness, and with it the professional respectability of psychological medicine compared with physical medicine, is wholly restored.

Broadly, therefore, given these three advantages, we can see that non-descriptivist ethical theory, while leaving intact the contribution of science to solving empirical clinical problems, is in its own right capable of making an important contribution to solving non-empirical clinical problems. Our view of medicine as a branch of ethics, illuminated by non-descriptivist ethical theory, is thus, at the very least, a clinically useful view.

BACK TO OUR INITIAL PARADOXES

The clinical usefulness of this view of medicine comes out more clearly still in relation to our three initial catch-22 paradoxes. For it allows at least first handholds on solutions to each of them. It allows a first handhold on our third paradox, because this was directly concerned with the recent increase in non-empirical problems; so any contribution of our ethics-based view of medicine to solving such problems is, by the same token, a contribution to resolving this paradox. Similarly, it allows a first handhold on our second paradox, because this was indirectly concerned with non-empirical clinical problems. It was concerned with patients' dissatisfaction with medicine, and these dissatisfactions both reflect and are embodied in non-empirical – that is, ethical, medico-legal, and political – clinical problems.

The contribution of our ethics-based view of medicine to resolving our first paradox – concerned with the displacement of the patient-as-a-person from the centre of medical attention – is less apparent. However, since this paradox is, in many ways, clinically the most important of the three, it merits rather closer attention. We can examine it by reference to the three advantages of non-descriptivist ethical theory outlined above.

Consider first, advantages one and two. By these, as we have seen, we are obliged to take seriously the evaluative part of medicine. And along with this goes the person – not for any high-powered philosophical reason, but because the person is, in medicine, bound up conceptually with the ethical, rather than the scientific, part of the subject. This is evident in our three paradoxes: the patient-as-a-person who, under our first paradox, was displaced by the patient-as-a-machine as scientific medicine advanced was the patient whose dissatisfaction with medicine had, under our second paradox, increased, despite medical-scientific progress; and under our third paradox, it was this dissatisfied patient-as-a-person around whom medical-ethical difficulties had been gathering. Therefore, anything which brings these medical-ethical difficulties, and the dissatisfactions they represent, back to centre stage medically will bring back with it the patient-as-a-person. And this is, I believe, what non-descriptivism – as a counter to the science-based illusion – does for us in a powerful, albeit rather non-specific, way.

The third advantage offered by non-descriptivist ethical theory brings the person back into medicine by way of a rather more specific effect – two rather more specific effects, in fact.

The first of these is what might be called its balancing-up effect. The third advantage of non-descriptivism as you will recall, is that it restores the logical respectability of the concept of 'mental illness' compared with that of 'physical illness', and along with it the professional respectability of psychological medicine compares with that of physical medicine. But you will remember from what I said at the start, that in psychological medicine, as against physical medicine, the patient-as-a-person is more immediately at the focus of clinical attention. Hence, in restoring the respectability of psychological medicine, non-descriptivism has the effect of restoring the patient-as-a-person to the focus of clinical attention. And this is its balancing-up effect. It balances up, within medicine as a whole, the patient-as-a-machine in physical medicine, with the patient-as-a-person in psychological medicine.

Its second effect is more specific still. It is what I shall call, taking my cue from J. L. Austin,[6] a 'who-wears-the-trousers' effect. It is one which reinforces the first effect.

Thus, the first effect I described a moment ago as operating through the 'restoration' of the logical respectability of the concept of 'mental illness'. It was natural that I should have described it in this way, because it is the value-laden concept of 'mental illness', rather than the apparently value-free concept of 'physical illness', the respectability of which has tended to be called into doubt. This is all part of the science-based illusion under which medicine has been operating. But now think about this from the opposite direction, from the point of view not of medicine as a branch of science but of medicine as a branch of ethics. From the first point of view, that of medicine as a branch of science, it is the apparently value-free concept of 'physical illness' which wears the trousers. But from the point of view of medicine as a branch of ethics, it is the other way round: it is the relatively value-laden concept of 'mental illness' which wears the trousers. For in being value-laden, it actually displays, where the concept of 'physical illness' conceals, the essentially evaluative nature of the concept of 'illness'. From the ethics-based point of view, therefore, the concept of 'mental illness', far from being a concept that is somehow *de*fective compared with the concept of 'physical illness', must be considered, by virtue of its evaluative connotations, to be the more *e*ffective of the two. And it is in this way that this 'who-wears-the-trousers effect' reinforces the balancing-up effect by which the patient-as-a-person is restored to the focus of clinical attention in medicine.

Mark you, having got the patient-as-a-person back to centre stage in medicine, we are left with the job of knowing how to handle him. And I suspect that it is only when we know how to handle him, and with the same efficiency as we now handle the patient-as-a-machine, that we will be able to manage more than just first handholds on any of our three initial catch-22 paradoxes.

But as yet we have no methods available for dealing with the patient-as-a-person that are comparable to the scientific method which is available for dealing with the patient-as-a-machine. The psychologists are interested mainly in personalities, not in persons. And as for the philosophers, they have little in the way of ready-made philosophical 'theory of the person' to offer us. Indeed, in this regard, medicine could well have as much to offer philosophy as philosophy medicine. For with the reappearance of the person at centre stage in medicine goes a considerable pressure of necessity to resolve the philosophical problems with which the concept of the person is associated . . . and necessity, of course, is the mother of invention. Furthermore, given the links which exist in medicine between the person and medical-ethical difficulties – the links running through our three initial paradoxes – it seems reasonable to suppose that progress in handling the patient-as-a-person will eventually be made (if at all) by a medicine–philosophy hybrid the attention of which is directed towards just these links – the links, that is, between concepts of the person and their ethical implications.

DISCUSSION

BASIL MITCHELL. I wonder whether you could give us some examples of the way in which your approach would work out in practice.

WILLIAM FULFORD. First of all, I must emphasize that it is still only an approach, and an approach which at this stage is intended only to change a little the posture of medicine. Also, I think that one of the mistakes – if I may say so – that philosophers have made as they have become involved in medicine is to try to arrive at answers rather too quickly. However, having said all that, I believe that my approach, just as an approach, can be helpful by giving doctors a broader frame of reference within which to work – more elbowroom, as it were. This has been brought home to me recently in discussing my approach with groups of general – that is, family – practitioners. Hospital doctors, by and large, don't need my approach because they deal mainly with patients whose problems fall into one or more of the well defined empirical areas. But general practitioners see medicine in the raw; they see an unselected mixture of empirical and non-empirical clinical problems. And their reaction to my approach is to say, 'Ah! I see. So it is not all a matter of science after all. No wonder I find so much of my practice so intractably difficult!' Of course, I would hope that in developing my approach, something more substantive in the way of actual answers to some of the non-empirical problems of clinical practice would come along; in fact, I hope to go on now to do more detailed work in some particular problem area, probably involuntary psychiatric treatment of depressed patients. But in showing the possibility of such answers coming along, how we might get to them, and so on, my approach does seem to be helpful.

GRANT GILLETT. There is a very concrete example, namely, the rise of cognitivism in psychiatry. Its ruling assumption is that the way persons reason about what is going on in their lives, and the degree of cognitive and rational responsibility they are prepared to take for their own lives, has got to be a guiding light in the therapeutic process. In no way can a person's active cognitive self as subject be bypassed by simply manipulating mental functions in an attempt to restore some functional conception of normality.

FULFORD. Yes, the agent-patient distinction is certainly much less clear-cut in psychiatry than in physical medicine, and an important part of what is involved in actually treating psychiatric patients is helping them to see themselves as agents and not as patients! Part of what I was saying at the end of my paper is that we could do with a more rigorous way of understanding this process.

ROGER TRIGG. I have some sympathy with what you say, but your approach is spoilt for me because what you are saying rests on an old-fashioned distinction between facts and values. This runs right the way through the prescriptive-descriptive debate, and it seems to me that in much contemporary philosophy of science we find a rather disturbing suggestion to the effect that there are no 'facts'. However, I am an unrepentant realist. Many philosophers of science point out the priority of theory, and the way in which values are incorporated into theories and so into what one counts as facts and evidence. This suggests that at the roots of every move in science, there are what might be called 'values', though the use of that word itself suggests a contrast with facts. There are no pure values, and there are no pure facts: every decision, whether in science or in ethics, is going to be a mixture of both. There is no clear contrast between the empirical and the ethical, between science and ethics.

FULFORD. But everything that you say strikes me as suggesting that that very distinction, old-fashioned as it may be, is still firmly there in our conceptual scheme. Certainly, fact and value *are* mixed together in medical talk, even in scientific talk, as they are in everyday usage. And our job is to disentangle them.

TRIGG. But there is still the illusion that there are pure facts and pure data, and that is an empiricist delusion.

MICHAEL LOCKWOOD. I wish to defend what Fulford said. I am old-fashioned enough to believe that the fact–value distinction is perfectly genuine and absolutely crucial. Clear thinking seems to me to demand that one separate out the factual claims one is making from the evaluative ones. That does not mean, of course, that science is a value-free activity. But scientists *ought*, I would maintain, to conduct their activity in a way that is as far as possible dispassionate, taking care to avoid ideological prejudging of what are essentially factual issues.

Fulford has raised the much vexed philosophical question of how we are to understand disease, illness, and so on: the question of what, exactly, these terms should be taken to mean. If we use 'ailment' as a collective term for illness, injury, and so on, then it seems to me that what we really have in mind here is a malfunction of the human being; and I see no reason for excluding mental malfunctions, regardless of whether one happens to believe (as I do) that there is invariably a material basis for what goes on in the mind. I would argue – and here I have been influenced by C. M. Culver and B. Gert[7] – that we only think of something as an ailment if it involves a malfunction in the absence of an external sustaining cause. If I take somebody and hold him forcibly to the floor, so that he cannot move, then he is undoubtedly suffering from a malfunction. But it is not an ailment, because immediately I let go, he is able to move again. That is what distinguishes him from someone who is paralyzed. Equally, in the mental sphere, one can distinguish a person who has a persecution complex from a person who is actually being persecuted. There is, in one sense, a malfunction in both cases. But in the case of the persecuted person, it is sustained by an external cause: the actions of his persecutors. Hence we do not say that there is anything wrong with him, just with his situation. By contrast, the person with the persecution complex is suffering from a malfunction which has as its cause something internal to his own workings. Of course, the term 'malfunction' already implies something that is bad, something that, in general, it is in people's interests not to have (though, of course, it may not be bad in the particular case; a broken leg may be an excellent thing to have if it prevents one from being sent into battle). To this extent, it is perfectly true that terms such as 'ailment', 'illness', 'disease', and 'injury' are evaluative. I think this is in some ways regrettable, because it often allows doctors to present what are in part value-judgements as though they were purely scientific ones. It allows value-judgements to masquerade as applications of purely technical expertise, when it is highly desirable to keep matters of fact and of value separate from each other. Awareness of this, it seems to me, is one of the things that has helped spur the recent upsurge of interest in medical ethics.

FULFORD. Compulsory psychiatric treatment illustrates the importance of recognizing this. Compulsory treatment hinges on the notion of 'illness'. The decision whether or nor to take away a person's freedom, his status as an agent, and make him a patient hinges on the decision as to whether or not he is ill. And this decision, which is an everyday clinical decision, is not *purely* scientific. The facts are important, but it also involves a value-judgement. And what I am saying is that the sooner we recognize this the better.

MITCHELL. I would like to have clarified the relation between what you have just said about terms in medical usage being value-laden and what you were saying in the main part of your paper about descriptivism and non-descriptivism. In your paper you said that it was important to see the value-judgements involved in medicine as being ethical value-judgements. But the sort of value-judgements that you have just referred to as being medical value-judgements are not ethical ones. It is an ethical question whether, given that someone is going to be ill, one ought or ought not physically to restrain that person; but it does not seem to be an ethical judgement whether or not that person is medically ill. It is not quite clear how your distinction between descriptivist and non-descriptivist theory, which was drawn up in relation to ethics, refers to the special cases that interest us in relation to medical terms.

FULFORD. Thank you. I was really talking about evaluation when I was discussing descriptivism and non-descriptivism. Certainly, medical value-judgements differ not only from ethical and moral value-judgements, but also, for example, from aesthetic value-judgements. And the next step, in the approach that I am suggesting, is to focus on what is involved in specifically medical value-judgements. First you explore how far you can get by considering medical usage in the light of what is known of the logic of value-terms. Then you go on to consider how medical value-judgements are marked off from value-judgements of other kinds. But I didn't try to go into all that in this paper.

RICHARD DAWKINS. I was a little worried about your use of the term 'non-scientific'. I accept that ethical questions are non-scientific questions, but at the beginning of your talk you rather implied that there was a tendency for treating the patient-as-a-person as secondary to treating the patient-as-a-(bodily)-machine, with scientists seen somewhat as shallow, simplistic fellows who thought of machines as being somehow in contrast to persons. Doesn't that rather beg the question? I would prefer to make a distinction between the patient as *simple* machine and the patient as *complex* machine. The patient as the latter may be very much the same as the patient as a person. You also referred to art and intuition; yet, if there is one field of human endeavour where art and intuition are absolutely paramount, it is surely science. In any of the great scientists, the crucial edge that they had over lesser scientists was the superiority of their art and their intuition. You seem to me to have too negative a conception of what science means.

FULFORD. I did not mean to imply that there is no art or intuition in science, let alone that scientists are shallow, simplistic fellows! Perhaps I did push some of my distinctions too hard. But the distinction between the patient as a simple machine and the patient as a complex machine is certainly not what I was after.

My intuition, if you will, is that the patient-as-a-person differs qualitatively from the patient-as-a-machine. And what I was saying is that one strategy for getting a clearer understanding of this difference is to examine medical usage – 'illness', 'disease', etc. – from the point of view of moral philosophy and of what is known of the logic of value-terms, rather than from that of the philosophy of science.

9

Jung's Concept of Personality

ANTHONY STORR

All concepts of personality are, to a varying extent, subjective. Jung's concept is no exception. It was influenced by his family background, by the period in which he lived, by his reading and education, and by the fact that he was a Swiss who was strongly influenced by German culture. I shall therefore give a brief account of his early life.

Carl Gustav Jung was born on 26 July 1875. His father was a minister in the Swiss Reformed Church. The greater part of his early childhood was passed at Klein-Hüningen, near Basel, to which the family moved in 1879. For his first nine years, Jung remained an only child who lived primarily in his imagination and who spent much of his time in solitary play. The birth of a much younger sister did little to alleviate Jung's isolation. He attended the local school; but, being more intelligent than most of his schoolfellows, attracted some competitive hostility. In his eleventh year, he was sent to the Gymnasium in Basel. From 1895 to 1900, he studied at Basel University. Jung originally wanted to be an archaeologist; but there was no teacher in this subject at Basel, and, since the family was far from rich, he was dependent upon a grant which applied only to the local university. He therefore decided to study medicine, but continued to feel that this choice was something of a compromise. However, his interest in the past found fulfilment in the study of evolutionary theory and comparative anatomy. He came to think of the mind as having an immensely long history, and as functioning along lines laid down in the remote past. It seems probable that this view of mind took origin from his anatomical studies. If the structures of the body had been adaptively evolved over many centuries, it was reasonable to assume that the structures of the mind had evolved in similar fashion.

As he approached the end of his medical studies, Jung was in debt, and realized that he would have to earn a living as soon as possible. At first he was inclined towards surgery. Then he happened to read a textbook by the Viennese psychiatrist Krafft-Ebing, and at once realized in what field his future lay. In December 1900, he became an assistant at the Burghölzli mental hospital in Zürich, which was then under the direction of Eugen Bleuler, the pioneer investigator of schizophrenia. In 1902, his MD dissertation entitled *On the Psychology and Pathology of So-Called Occult Phenomena* was published. During the winter of 1902–3, Jung spent a term at the Salpêtrière in Paris in order to study psychopathology with Pierre Janet. This was the famous hopsital at which Freud had attended Charcot's clinic during the winter of 1885–6. In 1903, Jung married Emma Rauschenbach. They had a son and four daughters. In 1905, he became senior staff physician at the Burghölzli and was also appointed a lecturer in psychiatry at the University of Zürich. In 1907, Jung published his pioneering book on schizophrenia, *The Psychology of Dementia Praecox*. He sent a copy to Freud, whom he met for the first time in Vienna in March of that year. In 1909, Jung visited the United States with Freud and Ferenczi, and was given an honorary degree by Clark University. In the same year, he relinquished his post at the Burghölzli in favour of his growing private practice. After his break with Freud in 1913, he went through a period of intense personal crisis, and resigned his lectureship at the University of Zürich. He continued to write and practise at his house on the Lake of Zürich until his death in 1961.

Although Jung was, for a time, strongly influenced by Freud, it is important to realize that he had carried out a great deal of original work before he encountered Freud. The main ideas which coalesced to form Jung's concept of personality can be traced to earlier periods in his own development. Jung was never a whole-hearted Freudian disciple: the differences between the two men were evident from the beginning.

Jung's earliest work and his later writings have more in common than is generally realized. They are linked by the theme that mental illness is characterized by disunity of the personality, while mental health is manifested by unity. Jung's doctoral thesis was a study of his 15½-year-old cousin, Hélène Presiwerk, who, claiming to be a medium, stated that she was 'controlled' by a variety of different personalities. Jung interpreted these as being personifications of unconscious parts of herself – subsidiary, incomplete personalities which could temporarily take over. At the turn of the century, psychiatrists were fascinated by cases of so-called multiple personality like Morton Prince's famous case of Sally Beauchamp. Pierre Janet was particularly interested in cases of this kind, had described several cases of his own, and had reviewed the literature. Janet believed that neurosis was due to some physiological deficiency in the nervous system which prevented cohesion of the various aspects of personality. This lack of integration resulted in aspects of consciousness becoming split off and dissociated. Jung was at least as much influenced by Janet, with whom he had studied, as he was by Freud, whom he had only read. He continued to think of personality as being capable of dissociation into subsidiary personalities. In hysteria, for example, the patient might behave like his young cousin; as if she were two or more different persons who had no cognizance of each other. It followed that cure of this type of neurosis depended upon making these divided selves aware of each other, thereby creating a new unity of personality.

In Schizophrenia, it appeared to Jung that the personality was fragmented into many parts, rather than into two or three, as in hysteria. Jung wrote: 'Whereas in the healthy person the ego is the subject of his experience, in the schizophrenic the ego is only *one* of the experiencing subjects. In other words, in schizophrenia the normal subject has split into a plurality of subjects, or into a plurality of *autonomous complexes*.'[1]

Jung's next group of studies was based upon the use of word-association tests. A list of a hundred words is read out, and the subject is asked to respond to each with the first word that occurs to him. By timing the interval between stimulus and response with a stop-watch, it became possible to demonstrate that, unknown to themselves, subjects are influenced by words which arouse emotion, because such words slow down their responses. Often, groups of words were linked around a theme; and to such a collection of associations Jung gave the name 'complex', a term which he introduced into psychiatry. These experiments were important in that they demonstrated objectively, in ways which could be measured, the dynamic effects of unconscious mental processes. Here is an example given by Jung himself. He was testing a normal man of 35.

To begin with, it was the word *knife* that caused four disturbed reactions. The next disturbance was *lance* (or *spear*) and then *to beat*, then the word *pointed* and then *bottle*. That was in a short series of fifty stimulus words, which was enough for me to tell the man point-blank what the matter was. So I said: 'I did not know you had such a disagreeable experience.' He stared at me and said: 'I do not know what you are talking about.' I said: 'You know you were drunk and had a disagreeable affair with sticking your knife into somebody.' He said: 'How do you know?' Then he confessed the whole thing. He came of a respectable family, simple but quite nice people. He had been abroad and one day got into a drunken quarrel, drew a knife and stuck it into somebody and got a year in prison. That is a great secret which he does not mention because it would cast a shadow on his life.[2]

The group of words connected with the incident constitutes a complex, which Jung defined as 'the *image* of a certain psychic situation which is strongly accentuated emotionally and is, moreover, incompatible with the habitual attitude of consciousness. This image has a powerful inner coherence, it has its own wholeness and, in addition, a relatively high degree of autonomy, so that it is subject to the control of the conscious mind to only a limited extent, and therefore behaves like an animated foreign body in the sphere of consciousness.'[3] Jung referred to complexes as being fragmentary personalities. Often, they interfere with what the person consciously wants to do. They are responsible for those slips of the tongue and other errors which Freud described in his book *The Psychopathology of Everyday Life*. Jung writes: 'They slip just the wrong word into one's mouth, they make one forget the name of the person one is about to introduce, they cause a tickle in the throat just when the softest passage is being played on the piano at a concert, they make the tiptoeing latecomer trip over a chair with a resounding crash.'[4] Jung goes on to say that complexes appear in personified form in dreams, and also as hallucinatory 'voices' in schizophrenia. He found that the extremes of dissociation and splitting occurred in the psychotic; but even normal people suffered from 'complexes', and in this way demonstrated some degree of dissociation within the psyche.

Jung was deeply influenced by his clinical experience at the Burghölzli mental hospital. Although, after 1909, when he gave up his hospital post, he was principally concerned with the treatment of ambulant neurotics, he remained fascinated by schizophrenia. His last paper on the subject appeared in 1957, only four years before his death. Many of the disagreements which led to the rift between Jung and Freud can be traced to the difference in their clinical experience. Freud only ever worked in a mental hospital for three weeks as a locum. His experience with psychotic patients was minimal; and, although he wrote a famous paper on Schreber, the judge with paranoia, his interpretations were based upon the patient's own writings, not upon any actual encounter with him. Jung was the first psychiatrist to apply psychoanalytic ideas to the study of delusions and hallucinations, and to demonstrate that such phenomena, hitherto dismissed as incomprehensible, could be shown to have a psychological origin and meaning. He believed that many cases of obsessional neurosis and hysteria were really cases of latent schizophrenia, and warned against the danger of precipitating psychotic breakdown by unwise psychotherapeutic intervention. On the other hand, Jung considered that psychotherapy did have a limited part to play in the treatment of schizophrenia and gives examples of cases which he treated with partial success.

It was Jung's experience with psychotic patients which led him to postulate a 'collective unconscious'. He found that delusions and hallucinations could seldom be explained as products of the patient's personal history. Jung's extensive knowledge of comparative religion and of mythology led him to detect parallels with psychotic material which argued a common source, a myth-producing level of mind which was common to all men. Jung described the collective unconscious as consisting of mythological motifs, or primordial images, to which he gave the name 'archetypes'. Archetypes are not inborn ideas, but 'typical forms of behaviour which, once they become conscious, naturally present themselves *as ideas and images*, like everything else that becomes a content of consciousness'.[5]

The kind of observation which led Jung to this conclusion is illustrated by the case of a man in his thirties who was suffering from paranoid schizophrenia. Jung encountered him in the corridor of the hospital. He writes:

> One day I came across him there, blinking through the window up at the sun, and moving his head from side to side in a curious manner. He took me by the arm and said he wanted to show me something. He said I must look at the sun with my eyes half shut, and then I could see the sun's phallus. If I moved my head from side to side the sun-phallus would move too, and that was the origin of the wind.

Four years later, Jung came across a Greek text, thought to be a liturgy of the Mithraic cult, in which a vision is described:

> And likewise the so-called tube the origin of the ministering wind. For you will see hanging down from the disc of the sun something that looks like a tube. And towards the regions westward it is as though there were an infinite east wind. But if the other wind should prevail towards the regions of the east, you will in like manner see the vision veering in that direction.[6]

Jung goes on to point out that certain mediaeval paintings depict the Virgin as being impregnated from heaven by means of a tube down which the Holy Ghost descends. The Holy Ghost was originally imagined as a rushing mighty wind, the *pneuma*.

Freud thought of the unconscious as chiefly derived from repression, a kind of dung-heap of the personally unacceptable. Jung thought that, while the unconscious certainly contained elements of personality which the individual might repudiate, it also contained the germs of new possibilities, the seeds of future, and possibly better, adaptation. Freud thought that neurosis originated in early childhood; that it derived from the patient having become fixated at one or other stage of emotional development. Jung agreed that material from childhood was often evident in neurosis, but considered that the appearance of such material was secondary to a failure of adaptation in the present. He wrote: 'The psychological determination of a neurosis is only partly due to an early infantile predisposition; it must be due to some cause in the present as well.' 'The moment of the outbreak of neurosis is not just a matter of chance; as a rule it is most critical. It is usually *the moment when a new psychological adjustment, that is, a new adaptation, is demanded.*'[7] Jung continues: 'I no longer seek the cause of a neurosis in the past, but in the present. I ask, what is the necessary task which the patient will not accomplish?'[8]

In Jung's view, therefore, the development of neurotic symptoms was not simply the onset of an illness, but a signal for the person to re-examine himself and his values in order to attain a new and better adaptation. This was particularly true of certain transitional periods of life; of, for example, the passage from adolescence to adulthood. Jung was fond of saying: 'Thank God he became neurotic!', meaning by this that depression or whatever symptom the person had developed had had the positive function of compelling him to look inward.

Freud and his followers were primarily concerned with the childhood determinants of neurosis. The task of psychoanalysis was to facilitate recall of the patient's earliest memories. The older the patient, the harder this task became. Therefore, in the early days of psychoanalysis, analysts were reluctant to take on middle-aged patients. Jung, on the other hand, came to specialize in the treatment of the middle-aged. Jung's major contribution to psychology is in the field of adult development. His interest in this undoubtedly originated from the period of psychological distress which he experienced after his break with Freud. This upheaval was so intense that Jung described himself as being 'menaced by a psychosis'. The sad story of the estrangement between the two men can be traced in *The Freud-Jung Letters*. In 1912, Jung published the first edition of what became known, in English translation, as *The Psychology of the Unconscious*, and, when published in 1956 as volume 5 of the Collected Works, as *Symbols of Transformation* (published in German as *Wandlungen und Symbole der Libido*, revised in 1952 as *Symbole der Wandlung*). In his autobiography, he described how he was unable to write the end of the penultimate chapter of this book for two months, because he knew that it would cost him his friendship with Freud, as indeed it did.

In July 1913, Jung reached the age of 38; a time of life in which so-called mid-life crises often occur. Jung was the first psychiatrist to draw attention to this phenomenon, which sprang directly from his own experience. By this time, Jung had married, fathered a family, and achieved professional recognition and a position in the world. His conscious attitude had been that, together with Freud, he could develop a new science of the mind. But something within him forced him, against his conscious inclination, to assert his own individual point of view, even though he knew that this would be treated by Freud as a betrayal. During the four years of the First World War, Jung went through a personal crisis which was both extremely disturbing and, in the end, rewarding. He conducted a self-analysis in which he recorded his own dreams and visions, many of which were alarming. For example, he thrice dreamed that, 'in the middle of summer an Arctic cold wave descended and froze the land to ice. I saw, for example, the whole of Lorraine and its canals frozen and the entire region totally deserted by human beings. All living green things were killed by frost.' In a later dream, this scene of desolation was relieved by the appearance of 'a leaf-bearing tree, but without fruit (my tree of life, I thought), whose leaves had been transformed by the effects of the frost into sweet grapes full of healing juices'.[9]

Jung wrote: 'The years when I was pursuing my inner images were the most important in my life – in them everything essential was decided.'[10] It was certainly out of the experience of those years that his view of the development of personality originated. His self-analysis convinced him that the important thing in life was to discern and make manifest one's own, individual point of view. Men became neurotic when they were in some sense false to themselves; when they strayed from the path which Nature (or God) intended them to follow. By listening to the inner voice, which manifested itself in dreams, fantasies, and other spontaneous derivatives of the unconscious, the lost soul could rediscover its proper path. This is, of course, a religious point of view, but one which does not necessarily postulate a God 'out there'.

The end of Jung's mid-life crisis was signalled by his writing one of the books by which he is best known to the general public, *Psychological Types*. Jung's concept of 'extravert' and 'introvert', terms which he introduced, derived from his observation that Freud and Adler could each confront the same psychopathological material and yet interpret it in different ways. Jung wrote:

> Since both theories are in a large measure correct – that is to say, since they both appear to explain their material – it follows that a neurosis must have two opposite aspects, one of which is grasped by the Freudian, the other by the Adlerian theory. But how comes it that each investigator sees only one side, and why does each maintain that he has the only valid view?[11]

Jung goes on to point out that Adler's psychology emphasizes the importance of the subject at the expense of the object; whereas Freud's psychology sees the subject in perpetual dependence upon significant objects. Introversion and extraversion have become familiar ideas to most people, and have been taken over by experimental psychologists like Eysenck. The importance of the dichotomy in Jung's view of personality takes us back to his days as a medical student. Since the time of the physiologist Claude Bernard, scientists have accepted the idea that the body is a self-regulating entity. Human physiology is a system of checks and balances, which ensures that any tendency to go too far in one direction is compensated by an opposing swing in the other. These so-called homeostatic mechanisms are dependent upon negative feedback; that is, upon fluctuations in some property like the level of blood sugar being reported to a central control, whence compensatory changes are set in motion to restore the normal balance.

Jung's delineation of extraversion and introversion enabled him to advance the notion that personality could be distorted by what he called 'one-sided development'. A man could be so extraverted, so totally involved in the external world, that he lost touch with the inner world of his own psyche. On the other hand, an introverted eccentric could be so preoccupied with the workings of his own mind that he failed to adapt himself to external reality. Jung postulated that the mind was self-regulating in the same way as the body. An outbreak of neurotic symptoms should be taken as a signal indicating that a compensatory process was beginning in the unconscious. If a new patient turned to Jung, asking what he should do, Jung would reply: 'I have no idea; but let us see what the unconscious has to say. Let us examine your dreams and fantasies.'

In case this seems a peculiar way of proceeding, let me illustrate what Jung meant by a case from my own practice, which I quote in my book on Jung. A girl came to see me because, although happily engaged, she could not face leaving home and embarking upon marriage. She developed acute anxiety symptoms. The onset of her symptoms at this particular time aptly illustrates Jung's statement that neurosis usually appears when some new adaptation is needed. It turned out that the girl was very much attached to her mother. In early childhood, she had suffered from a complaint which made it difficult for her to swallow. She had required special feeding and a great deal of extra attention from her mother, who had cared for her with devotion. She had nothing but good to say of her mother. Yet she had the following dream. 'I was being pursued by a steam-roller. As I reached the fence at the bottom of the garden and was about to be crushed, my mother appeared on the other side of the fence laughing with hideous glee at my predicament.' [12]

The dream paints a picture of the mother as a menace; a destructive person who is 'steam-rolling' the subject's individuality out of existence, or at least acquiescing in her being crushed. It is exactly the opposite picture to that held consciously by the girl. The truth was that her childhood illness had made her unduly dependent upon her mother, who, through no fault of her own, had become an obstacle to her daughter's development as an independent individual.

This is a very simple example of what Jung meant by compensation and self-regulation. He believed that, if patients paid serious attention to the spontaneous activity of their own psyches, they would be able to return to the true path of their own development, from which their one-sided attitudes had made them stray.

The analysis of dreams became one of the main techniques of treatment used by Jung and his pupils. Freud considered his book *The Interpretation of Dreams*, published in November 1899, to be one of his major achievements. As late as 1931, he wrote a Preface to the Third (Revised) English Edition in which he said: 'It contains, even according to my present-day judgement, the most valuable of all the discoveries it has been my good fortune to make. Insight such as this falls to one's lot but once in a lifetime.'[13]

However, posterity has not supported Freud's claim to have discovered the secret of dreams. In 1931, Jung wrote:

> The view that dreams are merely the imaginary fulfilments of repressed wishes is hopelessly out of date. There are, it is true, dreams which manifestly represent wishes or fears, but what about all the other things? Dreams may contain ineluctable truths, philosophical pronouncements, illusions, wild fantasies, memories, plans, anticipations, irrational experiences, even telepathic visions, and heaven knows what beside. One thing we ought never to forget; almost half our life is passed in a more or less unconscious state. The dream is specifically the utterance of the unconscious.

Jung goes on:

> The fundamental mistake regarding the nature of the unconscious is probably this: it is commonly supposed that its contents have only one meaning and are marked with an unalterable plus or minus sign. In my humble opinion, this view is too naïve. The psyche is a self-regulating system that maintains its equilibrium just as the body does. Every process that goes too far immediately and inevitably calls forth compensations, and without these there would be neither a normal metabolism nor a normal psyche. In this sense we can take the theory of compensation as a basic law of psychic behaviour. Too little on one side results in too much on the other. Similarly, the relation between conscious and unconscious is compensatory. This is one of the best-proven rules of dream-interpretation. When we set out to interpret a dream, it is always helpful to ask: What conscious attitude does it compensate?[14]

Jung's view of personality, as I have so far expounded it, is derived very largely from his experience with psychotic and neurotic patients. As his reputation grew, he came to be consulted by a variety of people who did not present obvious neurotic symptoms. Jung's later work is primarily concerned with what he called 'the process of individuation'; that is, with the development of personality in persons who were not 'ill' in any obvious sense. Jung wrote:

> The clinical material at my disposal is of a peculiar composition: new cases are decidedly in the minority. Most of them already have some form of psychotherapeutic treatment behind them, with partial or negative results. About a third of my cases are not suffering from any clinically definable neurosis, but from the senselessness and aimlessness of their lives. I should not object if this were called the general neurosis of our age. Fully two-thirds of my patients are in the second half of life. This peculiar material sets up a special resistance to rational methods of treatment, probably because most of my patients are socially well-adapted individuals, often of outstanding ability, to whom normalization means nothing.[15]

These were the people who most interested Jung: exceptional individuals whose natures compelled them to reject convention and discover their own path. In Jung's view, 'Nature is aristocratic, and one person of value outweighs ten lesser ones.' It is the individual who is the carrier of culture. 'All the highest achievements of virtue, as well as the blackest villainies, are individual.'[16] Jung thought that aiding the development of personality in these exceptional individuals was a quest of vital significance.

Jung defined personality as 'the supreme realization of the innate idiosyncrasy of a living being'. It is essentially an *adult* ideal, which is why I earlier made the point that Jung's main contribution was in the field of adult development. Jung wrote: 'It is not the child, but only the adult, who can achieve personality as the fruit of a full life directed to this end. The achievement of personality means nothing less than the optimum development of the whole individual human being.'[17]

This optimum development tends toward a goal called 'wholeness' or 'integration': a condition in which the different elements of the psyche, both conscious and unconscious, are welded together indissolubly: a condition which might be described as the opposite of the fragmentation and splitting found in schizophrenia. The person who approaches this goal, which can never be entirely or once and for all achieved, possesses what Jung called 'an attitude that is beyond the reach of emotional entanglements and violent shocks – a consciousness detached from the world'.[18] This search for integration is essentially a religious quest, though not one which is concerned with any recognized creed. It is religious because it involves a change within the individual from an attitude in which ego and will are paramount to one in which he acknowledges that he is guided by an integrating factor which is not of his own making. Jung describes people as achieving peace of mind after 'long and fruitless struggles'. He wrote:

> If you sum up what people tell you about their experiences, you can formulate it this way: They came to themselves, they could accept themselves, they were able to become reconciled to themselves, and thus were reconciled to adverse circumstances and events. This is almost like what used to be expressed by saying: He has made his peace with God, he has sacrificed his own will, he has submitted himself to the will of God.[19]

Jung described the symbols in which this new unity of personality expressed itself: circular forms indicating wholeness which are comparable with the so-called mandalas used in Tibetan Buddhism as ritual instruments to assist meditation. Jung wrote:

> If the unconscious can be recognized as a co-determining factor along with consciousness, and if we can live in such a way that conscious and unconscious demands are taken into account as far as possible, then the centre of gravity of the total personality shifts its position. It is then no longer in the ego, which is merely the centre of consciousness, but in the hypothetical point between conscious and unconscious. This new centre might be called the self.[20]

The self, of which the mandala is a symbol, is the archetype of unity and totality. Jung believed that this archetype was the underlying reality manifesting itself in the various systems of monotheism. The self, therefore, is the God within; and the individual, in seeking self-realization and unity, becomes the means through which, as Jung put it, 'God seeks his goal'.[21]

I mentioned earlier that Jung was the son of a pastor in the Swiss Reformed Church. Two of his paternal uncles were also clergymen, and there were no less than six parsons in his mother's family. What I did not mention was that, at an early age, Jung developed serious doubts about the conventional faith professed by his father. He began to think of religion as a personal matter which had little to do with accepted creeds. He tried to discuss some of these doubts with his father, but found the latter unwilling to enter into argument. Jung found himself in the position of being unable to subscribe to the faith in which he had been reared, while at the same time continuing to believe that individuals could neither be happy nor healthy unless they acknowledged their dependence upon some higher power than that of the ego.

In the letters between himself and Freud, the question of whether they should join a new International Fraternity for Ethics and Culture is discussed. In a letter dated 11 February 1910, Jung wrote:

Is there perchance a new saviour in the I.F.? What sort of new myth does it hand out for us to live by? Only the wise are ethical from sheer intellectual presumption, the rest of us need the eternal truth of myth. You will see from this string of associations that the problem does not leave me simply apathetic and cold. The ethical problem of sexual freedom really is enormous and worth the sweat of all noble souls. But 2000 years of Christianity can only be replaced by something equivalent.[22]

A critic might allege that the whole of Jung's later work represents his attempt to find a substitute for the faith which he lost when a child. He might go on to say that Jung substituted the analysis of dreams and fantasies for prayer. Jung urged his patients to draw and paint their dreams and fantasies. Moreover, he encouraged them deliberately to set aside part of the day for reverie; for what, in Jungian technique, became known as 'active imagination'. This is a state of mind not unlike that described in some forms of meditation, in which judgement is suspended, but consciousness is preserved. The patient was enjoined to note what fantasies occurred to him. In this way, he might be able to rediscover hidden parts of himself, as well as portray the psychological journey upon which he was embarking. The parallels with the stages of Recollection, Quiet, and Contemplation described by the mystics are striking.

The state of reverie is also the one in which most creative discoveries are made. In a paper on 'Individuation and the Creative Process', I pointed out many similarities between the two processes.[23]

Jung's concentration upon changing dynamics within the charmed circle of the individual psyche is interesting, in part because it is so unfashionable. During the last 30 years or so, we have witnessed the rise of the so-called object-relations school of psychoanalysis, dominated by Melanie Klein, Ronald Fairbairn, and Donald Winnicott, and later reinforced by John Bowlby. Whatever disagreements still divide the various psychoanalytic camps, there has been a consensus of opinion that, if one wants to understand the growth and development of human beings, one must first study their interpersonal relationships. It has been assumed that, from the baby's earliest relationship with its mother onwards, human happiness and fulfilment depend upon inter-personal relationships, and that treatment of neurotic problems largely consists in helping patients to improve their relationships by means of understanding and improving the way in which they relate to the analyst.

Yet, here is Jung saying that what really matters is the patient's relationship with the unconscious, and the dynamic changes which take place within the individual psyche as a result of the process of individuation. Jung was perfectly well aware of the significance of interpersonal relationships, but his emphasis is quite different from that of contemporary analysts. I myself am inclined to think that our present elevation of interpersonal relationships into the be-all and end-all of human existence has been overdone, and that Jung's point of view might be a starting-point for a compensatory swing of the pendulum away from object relations.

Jung's later work is principally concerned with the elucidation of the symbols in which the process of individuation is expressed. His interest in alchemy, which often seems to puzzle people, arose because he found parallels between the alchemists' description of their 'Work' and what seemed to be happening in his patients. In Jung's view, the alchemists' quest for the philosopher's stone, or for the means of transforming other substances into gold, was not so much a series of chemical experiments as a spiritual journey. More particularly, the alchemists were concerned with the transformation and combination of opposites, using chemical interaction as a symbol of psychic processes. Because, scientifically, there was nothing in alchemy, it acted as a gigantic projection test; a kind of Rorschach ink-blot, in which anything that was seen actually originated in the mind of the observer.

Part of Jung's rejection of conventional Christianity seems to have been based upon his impatience with what might be called the Pangloss element. He felt that orthodox Christians were disinclined to accept the reality of evil. In adolescence, therefore, it was reassuring for him to encounter Schopenhauer, of whom he wrote:

> Here at last was a philosopher who had the courage to see that all was not for the best in the fundaments of the universe. He spoke neither of the all-good and all-wise providence of a Creator, nor of the harmony of the cosmos, but stated bluntly that a fundamental flaw underlay the sorrowful course of human history and the cruelty of nature: the blindness of the world-creating Will.[24]

The problem of evil continued to preoccupy Jung throughout his life. His insistence upon the equal reality of evil and good led to an interesting series of exchanges with Victor White, a Dominican priest who was professor of Dogmatic Theology at Blackfriars in Oxford and author of *God and the Unconscious*. White was a close friend of Jung; but the differences between them on the problem of evil led to an estrangement. White maintained the Catholic doctrine of the *privatio boni*, which alleges that evil is the absence of good and has no substance or reality of its own. Jung strongly objected to this view. For him, good and evil were equally real as polar opposites.

A good deal of Jung's thought seems to have been directly derived from Schopenhauer. Schopenhauer considered that individuals were the embodiment of an underlying Will which was outside space and time. Jung begins his autobiography by writing: 'My life is a story of the self-realization of the unconscious.'[25] Jung took the term 'individuation' from Schopenhauer. Schopenhauer considered that the very notion of individuality, the *principium individuationis*, is dependent upon the human categories of space and time, which force us to be conscious of individual objects and which prevent us from seeing the original unity of the Will of which individuals are a manifestation. Jung also believed in a realm outside space and time from which individuals became differentiated. Borrowing the Gnostic term, he referred to this spiritual realm transcending consciousness as the *pleroma*. In the pleroma, all is one, and there is no differentiation between opposites. Jung gives as examples of opposites, good and evil, light and darkness, time and space, force and matter, beauty and ugliness, and so on. But, whereas Schopenhauer's philosophy is governed by the ideal of deliverance from the bonds of individuality by means of denial and asceticism, Jung's philosophy is governed by the idea of affirmation of individuality.

Jung's belief in the underlying unity of all existence led him to conclude that physical and mental, as well as spatial and temporal, were human categories imposed upon reality which did not accurately reflect it. Through his collaboration with the physicist Wolfgang Pauli, Jung came to think that the physicist's investigation of matter and the psychologist's investigation of mind might be different ways of approaching the same underlying reality. Perhaps mind and body were simply different aspects of a single reality viewed through different frames of reference.

Jung claimed that there were 'sufficient reasons' for believing that 'the psychic lies embedded in something that appears to be of a non-psychic nature'.[26] Pauli also postulated 'a cosmic order independent of our choice and distinct from the world of phenomena'.[27] Jung wrote: 'The background of microphysics and depth-psychology is as much physical as psychic and therefore neither, but rather a third thing, a neutral nature which can at most be grasped in hints since in essence it is transcendental.'[28]

Jung's later thought extends beyond the personal to realms where many of his readers will not follow him. But his contribution to our understanding of the development of personality is both original and of outstanding interest, and has had considerable influence on the technique and practice of psychotherapy.

10

Personality and Poetry

ANTHONY NUTTALL

THE PSYCHE

In Plato's *Phaedo*, Socrates, before taking the hemlock and dying, in obedience to the laws of Athens, draws his friends together and talks to them about immortality. He looks back on his life and remembers how in his youth he was tremendously attracted by physical explanations, and then how, as time went by, these became less and less satisfactory to him. It is as if, he says, in response to the question 'Why am I sitting here now' he were to be told, 'Ah, that's because your legs are flexibly constructed of bones and muscles so that they can be put in what is called a sitting position.' But, by the god of Egypt, says Socrates, that's no use at all. I'm sitting here 'because the Athenians have condemned me and I think it right not to run away – *that*'s why I am sitting here.'[1] Socrates thus steps from the material to the ethical, and suggests that the mere enumeration of physical conditions will never begin to explain any action of which the essence is ethical or moral. But actions of human personality are commonly thus. Much of the rest of the dialogue is taken up with discussion of the *psuchē* (psyche), often translated 'soul', but in some ways closer to 'personality'. *Psuchē* covers mind, intelligence, character, the subject-matter of psychology, which 'soul', with its increasingly restricted religious signification tends not to do. So let us use the term 'psyche'.

The principal question asked in the dialogue is whether the psyche is mortal. Socrates offers a number of arguments for immortality, some of them very ingenious, and persuades almost no one. Among these arguments, which almost claim the status of proofs, is one which is nothing like a proof, looks hopelessly vague, but, to my mind, is the most persuasive of the lot. This is the one commonly known as the 'argument from affinity'.

Socrates says that visible things manifestly decay, but that anybody with any intelligence can see that the catalogue of visible things does not exhaust reality. Circularity (as distinct from 'that round wheel', say,), justice (as distinct from so many bodies exchanging equal-sized objects), and so forth may be classed as illusions or culturally relative fictions by materialist philosophers with their backs to the wall, but they are never construed in this way by ordinary intelligent people in real life. It follows that the fabric of reality is in part physical, in part something else. Now if you look at the class of things which are not visible, these do not seem to be subject to decay in the same manner as visible things. The body of a particular judge may perish, but the justice of his one correct decision does not. Notice that the language here need not take on any sort of mystical resonance; there is no need for any special assertion of justice glowing through eternity or anything like that; all that is needed is an ordinary acknowledgement that certain sorts of universals operate achronically, without any involvement in the time sequence. Given this loose division into things that you can see and those that you can't see, says Socrates, which group does the psyche belong to? Socrates decides that it belongs with the invisibles, since you can see a person's body but never his psyche. I think Plato knows that there is a difficulty here, which arises from the fact that an individual's psyche is not a universal like circularity; on the other hand, the pysche of Michael Dummett is not as firmly removed from the universal Dummettishness as say, that wooden wheel is removed from circularity. Plato implicitly grants, however, that there is some lack of fit. Otherwise he would have had another 'proof' of the form: invisible universals are timeless; the psyche is an invisible universal; therefore the psyche is timeless. But he does not presume to say that. Instead, more modestly, he suggests a certain, strange kinship between personality and timeless universals, a kinship in which the ever-decaying physical world cannot share.

Now I think I should say that I am not nearly as confident as Plato (who is himself less than certain) that the human psyche is immortal; I do feel, however, that the full idea of a person, or rather of any one person we know, is necessarily richer than almost any other idea in operation. If we fully attend to it, there seems to be more there than can be confidently assumed to fall under the ordinarily observable processes of death and decay. We feel this especially with people we love. After the death of his great friend Charles Williams, C. S. Lewis said that when the idea of Williams and the idea of death met in his mind, it was the idea of death that was changed. Mind you, when Lewis's wife died later on, it apparently didn't feel like that, because the sheer pain of loss of was so great.[2] We late-born folk cannot but be aware of the various artillery brought to bear on the religious conception of immortality in the ages after Socrates. What does strike me though, is that many of the seemingly 'hard-headed' rebuttals of the Platonic view could, in a matter of two or three decades, come to appear positively weak-minded.

THE DISSOLUTION OF THE PSYCHE

Consider for example, Watsonian/Skinnerian behaviourism, in which the concept of the psyche is construed as a shorthand description of externally observable actions of bodies. The general idea was that if psychology was to be scientific, it should not concern itself with interior, 'introspectible' states of mind, but with external behaviour; most descriptions of individual human natures are based in practice on the things people visibly and audibly *do*, and not on their mental states. When we say that John is angry, we are not guessing at some inaccessible mental state; we are summing up the facts – for example, that he has just punched Fred on the nose and kicked his cat. At its most extreme, this form of behaviourism led to an actual denial of the very existence of thoughts and private mental states, leading some bahviourists to adopt an exaggeratedly nominalist view of universals. Skinner offered a violently reductive account of the universal 'probability', saying that those propositions (bits of verbal behaviour) were 'probable' which were uttered most loudly and most frequently by most people. Chomsky, in his famous review of *Verbal Behaviour*, mildly observed that perhaps Skinner could make his theories probable by training machine-guns on huge crowds of people in city squares and getting them to chant over and over again the basic principles of Skinnerian psychology.[3] Or, think of the old joke about the two behaviourists who make love, after which one says, 'That was marvellous for you; how was it for me?' What this brings out is the fact that inner experience is really quite different from experience of objects in the public world, not so much in Plato's sense as between the empirical and the non-empirical, as between different *modes* of the empirical (for if we divorce the psyche too firmly from experience, we shall end up with the mystified insulated conception *soul*, about which I was complaining earlier). My sense, nevertheless, is that Plato's argument continues to nag, to pluck at the sleeve of the mind, so to speak; for though it rapidly rises to an unmanageable vagueness and confusion, it has a surprisingly strong foundation.

In a word, I agree with Plato that if we confine ourselves rigorously to physical particulars, we cannot achieve anything like an adequate account of the real world. I would further agree that there is some sense, not yet adequately analysed by anyone, in which being human peculiarly and essentially involves a participation, as it were, in both the material and the non-material. Planets burn and then grow cold; but they never know that they do these things, never know what warmth is, what coldness. Clearly, a binary division into universals and physical particulars is far from adequate. There are too many intermediate entities. Compare a lump of coal with a clear view of a lump of coal; compare the view with a sensation (of being hit by the lump of the coal say); compare that with a particular memory of a lump of coal, and that with the thought of coal, and that with the concept of coal, and that with intelligence or memory as such; or compare circularity with love, love with Beethoven's Eighth Symphony (Beethoven's Eighth Symphony exists all right; but where is it?). Now cross-compare; if you have been considering triangularity, say, the sensation of the lump of coal hitting you will seem physical; but if you have been comparing the sensation with the lump of coal itself, the sensation may appear to be a merely mental thing.

In all this the psyche is obstinately elusive, as ordinary universals are not. The relation between baldness, for example, and an actual bald head is perspicuous. Philosophers may argue about the ontological status of baldness, but there is a sense in which we understand the distinction between baldness and a particular bald head perfectly. But with the psyche, or personality, it is more difficult. I have already disparaged the attempts of early behaviourists to construe the psyche in terms of summary descriptions applied to complex behaviour, suggesting that they acknowledge a certain autonomy of inner experience. But then one thinks of Hume, who, with his usual candour, professed that he was very willing to look within for this thing called a 'self', or a 'soul'; but that when he did so, he never saw it.[4] Try as he might, all he got from introspection was bits and bobs, particular sensations, fragments of remembered conversation, appetites, resentments but never a unified 'self'. So here we have someone who was fully prepared to acknowledge and explore inner experience, but who, after a thoroughly honest endeavour, came up with precisely nothing. For Hume, the effect of introspection was not to discover the self, but to de-construct it. We are left, it might be thought, in some disarray.

THE DISSOLUTION OF THE POEM

At this point, cued by the word 'disarray', I want to discuss the present state of English literary studies. At present a battle is being fought – a battle of Byzantine intricacy and Cimmerian obscurity. Every so often, journalists scent drama and conflict, and try to run articles explaining what is going on to the world at large. One is rung up by baffled, hard-pressed columnists, and the conversation usually ends with them saying, in a despairing way, 'You mean they are arguing about *that*?'

Roughly speaking, it is all about the replacement of New Criticism by a revived structuralism and the subsequent replacement of structuralism by deconstructionism. In the interest of brevity, I will use artificially simplified terms here; but in fact, it is characteristic of the debate that members of any party tend to see the opposition in precisely these simplified terms.

The New Critics believed by and large in a sort of autonomy of the poem. Study of the lives of poets, the history of ideas, and the like were all, strictly speaking, forms of truancy from literary criticism, which, in its purest form consisted of a close analytic reading of particular poems. They saw the authority of the poem as necessarily higher than that of the poet as a historical person. They delighted in test cases in which poets had said silly things about their poems, whereas the texts themselves demonstrably conveyed a richer, more coherent meaning. They liked to quote D. H. Lawrence's words, 'Trust the tale, not the teller.' Each poem was held to propose in effect the terms on which it should be read, as a separate work of art, unrelated to any other. It was this notion of separateness which was subverted by the new structuralism.

Structuralism initially grew out of Russian formalism, Lévi-Strauss's anthropology of differing cultural codes (usually binary systems), and Saussurian linguistics, with its stress on context as that which confers meaning (a mere noise usually means nothing; only as it forms part of a relational sequence does meaning begin to come through). The general thrust of this movement is to locate meaning in the relations rather than in the given chunks of a system. As we move up the hierarchy from linguistic to literary analysis, the effect of this relocation is to cast doubt on this very possibility of reading a poem as a thing-in-itself, an insulated thing. If the poem carries a meaning, it is by virtue of its relation, echoic or contrasting, to other poems, for literature is really a huge, ever-growing web; and what we call particular poems are merely points of intersection. So addressing the cultural context, far from being a form of truancy from literary criticism, is its primary task.

Of deconstructionism I will say very little. At one stage, structuralism had high, almost scientific, hopes. Just as in languages, according to some theorists, there are 'deep structures' which generate the variously differentiated systems of French, Italian, and so on, so in literature, it was thought, certain primary oppositions (of light and dark, say,) or simple narrative sequences (injunction followed by transgression, for example) formed a matrix from which the richly differentiated structures of an actual literature might be derived. The idea was to analyse and set forth this generative grammar of literature, so that the phylogeny of art would be seen in its ultimate, necessary form; the codes of the great game in which individuals had participated for centuries without any general understanding would be identified and understood; and the deep structures permitting the formation of all the proliferating structures would be intelligible at last. What the deconstructionists did was to cast doubt on the dream of terminal understanding, often by showing that the very features which the structuralists supposed they were discovering were themselves merely the fluid product of yet another set of varying cultural codes. If meaning is located in context, it is endlessly deferred, because there is always a further context, and all definitions presuppose other definitions *ad infinitum*. In such an environment, one can no longer hope for certainty or truth but only throw oneself into the maelstrom with a sort of joyous despair. Deconstructive criticism, (some of which is tremendously clever) is characterized by a most peculiar Nietzschean nihilist hilarity which I cannot hope to convey.

REAL PEOPLE AND REAL POEMS

What is very noticeable in all this is a repeatedly applied process of dissolution. The New Critics set aside the living author as irrelevant: the poem was the thing. The structuralists actually 'dissolved the author outright and then merged the poem with its context: not the poem, but literature – which essentially propagates itself – is the thing. Deconstructionism dissolves the author, the reader, and the text, and also, in its metaphysically extreme moments, the very notions of meaning and truth. I should stress that it is only at these extreme moments that this fundamental dissolution occurs, for there is, so to speak, a house-trained deconstructive criticism which contents itself with emphasizing detectable incoherence in literary works, rather than eliciting coherent patterns as previous criticism had done. This is all thoroughly cognitivist, in that it presupposes existence of a text about which certain true statements can be made. But the metaphysical extreme is my concern at present.

I will now try to pull the two bits of this paper together – the story of the philosophical investigation of the psyche, or soul, which seemed to end with losing the soul, and the story of the analysis of poetry, which seemed to end by losing the object of inquiry. It is as if the analytic intelligence, for considerable stretches of human history, operates as a sort of death-ray, withering all that lies in its path. Hume's method of highly focused introspection yielded no sort of 'self', but only a succession of bits. But the behaviourists' wild swing to the opposite extreme yields mere bloodless patterns of behaviour which no ordinary person finds adequate if an account of what it is to be human is being sought. In literary studies, the too highly focused work of certain New Critics presented isolated poems as intricate, yet somehow dessicated, things. The proper nourishment of cultural context was being denied. But the structuralist fled too abruptly to the opposite extreme, where there is in effect nothing but context. Something keeps going wrong, and it seems to be something to do with the artificial separation of different orders of being or discourse, and the subsequent wanton privileging of one order over all the rest. Certainly the basic philosophical challenges always seem to be readily reversible. 'Look,' says the structuralist, 'identity presupposes relation. You can't describe anything without describing its relation to other things; it's the relating that carries the meaning.' But, equally, relation presupposes thing, for a world in which nothing was related to any other thing would be a world without relations. The notion of relationship *in vacuo* is philosophically incoherent.

In ordinary life we operate not simply with primary atoms and their relations, or with ultimate particulars and pure universals, but with all kinds of inter-mediate wholes, two very important examples of which are persons and poems. These can be shown to be complex, involving different orders within them. But it does not follow from such analysis that they are, so to say, exploded. As we analyse, we must remember the necessity of integration, and here I am referring to an utterly fundamental necessity; indeed, the hardest analytic thinkers always use existing integrations at some point in their thinking, though not of course where the searchlight is shining most brightly. The intellectual purist may say that there is no method for weighing the importance of main-taining a cathedral, say, against a programme for improving council houses, because the arguments on each side are strictly incommensurable. They belong to different language games, to use Wittgenstein's term. But they occur, endlessly enmeshed, in one world. Outside the lecture room, we know that we must, can, and do weigh such considerations against each other within the complex whole called stewardship.

It seems to me that in certain, quintessentially human fields the analytic intelligence becomes nothing more nor less than a technique for losing the goods – unless it is accompanied by a sense of the necessary integrations or wholes. This might sound like an attack on science which is not at all what I intend – not even an attack on scientific psychology. Occam's razor, controlled experiments, definition of the field of inquiry, specification of testable predictions, all these are of proven – indeed spectacular – intellectual utility. The danger is metaphysical: that when we hear the specified terms suddenly characterized as alone real, we acquiesce in the implication that all the rest is some sort of illusion. Good literature is not just an analogy, a secondary echo of the properly human, that retains both the complexity and the wholeness of personality; it also engages explicitly with meaning, and addresses the human in a manner quite different from that of analytic philosophical psychology.

Hume excluded from his picture the temporally diffuse awareness of continuous 'personal colour', duration, predisposition, and so on, which for most of us gradually grows into an awareness of selfhood. Or, at least, he does so in the famous passage in which he employs the fierce introspective searchlight. To be fair, there are signs in *The Treatise* that he recognized this, as when he says: 'In thinking of our past thoughts we not only delineate the objects of which we were thinking, but also conceive the action of the mind in meditation, that certain *je-ne-sais-quoi* of which 'tis impossible to give any definition or description, but which everyone sufficiently understands.'[5] And of course this more diffuse awareness is itself irremediably mixed up with our relationship to others – not with introspection, but with extrospection. But the self is not dissolved by this. Set against Hume (perhaps the greatest British philosopher) the greatest English poet. In *Hamlet* Shakespeare shows us a person who so thoroughly withdraws from ordinary relationships that his psyche, or soul, begins to decay. We see Hamlet engaging in introspection to the point of psychic self-destruction; whereas an actor can weep real tears for a fictitious Hecuba, Hamlet can feel nothing for a real dead father. It is a study in artifically intensified introspection. But because we are in the world of drama, in which, contrary to the principle of Occam's razor, entities are endlessly multiplied beyond a single immediate necessity, we can see what is surely a possibility, a person living as all persons must, among other human beings, but with an inner life that is going seriously wrong. Elsewhere, I have compared the plays of Shakespeare to Occam's beard.[6] Because of the context and an equally intense preoccupation with both a properly relative and an isolated inwardness, *Hamlet* the play (as opposed to Hamlet the person in the play) remains sane, so to speak. It corroborates and strengthens our sense of humanity. There is never any danger of that sense being lost. It takes – I won't say a scientist – a philosopher to do that.

11

A Theology of Personal Being

JOHN MACQUARRIE

The question of what it means to be a human person, theologically speaking, can be approached in a number of different ways. Karl Barth, for instance, devotes one of his many volumes to anthropology, and uses the biblical and Christian witness as the foundation for his whole exposition. To my way of thinking, this is a little bit too dogmatic, for the theologian should also take into account what people in other disciplines are saying about human nature and human being.

This is a vast subject, of course; there is hardly anything that does not in one way or another tie in with the problem of the human person. So I will simply select three aspects, aspects that are fairly central and regarding which there is a definite Christian, and indeed biblical, teaching. Moreover, each can be linked with the human situation at the present time, and with the views of personhood that are being put forward in this century.

BEINGS-ON-THE-WAY

The first point that I wish to make concerning Christian teaching on the subject is that a human person is a being-on-the-way – that is to say, persons are always unfinished; and, even more, communities of persons are unfinished. We see the human person and the human community as transitional, as on its way. Human nature is something that is in process of change, and that of course contrasts with many traditional views which regard human nature as fixed. This view that human nature is in process of change is, I believe, very much in accord with biblical teaching.

The foundations of biblical anthropology are perhaps to be found in the Abraham stories. We see Abraham leaving his settled community and going out into the wilderness, where he has the task of establishing a new community. And even in the New Testament, where you might see the Church and the figure of Jesus Christ as standing at the end of the development set in motion by Abraham, we read in one of the Johannine epistles: 'now we are God's children, it does not yet appear what we shall be' (1 John 3: 2). Again, there is the idea of humanity as in a process of transition, but moving towards a goal that is still unknown.

This notion of humanity as on the way, unfinished, in process of change, is implicit, I think, in the creation stories at the beginning of the Bible, although it is possible to interpret these stories in a somewhat different way. St Augustine, for instance, thought that Adam had been created as already an adult at the height of his powers – sixty years of age, let us say! That was St Augustine's view. But some of the Greek theologians took a very different view. Irenaeus, for example, said that Adam had been created like a child and had had to grow, which is a much more profound insight, I think, because it shows that Irenaeus recognized that there could be no personhood without experience, without history. Having said that Adam was created like a child, however, he went on to read into the creation story an exegesis which my Hebrew scholar-friends tell me is not really there. In the first chapter of Genesis we read that, in creating the human being, God said; 'Let us make man in our own image and likeness'; now it is said that the words 'image' and 'likeness' mean the same – this is just the parallelism of the Hebrew language. But Irenaeus thought that they were to be taken differently, and that the image of God was a kind of potentiality that was given to the human being, and likeness to God the realization of that potentiality, the state reached when the human being had come closest to God. Incidentally, Irenaeus and many other early theologians did not hesitate to use the word 'deification' for this process of human development. They saw the human pilgrimage as beginning in immaturity and imperfection, and progressing through various stages to greater and greater manifestation of the image, and ultimately to likeness with God. Of course, there has been a great deal of argument as to what that likeness or image might be. Some people have seen it in terms of dominion, but I think that this is a very superficial reading. Others have seen it in terms of freedom, which I think comes somewhat nearer to the truth – that as free agents we have the rather awesome responsibility of being able to bring something new into being, that in some sense the human being has some share in the divine creativity. In our responsible acts we are actually creators, for we are creating a history; in fact, we are creating ourselves and our world. It is clear that his biblical view of the human being as a being-on-the-way, a being in transition, who is moving towards some goal, even if the goal is hidden, is very close to some of the modern anthropologies that have evolved during the last century or so. Many modern thinkers have been telling us that man is in process of change, that his nature is not fixed, but is something that is developing; and they have used the word 'transcendence' in describing that process.

'Transcendence' is a word that is often used of God, and when used of God, it refers to the fact that God is above this world and in control of it. When we use it of humans, however, we are using it more in its original sense, as signifying the crossing of boundaries, of going forward; it is that sense which is intended when modern thinkers say that the human being is in a process of transcendence. That is very true for instance, of Marxism and especially, perhaps, of such neo-Marxists as Bloch and Marcuse. Marx taught that, by his work and his labour, man makes both himself and the world in which he lives. It is a teaching that is also common among existentialists; Sartre's view of the human being as surging up from nothing and then making himself recalls the story of Abraham going out into the wilderness. And recently, Roman Catholic philosophers in the Thomist tradition have been taking the same view of the human being as in process of transcendence, although they give it a more intellectual tone. For example, Bernard Lonergan said that transcendence consists of asking questions, each question giving rise to a new question, in a never-ending progression.

Most of these thinkers do not give the word 'transcendence' a moral valuation; they see it as describing a process of change, but not necessarily change for the better. Thus, it is not a doctrine of progress in the old sense. The change they are talking about seems to come about in two different ways, inwardly and outwardly. It is an inner change, a change in the human being's conception of himself or herself – that is to say, it involves new images of what it is to be a human person. The interesting thing is, of course, that although we can have theories about the cosmos – theories about quasars, and obviously the theories do not in the slightest degree affect the realities in question (quasars remain quasars, no matter what cosmologists think about them), it is different with theories about human beings, because in that case our theories make a difference to who and what we are. For instance, if I strongly adhere to the theory that man is best conceived as a naked ape, as Mr Morris had it, then that affects the way in which I live and the way in which I esteem my fellow human beings. A very good illustration of this is the contrast between Thomas Hobbes and John Locke. Hobbes said: 'The state of nature is the state of war.' Now if you believe that, it actually changes the human reality, for you think it is a good idea to have a large army, lots of armaments, and so on. But if, like Locke, you believe that the state of nature is men living according to reason, then you take a different approach: you act differently, and you become a different kind of human being. So the images we have of ourselves are very important; they become part of ourselves and actually affect the reality.

The other way in which human beings change is, of course, in their outward being. We not only project different images of ourselves, but we mould our environment and create new physical conditions for life. Let me give you one or two illustrations of this kind of thing, which, I would say, amounts to a change in human nature. If I want to travel from New York to San Francisco, then it is natural that I should get on an aeroplane at LaGuardia Airport and do the journey in five yours; it would be most unnatural to get on an ox-wagon to cross the continent – and I could find considerably harder ways to do it – and end up in San Francisco about six months later. Likewise, it is natural to be able to see what is going on in Brussels, Ethiopia, or wherever, because television has become a part of us, part of human nature if you like. The big difference between ourselves and the animals is this: that animals have bodies that are pretty much determined; and they are able to do certain things, and often to do them supremely well, much better than we could do them, for we have only very clumsy, undifferentiated bodies. But we add extensions to our bodies – television sets, jet aircraft, and so on – and these have become incorporated into the human reality; they have become natural in some sense, part of what it is to be a human being. Nowadays, it is probably true to say, television, the ability to see things happening on the other side of the globe, even as they are happening, is part of our human equipment. I suppose that explains why many countries around the world which cannot afford to feed their inhabitants nevertheless operate television services.

To give a more controversial example, I would say that the contraceptive pill has now been incorporated into human nature. By separating the functions of sexual intercourse and reproduction, which, for most of human history have been a single function, it has revolutionized sexual mores. But this is a mixed blessing, and it is arguable whether it is progress; this is something which in some ways and from some points of view could be regarded as a good thing, and yet is obviously open to a great many abuses. If one accepts that the human person is a being in transition, a being-on-the-way, then questions arise as to what kind of changes are desirable, what kind of changes enhance our human personhood. It is not at all easy to answer these questions.

BEINGS-IN-THE-WORLD

The second aspect which I want to look at is also biblical and Christian, although here the Christian position is unclear. The human person is not only a being-on-the-way; it is also a being-in-the-world – that is to say, it is embodied. To be a person is, among other things, to be or have a body, to be inserted in a physical universe. We are not just spirits; we are not simply souls. Now Christianity has perhaps been a little bit confused about this. At a very early stage, Christian theology was influenced by Platonism, and, by the end of the first century, the doctrine of an immortal soul had been brought into the Christian frame of belief. In the writings of Clement of Rome, for instance, we read that when Peter and Paul arrived in heaven, they found that some blessed spirits had already preceded them; so, even at this time, there was the thought of an immortal soul going to heaven after the death of the body.

However, authentic biblical teaching is different. It takes the position that to be a human person, you need a body. Again, let us go back to the creation narratives in Genesis. In chapter 2, we read that, when God created Adam, he 'formed him of the dust of the ground' and then 'breathed into him the breath of life'. Thus, 'dust', or matter, I suppose you could say, was an essential constituent of the being of Adam. This is in contrast to the views of the Gnostics and some other middle-easterners who held that, initially, human beings were purely spiritual, and that the tragic fall into matter came later. This is a view that is still propagated by some Eastern religions of the present time, which regard salvation as consisting in the escape of the soul, the spiritual part of man, from its material prison, the body. Now this view is not found in the Bible, where man is said to have been created out of the dust before there is any talk of a fall or of sin. In any case, sin is not associated particularly with the body; it has often been said that the first sin of our forefathers, as recorded in Genesis, was a purely spiritual sin, the sin of pride – 'you shall be as God.'

Now the view that the human being is both material and spiritual and that you cannot have the one without the other was reinforced at a later stage by the doctrine of the resurrection of the body. That doctrine seems to have arisen among the Jews about the time of the Maccabean wars, when so many young men were dying in patriotic struggles. It developed in response to the question of the justice of God. Could it be that the people who died in these wars had simply ceased to be? The answer was a doctrine of the resurrection of the body. Notice that it was not a doctrine of the immortality of the soul. So you could say that this theological view of the human being is opposed to materialistic views, which regard man as simply an organism, albeit a higher organism; but is equally opposed to idealist or spiritualist views, which see the real person as a soul or spirit, and the body as a mere appendage. The biblical teaching is quite clearly, I think, that man is a psychosomatic unity, with both physical and ideal aspects. And the dignity of the body and of the material side of human existence is emphasized in the New Testament in the account of the Incarnation and later in the Church through the rise of sacramentalism.

As for the ethical implications of this view of man as a being-in-the-world, we get a good clue from the encyclical *Progressio Populorum* of Pope Paul VI. In that encyclical we read that 'Man must know something, and have something, if he is ever to be something,' which is a very interesting statement. It moves away from any purely spiritualistic ethic, and shows a recognition that our bodily life is constitutive of our humanity. In some ways, of course, it contrasts with some earlier Christian views, which were more ascetic in tone, and more or less said that the body does not matter and that what we have to do is to save our souls. What Paul VI is saying in effect is that if you are going to be a whole human being, if you are really going to achieve something like personhood, then you must *have* something. The New Testament, of course, teaches that it is more difficult for a rich man to enter the kingdom of God than for a camel to go through the eye of a needle, and undoubtedly there is a concern with the material, a concern with having, which can become detrimental to human life. But surely we have to strike some sort of mean. There is a degree of human deprivation which precludes the attainment of truly personal being, and there is a level of affluence at which people may become so concerned with material goods and material comforts, that true personal being is threatened.

So when we consider this aspect of the Christian view of man, we see that whatever ethic we hold must take account of our physical well-being, which means that, among other things, it should call for a fair distribution of the world's resources.

BEINGS-WITH-OTHERS

The third aspect I want to consider is that, according to the theological view, a human person is a being-with-others, not an isolated being. I have already cited the verse in which God says, 'Let us make man in our own image and likeness' but the text goes on to say that he did make man in his own image and likeness, 'male and female created he them.' There is a very interesting play on a singular and plural in these verses. The Hebrew word for God is itself a plural word, although it is construed as a singular noun. What does it mean, then, to say, 'Let us make man in our own image. . . . Male and female created he them'? It means, obviously, that the image of God cannot be formed in an individual human person. It needs at the very minimum the human couple, male and female. And one can say that in the mystery of the divine being, there is also sociality, that God is not merely an individual, but is somehow within himself a social being. Eventually, of course, the doctrine of the Trinity developed, a doctrine which, among other things, puts forward this notion of relationships within God. Here, though, we are simply concerned with the fact that the divine image cannot be represented by one human person. It needs at the very least two, the smallest human society, the couple. And this point is reinforced in the second creation story, in the second chapter of Genesis, where, after God has formed Adam from the dust of the earth, breathed into his nostrils the breath of life, set him in the garden, and so on, he decides that somehow Adam is incomplete and is unhappy; so he brings all the animals along, and Adam gives them names, but even so, he cannot find a 'helpmate'. Incidentally, the noun 'helpmate' is a kind of barbarism, because what it actually says in Genesis is a 'help meet for him'; but it has been turned into 'helpmeet', and then into 'helpmate'; nevertheless, you see how bad grammar, like bad exegesis, can produce good theology – if only occasionally. And so Adam needs a 'helpmate', if I may use that form of the word. And he cannot find one; even man's best friend, who was presumably in that parade of animals, did not seem to satisfy his need. So another human being is brought into being, namely the woman. And now man, who is incomplete in himself, becomes complete, as it were. He finds his completion in this other human being; and in this particular case, the notion of sociality is combined with that of sexuality in the forming of the most intimate and natural kind of human community.

Now it is not too difficult to go from that story to the conception of the essentially social nature of man taught by Feuerbach in the nineteenth century, and by Martin Buber more recently. 'There is no I without a thou' – no person without relationships to other persons. And both these thinkers say, I think rightly, that there is no more absurd notion than that of individual salvation. There can be no salvation of an individual while the rest of humankind is left to perish; we are either saved – that is to say, made whole – together, or we simply go under. Here we see the foundations of the idea that what we call the individual is a mere fragment, abstraction. The English philosopher Bernard Bosanquet was saying this eighty years ago, that the true individual, the only reality which can be absolutely whole and undivided, is the human race in its solidarity, for we are bound together in this web of life.

This obviously has important ethical implications. Traditionally, ethics has been very much concerned with the individual. This is true of Christian ethics in general, and in particular of sexual ethics, which have been conceived on an individual basis. But nowadays, we really have to look at broader issues; we have to look much more than we have in the past at social ethics and the implications of our relatedness to other human beings. But this is a very difficult area indeed. Not long ago, in addressing a group in Oxford, I tried to explore the relationship between the individual virtue of love, which many people see as central to the whole Christian and biblical teaching and the social virtue – you might even call it the global virtue – of peace. We seem to be tolerably clear on the more individual aspects of ethics; most of us recognize that we have certain obligations and try as far as possible to fulfil them, and we have some idea of what love means. But love is an intimate kind of virtue, and when it comes to the larger questions, it is much more difficult to see one's way. What do we mean by peace anyway? What kind of obligations does it impose, not so much on individual human beings as on whole groups of human beings? What is the ethical context in which we should view the actions of, let us say, states, trade unions, and institutions of one kind or another? I remember Reinhold Niebuhr taking a somewhat cynical view of these questions when I talked to him in New York some years ago. He said: 'In individual ethics, with great difficulty, people may to some extent fulfil their obligations and manifest love and so on, but when you get to dealing with groups, whether it is trade unions or universities, shall we say, or anything of that sort, it is really the law of the jungle that prevails; self-interest is the only rule that guides conduct'.[1] Some younger ethicists in the United States have challenged Niebuhr and have suggested that he was being a little bit too cynical, though he called himself a realist. But certainly this seems to me to be one of the really difficult ethical questions at the present time. In the modern world, in which big associations, corporations, institutions, and so on are responsible for ordering so much of human life, how do we, as beings who are always beings-with-others bring in the ethical dimension?

12

Christian Theism and the Concept of a Person

ADRIAN THATCHER

Christian theists hold that there is a God who is personal. Too often, however, the credibility of theism suffers from a close association with Cartesian dualism. I will attempt to show that neither the Christian concept of God nor the Christian understanding of the human person requires such a dualism in order to be credible. In the first part of the paper, I draw attention to the use of philosophical dualism in some theological writing and develop some theological criticisms of it as it appears in the doctrines both of God and of humankind. In the second part, I draw on the new concept of matter, a gift of the physical sciences to theology, and inquire whether it can have any application to God. Finally, I suggest that conclusive grounds for ascribing personalness to God can be derived from the claimed identity of this God with the human being Jesus of Nazareth.

THEOLOGICAL DIFFICULTIES FOR PHILOSOPHICAL DUALISM

Let us begin by separating out some different uses of the concept of a 'person', starting with the ancient theological use, according to which the one God is said to consist of three Persons. The Latin 'persona' and the Greek 'prosōpon', despite their very human origins, soon came to be used for the divine Persons of the Trinity. The divine *personae*, said St Augustine, are understood 'in a mystery....When, then, it is asked what the three are, or who the three are, we betake ourselves to the finding out of some special or general name under which we may embrace these three; and no such name occurs to the mind, because the supereminence of the Godhead surpasses the power of customary speech.'[1] According to the second, or ontological, use, a person is defined by his or her identity, or essential difference from non-persons. Locke claimed that a person was 'a thinking intelligent being, that has reasons and reflection, and can consider itself as itself, the same thinking thing, in different times and places.'[2] Descartes, while not employing the term 'person', asked what kind of thing he himself was, and answered, 'a thinking thing'.[3] The third use is psychological, where the term 'personality' refers to the particular character that a person acquires. The fourth use is moral. Kant, we recall, observed that, rational beings are called *persons*, because their very nature shows them to be ends in themselves, that is, something which cannot be made use of simply as a means.'[4] The fifth use is existential, where the person is what he or she makes of him or herself. 'If man as the existentialist sees him', says Sartre, 'is not definable, it is because to begin with he is nothing. He will not be anything until later, and then he will be what he makes of himself.'[5] In order to counteract the bias towards individuality in much Western philosophy, let us postulate a sixth use that is *social*, a person-in-relation. 'Persons', wrote John Macmurray, 'are constituted by their mutual relation to one another. "I" exist only as one element in the complex "You and I".'[6]

As a preliminary move, let us concede that God can hardly be conceived of as a person in accordance with *any* of these six uses. God is a single essence, or being, and this essence is expressed in three modes, or forms, which are the Persons of the Trinity. But God is not a single Person of this first type. The other five concepts have been fashioned to single out some feature that has been claimed for the human being, and it would seem to be a grammatical mistake to apply these to God. The life of Jesus enables Christians to speak of God's character as self-giving love, but this is a claim for Christology, not philosophical theism. God, Christians say, treats men and women as ends in themselves; and God, for women and men, is supremely an end. But talk of means and ends belongs to moral, not theistic, discourse. The existential concept of a person, at least for Sartre, replaces God in an atheistic humanism. The social concept requires other persons to constitute 'me' as a person, but no such requirement could apply to God, who being self-existent, needs nothing to constitute him.

Given the apparent implausibility of speaking of God as a 'person', it may come as a shock to discover that in some recent debates in the philosophy of religion, theists and atheists have agreed to call God a 'person', albeit a person without a body. This might well be called 'the personalist consensus'. Within this broad framework of agreement about what 'God' means, disagreement about whether the concept is coherent and whether it has application to anything with real existence can go on and on. A previous generation of philosophers of religion conducted their polemics on this carefully chosen territory, and in the last decade the battle has resumed. The theist Richard Swinburne holds: 'That God is a person, yet one without a body, seems the most elementary claim of theism.'[7] The atheist J. L. Mackie eagerly accepts this position, adding that it is 'literally meaningful', readily conceivable, rightly immune to direct verification, and so on; but also that it is a 'miracle' that any rational person still defends it.[8] Many unfortunate consequences follow from dealing with what is at issue between theism and atheism in this way.

There are two principal formative factors in the personalist consensus: the constraints imposed on the idea of God by the doctrine of incorporeality, and the influence upon some post-Renaissance thought, both philosophical and religious, of Cartesian dualism. The notion of a person without a body derives from the ontological concept of a person, which divides into two substances, one mental, the other physical. It is easy to show how a succession of philosophers of religion have adopted a common procedure of selecting dualistic concepts of the person and, after purging them of all traces of materiality, have ascribed them, with varying degrees of literalness, to the divine being. This has been called 'the dematerialization procedure'.[9] In every case the procedure begins with pairs of concepts which already assume that the dualistic account of the person is true. These might be mind and body, self and behaviour, agency and performance, intention and action, P-predicates and M-predicates, and so on. Proper conceptual distinctions soon become improper ontological distinctions, with the result that whatever concept is applied eventually to God – whether Mind, Supreme Self, All-Agent, Person, and so on – it has become entirely detached from its material counterpart. It follows that these models or concepts of a 'person' are no such thing, for they have divided the person in two and then left no place for the material side. If we are to say that God is a bodiless person, we need prior agreement that persons are not bodies, which means that we must adopt a Cartesian concept of a person. But there are good philosophical and theological grounds for steering clear of such a concept.

The argument between dualists and non-dualists over the nature of persons is as lively now as it was in the time of Descartes and Hobbes. The ablest contemporary philosophers are at odds over the issue, with Swinburne, for example, arguing strongly for a Cartesian view,[10] and Derek Parfit holding that the problem about personal identity itself arises out of a mistaken dualist framework, and that 'the existence of a person, during any period, just consists in the existence of his brain and body, and the thinking of his thoughts, and the doing of his deeds, and the occurrence of many other physical and mental events.'[11] This philosophical stalemate is likely to perplex the theologian. Some theologians think that the re-emergence of dualism allows them to defend the doctrines of the image of God and life after death more plausibly. Although I favour a broad materialist position in the argument, I shall leave the topic to the philosophers for the present, and turn to a theological analysis of claims that a person is essentially an immaterial substance which can survive the death of the body with which it is associated.

There appears to be a rare unanimity among biblical scholars that the biblical picture of the person is non-dualist, and that the Bible gives little or no support to the idea that a person is essentially a soul, or that the soul is separable from the body.[12] Dualists, of course, may reply that, regardless of what the Bible said about the issue *then*, dualism offers a convincing framework for Christian teaching *now*. Even so, they cannot get around the fact that, from a biblical point of view, dualism is very odd. Lynn de Silva summarizes the position thus:

> Biblical scholarship has established quite conclusively that there is no dichotomous concept of man in the Bible, such as is found in Greek and Hindu thought. The biblical view of man is holistic, not dualistic. The notion of the soul as an immortal entity which enters the body at birth and leaves it at death is quite foreign to the biblical view of man. The biblical view is that man is a unity; he is a unity of soul, body, flesh, mind, etc. all together constituting the whole man. None of the constituent elements is capable of separating itself from the total structure and continuing to live after death.[13]

Despite growing confidence that the Bible supports a now fashionable holistic view of the person, biblical anthropology is not absolutely decisive. There are passages in which *sōma* and *psuchē* are contrasted, and in which the influence of the Greek idea of immortality can be readily detected for example Matt. 10: 28; 2 Cor. 5: 1–5; Phil. 1: 21–3. But more decisive perhaps is the sense of creatureliness and mortality, which seems incompatible with dualism. In biblical thought the entire human being, not merely the human body, is subject to death and decay. 'Dust you are, to dust you shall return', says God to the man in the garden (Gen. 3: 19).[14] 'All mankind is grass,' cries the prophet; 'they last no longer than a flower of the field. The grass withers, the flower fades, when the breath of the Lord blows upon them; the grass withers, the flowers fade, but the word of our God endures for evermore' (Isa. 40: 6–8). 'Your life, what is it?', asks St James. 'You are no more than a mist, seen for a little while and then dispersing' (Jas. 4: 14).

More important, the doctrines of creation, incarnation, resurrection, and ascension all favour the non-dualist view. To say that our souls are immortal is to blur the distinction between the Creator and the creature. What is created, as the biblical passages just quoted clearly show, has an end as well as a beginning: indeed, the whole point of these images in these verses is to draw attention to the brevity of human life, especially when compared with the eternal life of God. But this makes no sense if persons are immortal, appearances not-withstanding. The incarnation of God in Christ is a profoundly materialistic affair which allows the human nature of Christ in its totality – not merely Christ's human soul – to be taken up into the perfect unity of his single divine Person. Moreover, the resurrection and ascension of Christ seem clearly to exclude dualistic accounts of the human person. The death of Christ was a real and total death, not merely the death of his mortal body. The miracle of the resurrection is precisely that God raises Jesus from the dead, not that he raises Jesus' mortal body and reunites it with his immortal soul. What purpose does the resurrection of Jesus serve, we may ask, if Jesus was not really dead? Was it just to convince the disciples that the bonds of death were forever loosened? Hardly, for if the disciples had believed in immortal souls they would not have required assurance on that point; and if they had needed such assurance, a resurrection miracle would not have provided it; it would merely have created confusion. The ascension of Christ is also rendered superfluous by a dualist account of the person; for the soul of Christ, being alive after his physical death, would presumably have been capable of returning to the Father without its body. What then is the ascension? A highly visual way of saying cheerio? It is, rather, the return of the transformed, transfigured, glorified, yet still *embodied*, Christ to the Father. No particular historical version of the event is favoured by arguing thus. The point is that the theological convictions expressed by the resurrection and ascension narratives make much better sense on the assumption that all men and women are essentially bodily unities, *after*, as well as before, their bodily deaths.

Christian faith has nothing to fear from the suggestion that men and women lack a fixed non-bodily identity or essence. Indeed, that we have no permanent identity may well be why we seek the grace of God to confer unity and direction upon our lives. One writer, comparing the concept of 'self' in Christianity and Buddhism, even goes so far as to claim that 'Christianity goes beyond Buddhism in its doctrine of *annatā*, denying both an "ego-entity" and "exclusive individuality" to the human person.'[15] The modern concern, indeed obsession, with the self, which issues in talk about self-analysis, self-knowledge, self-presentation, self-realization, self-esteem, and the like, can usefully be contrasted with a Christian approach to these matters. In Christian teaching the self is supremely unimportant, for 'whoever cares for his own safety is lost; but if a man will let himself be lost for my sake, he will find his true self' (Matt. 16: 25). There is a surprising lack of emphasis on the self in Christian teaching, which actually liberates the individual from self-preoccupation and frees him or her for the love of God and of other people. This is another example of a non-dualist understanding of the person actually advancing traditional Christian teaching.

The account of the Christian hope based on the resurrection of Christ is also more *religiously* adequate than its Hellenized counterpart, which is based on the natural immortality of the soul. It emphasizes our finitude and our mortality; it allows death to be a total extinguishing event. Above all, the eternal destiny of all women and men is placed in the hands of a loving God who is trusted to confer on his creatures a new somatic existence; it certainly does not depend on the dubious powers of persons to survive their own deaths. One of Bishop Butler's problems in providing arguments for the immortality of the soul 250 years ago was, paradoxically, a result of their very success. For, once belief in natural immortality is established by reason, death has no religious significance, and trust in God to provide a future life is superfluous since it will happen anyway. By removing the need to believe without confirming evidence, religious dualists are in danger of imperilling the simple trust in God which they advocate elsewhere.

A Cartesian view of the person also seems irreconcilable with Christian theology on a variety of other grounds. It is the followers of Aristotle, rather than the followers of Jesus, who say that we are, or are primarily, thinkers; in biblical thought the heart is more central than the mind. In mind–body dualism, the human body is easily disparaged, because it is inessential to mind and to personal identity. Since, for Descartes, only the mind is conscious, the body is no more than an object, a machine governed by mechanical laws. Deprived of its soul, it is without religious significance. It is often blamed for being the source of sin, without regard for the fact that sins such as pride, malice, uncharity, and so on, if we are to assign sins to the different substances of the person, would have to be assigned to the non-bodily side. In Descartes' own method for establishing the certainty of his own existence, other people have no part, self-identity and self-certainty being established in isolation. Our feelings and emotions, essential ingredients of our moral and aesthetic awareness, are untrustworthy because of their bodily origins and are of no philosophical interest. Since only persons have an additional immaterial substance, the rest of creation is void of religious significance.

I thus conclude, first, that there are no religious reasons for preferring philosophical dualism over rival views, and that, in fact, there are strong religious reasons for rejecting it. There are also strong philosophical reasons, which I have not touched on, for rejecting it. Second, if we do not adopt Cartesian dualism in the first place, we are unlikely to find convincing any attempt to speak of God by means of it. In the light of these conclusions a different approach to the concept of the person seems warranted.

THEOLOGICAL IMPLICATIONS OF THE NEW CONCEPT OF MATTER

If dualism is rejected, what are the consequences for our understanding of ourselves and of God? With regard to ourselves, I can add nothing to the masterly treatment given by Arthur Peacocke in his *Creation and the World of Science*.[16] Summarizing how the concept of matter is understood today, he writes:

> The material units of the universe – the sub-atomic particles, the atoms and the molecules they can form – are the fundamental entities constituted in their matter-energy-space-time relationships, and are such that they have built in, as it were, the potentiality of becoming organised in that special kind of complex system we call living and, in particular in the system of the human brain in the human body which displays conscious activity. In man, the stuff of the universe has become cognizing and self-cognizing.[17]

Non-scientists like myself have great difficulty in even beginning to grasp the enormous shifts of understanding signalled here. For the last three centuries, a closed, mechanical, inert view of matter rendered almost inevitable a dualism of matter and spirit. Since there was no room in a closed material world for spirit, room had to be found elsewhere. It was located in Kant's 'noumenal realm' or the religious equivalent – the soul – or in a remote supernatural realm, as in deism. But in materialism it was located nowhere at all. Now, however, we have a concept of matter which is open, fathomless, emergent, and self-organizing. No longer are Christians driven to reify the soul or spirit in order to gain religious entry into the material world, for the material world emerges through a 'hierarchy of complexity' to humankind, in which conscious-ness, and mental activity and function 'are not an activity and function of some new thing or entity, the "mind", but are a new activity and function of the all-pervasive physico-chemical units that emerges when these units have evolved a particular kind of organized complexity'.[18] This view of matter seems entirely consistent with Christian theology (as Peacocke goes on to show), and gives rise elsewhere to views of the person which are variously called 'holist', 'compositionalist', 'organicist', and so on.

The deep-rooted conceptual problem about matter which remains is that it has always been an exclusive term involving contrast, either with form (as in Greek philosophy) or with mind (as in Cartesian dualism). The new concept of matter, however, is an inclusive term. It is inclusive of form, since it is self-organizing, and of mind, since mind is matter in an advanced stage of organization in the hierarchies of nature. If matter contrasts with anything, it is with the older concept of matter that preceded it. It is bound to take theology a little time to accommodate this remarkable change.

This shift from an exclusive to an inclusive concept of matter certainly helps to recast the doctrine of God's incorporeality, that element of theism which tempts some theologians to adopt Cartesian dualism. When we consider God's incorporeality from the point of view of a dualism which makes an exclusive separation between matter and spirit, then it is unthinkable that God should have a material body, inert, solid, and impenetrable. But once this exclusive concept of matter has been replaced by the inclusive self-organizing one that becomes organized in the form of living persons, there are no reasons why we should not posit, within the inclusive infinity of God, elements of matter. This is not to say that the material world should be posited as God's body. It is rather to say that the blurring of the distinction between spirit and matter also blurs the distinction between God and the world, and that theology is the better for it. If the finite world is lodged by its Creator in his infinite being, then we have the basis for a metaphysic in which the dynamism and directedness of living matter is fully consistent with its place in the life of the One who is the dynamic source of all that lives. God's incorporeality is fully consistent with whatever way he chooses to manifest himself in the material world that he has created. The prefix contained in the word 'incorporeal' may be taken to deny, not all materiality to God, but only that God's corporeality is finite. God is not corporeal as creatures are; nor could he conceivably be a Cartesian *res extensa*. But we now have a different understanding of what it means for something to be a *corpus*, or material body, and there is less difficulty in assigning to God a corporeality, provided it is of a form appropriate to his infinite being and to nothing else. To assign infinite corporeality to God may add to incarnational and sacramental theology a heightened emphasis on God's real presence in the world.

If God is not a person and Cartesian accounts of persons are not to be utilized in speaking of him, what may we say of God? The issue has been fully explored and developed by John Macquarrie and Keith Ward whose treatment can hardly be bettered.[19] I prefer to break into the theological circle with Anselm's prayerful attribution to God, and God alone, of necessary existence: 'You so truly are that you cannot be thought not to be. . . . Whatever else there is, except for you alone, can be conceived not to be. Therefore, you alone, of all things exist in the truest and greatest way, for nothing else so truly exists and therefore everything else has less being.'[20] The real existence of God cannot be deduced from our concept of him; it can be, and has to be, affirmed as an object of faith, which reason cannot show to be more than probable. God, then, is a real ontological subject, posited by faith, whom we identify and praise with our term 'God'. The contrast between necessary being and contingent being is well expressed by the contrast between 'being' and '*a* being'. To think of God as *a* being is to include him in a genus with other beings; better to call him being itself, from whom all beings derive. Although not *a* being, he is still identifiable, for he can be contrasted with all that he has made. The fundamental attribute of divine existence is love. Divine existence brings into being and nurtures an object for its love in creation, and units it with itself in redemption. Because of its love, while remaining eternal, it becomes temporal, and unites the temporal with itself. Its 'dynamic infinity' (Keith Ward's phrase[21]) is able to include finitude within itself. Its infinite love qualifies its infinite power. It always enables creatures, never coerces them, thus prompting their free response. Since all that is depends on God for its existence, God is the source of all power. His creatures are free, which is why he chooses not to control them. His providential action in the world is 'homeostatic' – that is, despite creaturely misuse of freedom, God can yet fulfil his purposes, however far from their realization his creatures may have strayed.[22]

God, then, is the source of personal being, for he creates a material, yet person-producing, world in which persons are the bearers of his image. Persons, therefore, more than any other created beings, can symbolize him, for, as Macquarrie says: 'The whole hierarchy of beings can be seen as an open series in which at each stage the tendency to be like God emerges more strongly.'[23] Since we have no firm knowledge of divine existence except what is disclosed to us, our speech is tentative, employing metaphor, analogy, and so on. There can hardly be any objection, therefore, to using human analogies in speaking of God and of his actions. Religious discourse takes it for granted that God speaks, acts, creates, saves, and so on. But any attempt by Christians to discuss the being of God is bound to remain woefully incomplete if it ignores the incarnation of God in Christ. This is especially true with regard to the personalness of God, since it is the incarnation which gives Christians their sole convincing grounds for claiming that God is a personal God.

CHRIST THE GROUND OF GOD'S PERSONHOOD

Christian theism is the only kind of theism which can substantiate belief in a personal God, and so give over to philosophical theism the concept of a divine person which it seeks to establish on other grounds. This is because God himself becomes a human person in Jesus Christ. Jesus of Nazareth was confessed as *vere deus, vere homo*: truly God, truly man. The force of *vere homo* was not merely to deny Docetism, according to which Jesus only *appeared* to be human; it was also to emphasize that Jesus was more fully human than anyone else, that in him is found true humanness. The last five of our six concepts of person can therefore be ascribed to Jesus quite readily. He too was a thinking, intelligent being with a mind, 'a reasonable soul and a body', as the Chalcedonian definition has it. He too regarded other people as ends in themselves; his finished life is more of an example of resoluteness and choice than Sartre ever understood. He too was a person-in-relation.

The Chalcedonian definition affirms that Jesus Christ was 'perfect in manhood, . . . truly man, . . . of one substance with us as touching the manhood, like us in all things apart from sin'. There is then a solidarity between the perfect manhood of the divine Son and ourselves, which is marred only by our wrongdoing. Jesus is fully and completely human, where 'completely human' is qualified by his unity with God. We, by contrast, are partially and fragmentarily human, missing the mark, failing to achieve the 'new pattern of humanness' which was lived and achieved among us. What entitles us to say that the Father of Jesus is a personal God is the other *homoousion* clause of the definition, 'of one substance with the Father as touching the Godhead'. The real identity between Jesus and God enables us to extend some of our predicates about Christ's perfect manhood and human nature to God the Son, and so to God himself. God is personal because God has become a person in Christ. Christ is already a Person in the first sense. But God the Son also becomes a person in our other senses, and, provided we preserve the careful distinctions which have been made, we are in no danger of re-introducing 'two Persons' to Christology. There are good grounds for associating the human nature of the divine Son more closely with concepts of the human person, in our last five senses.

Jesus shows both what it is to be God and what it is to be completely a person. We are now able to see how, despite earlier disclaimers, some features of human personhood, are, after all, directly attributable to God. The philosophical concept of a person which best enables us to visualize the unity of the divine and human natures in the one Christ is the double-aspect, or Strawsonian, type.[24] Just as a person is a single entity to which double sets of predicates must be ascribed, so the divine Person of the Son (in our first sense) is also a single entity to whom a double set of predicates must be ascribed, corresponding to his two natures. But one of the two natures is a *human* nature. Predicates ascribing godness and humanness are ascribed to the single divine Person in the first sense, just as predicates acribing material and psychological states are ascribed to the single person of Strawson's version of the second sense.

God's embodiment in Jesus confirms the suggestions made earlier about his corporeality. In uniting himself to a historical person, God willingly becomes subject to the conditions of time and space, confirming what was suggested about his dynamic infinity. Unlike a god who cannot change or suffer he thus becomes subject to physical pain and rejection. The outpouring of his love in creation is surpassed only by the outpouring of his love in redemption. God's character as love is seen in the human character of Jesus (our third sense). His self-giving love is the self-giving love of God; it also reveals a new understanding of what 'respect for persons' might mean. The cries from the cross, 'My God, my God, why has thou forsaken me?' (Matt. 27: 46 and Mark 15: 34 (RSV)), and 'It is finished' (John 19: 30), contribute to an existential understanding of the person (our fifth sense), to an actual completed life in which, isolated by the burden of his responsibilities, the human Jesus lays hold of his life in freedom and offers it to the Father, and the Father takes into himself the pain and uncertainty of human obedience to God.

Jesus is also a person in the sixth, or social, sense. About the social concept, Keith Ward observes: 'Co-operative and sharing love is one of the greatest values, as it is only in transcending self and relating to others that one truly becomes a person, a developing, self-expressive being discovering itself in the forms of its social relationships'.[25] However, it is God himself, rather than Jesus, to whom Ward refers, for he continues: 'Thus God can become a person, in this sense, only as he creates some community of rational agents in relation to which his own perfection can be expressed.' Ward says that God becomes a person in the sixth sense through making a world and then interacting with it. With this Christians can whole-heartedly agree, adding perhaps that the uniting of God with the human person Jesus of Nazareth is what gives us the ultimate ground for all our personal ascriptions to the deity. For, once God's personalness is grounded in Jesus, reverent speculation about it can begin.

DISCUSSION

STEVEN COLLINS. I have two questions. First, if Christ is a person in a full-bodied sense, where is he now? Second, if we are to believe that life after death involves some sort of bodily continuity with this life, how do you find enough bodies for everybody to have one in eternity? How do you find enough matter? Because, after all, we have been recycling it for a while, have we not? THATCHER. The main problem about the doctrine of the resurrection of the body is exactly how we are to take it. To speak of the reconstitution of the person is one way of doing so. My inclination is to leave the problem to God himself. That is a situation which is more religiously adequate; and beyond that, I do not think it is up to me to say. I do not think Christians want to depict God as searching out the former atoms of the decomposed bodies of the faithful! There is also an obvious philosophical problem associated with this. If we picture God as reconstituting persons as embodied beings after their deaths, would these beings be replicas of their former selves? Or would they, in some sense known to God, be the same person? As to where the body of Jesus is after the ascension, it is not here; it is a *transformed* body.

ROGER TRIGG. I find it worrying that this kind of question can be sensibly asked in this context, because it seems to me to be a caricature of Christianity to suggest that life after death involves reconstituted atoms as they are here and now. This is the kind of view that suggests that bodies suddenly just come up out of the graveyard, and that therefore we should not be cremated because of the problems that might create. To me, life after death is something to do with continuing in a completely different environment, outside space, outside time, in a completely different dimension. Whether we want to call that the immortality of the soul or the resurrection of the body, I don't mind. Because in this context 'resurrection of the body' refers to something that has become so transformed that perhaps it gets near to being equivalent to 'immortality of the soul'. St Paul talks about 'glorification' and 'transformation' of the body in the sense that the body then becomes something very different from what we experience here and now. You have been talking about something that goes on within our present type of existence. In my view, we can accept science, in so far as it indicates that all this is going to come to an end some day, and yet make substantial claims about resurrection and immortality.

RICHARD SWINBURNE. I wish to take up one point: your [Thatcher's] suggestion that dualism is not very consonant with the Christian tradition. I thought that you were oscillating between about four senses of 'dualism'. First, of course, there is what is known as property, or attribute, dualism – that is, the view that there is only one kind of thing, matter or energy, but that it has two sorts of properties, physical properties and mental properties. Second, there is a form of substance dualism which says, that there are two things, body and soul, but that the soul is dependent on the body, despite being a separate thing. The soul is the essential part of the person, in that it is the continuing of the soul that makes for the continuity of the person. In this form of substance dualism, there needs normally to be a body, at any rate to keep the soul operative and ticking over, but not necessarily the same body; and by special divine act, God may keep the soul operative temporarily without a body. This is the most modest form of substance dualism. Third, one can have a substance dualism which also says that there are two things, and that the soul is the essential part of the person, but that the soul is naturally immortal. The soul continues even if you destroy the body. Fourth, one can hold the third view together with the view that the body is not part of the person, or is not necessary for the full person. Now I do not think any reputable or orthodox Christian theologian has ever held this fourth position. They have all thought that in the general resurrection a body is necessary and would have to be joined to the soul in order to re-establish the full person. Many Christian theologians, as you rightly point out, have held, contrary to the Bible, that there is a natural immortality to the soul, that the soul will go on living for ever under its own steam, as it were. They include Butler, Descartes, and, alas, even Aquinas. They all get arguments from Plato. The only form of dualism which is biblical, and the one which I have wished to defend, is the second – that there are two things, soul and body, and that it is the continuing of the soul which is essential for the continuing of the person. But the soul, even though it *can* perhaps continue without a body, does not have any *natural* inclination to continue. The person can continue if the soul continues, but linked with a different body. So it would not be a particular body which was necessary for the continuity of the person. Christian theology does need a substance dualism in this form, and has to go beyond property dualism, since it is committed to the resurrection of the dead. As you rightly point out, the molecules which form this earthly body may be turned into energy and dissipated to the four winds. How can *I* be reconstituted when *they* are no more? Since Christian theology is committed to the view that *I* can continue, nevertheless, it must hold that what makes me *me* is something other than these molecules. I give that something else the name 'soul', and I do think that this is necessary for Christian theology, which does not have to maintain that there is a natural immortality and that the body is not necessary for the full life of a person. It holds that persons normally only continue when embodied, but that the same person does not have to have the same body. The doctrine of resurrection does need a modified form of substance dualism, and your attacks on dualism were really directed to the more extreme form of substance dualism.

A historical point: the Fathers asked how on earth a cannibal could be resurrected at the last day if that cannibal has lived on other people and all his molecules were necessary for the reconstitution of those other people? So they objected to the view that we can understand the person solely as material.

COLLINS. I do not see what discussion of the person of Christ and the nature of God has to do with human persons or vice versa.

THATCHER. There are two kinds of connection. First, there is a particular and distorted concept of a person which lies behind very much popular, and some philosophical, discussion of the Christian God. Second, I think Christians should exploit a lot more than they do their belief that Jesus Christ is truly man. He is an exemplification of what true humanness ought to be; this is implied in the doctrine of the incarnation.

MICHAEL RUSE. Is there anything that somebody like you can say intelligibly to someone in an austere, tough-minded materialist position? Or are you and such a person operating in two opposed paradigms and such incommunicable languages that there can be no meeting-point?

THATCHER. I have been speaking as a theologian from the presuppositions of Christian theology, just as Peter Atkins spoke from his different pre-suppositions. They are very different, and the difference has to be explored.

ARTHUR PEACOCKE. May I attempt to throw a lifeline between these two? We have to ask, is there something more to be said about the human person than a materialist account offers? What Thatcher is claiming is that it is possible to fill out the 'more-that-is-to-be-said' in terms of our perception of what the human person is in the light of the Jesus Christ of history.

MARJORIE REEVES. There are many different facets of human experience: our reactions in all sorts of ways to beauty, to tragedy, to love. I would also want to add that a distinctive feature of human experience in its breadth is its growth from childhood through to maturity as one sees perceptions, thoughts, and intentions developing and informing the soul. So I would wish to emphasize our need to consider the *growth* of persons – that is, their education.

ROBIN ATTFIELD. We need to clarify the basis of the theological account of the person. On the latter view, the explanation of these being anything at all is the agency of God, and God is understood to have the sort of character necessary for such an explanation. So we have to hold that God is necessarily omnipotent and omniscient – that is what it is to be God. I find it very difficult to accept that God might be a person in any of Thatcher's senses 2 to 6. God could not be a particular *human* because of the quite incompatible properties that a human person has – finitude, limited power and knowledge, vulnerability to change, and so on. Even if we can clearly say what sort of 'thing' God is (and I think we would have to say something in answer to that question), God cannot actually be 'a person'.

THATCHER. Discussions of the attributes of God do historically seem to have taken place apart from considerations of God's revelation in Christ.[26] Christians might want to begin with God as shown in Christ, and work from there to God's attributes. When that is done, then they usually recognize that 'omnipotent', 'omniscient', and so on have to be qualified by ways not stemming from purely philosophical considerations.

RICHARD DAWKINS. Some of the arguments that we have been having this evening have been about explanations of complex phenomena, and whether things like beauty, trust, and love can be reduced to scientific kinds of explanation. They are the kind of questions about which we are liable to find we do not actually disagree, but are only using words in different ways. There are several questions that are clear; for example, the question of whether the 'person' is something that survives death. I know what the proposition that I am going to survive my death means, and I think it is false., If you are not a dualist, then I do not really see how you can dodge the seemingly very naive question that, if a person is to survive, where will he be? Do you literally believe that you are going to survive death?

THATCHER. I am not the least bit interested in that question.

DAWKINS. But how can you say that as a Christian theist?

THATCHER. I would say that in life, as in death, we are in the hands of God. The actual form that I shall take, if I shall take any form at all, after I physically cease to be is simply not my problem. If there is a loving God who chooses to confer a new life upon his children, then that is up to him. I happen to believe that that will happen. But *how* it will happen is something that we can only speculate about: ideas about the immortality of the soul, the resurrection of the body, and so on seem to me to be word-pictures on the very fringes of our language and understanding.

TRIGG. Can I ask where you draw the line between problems that are God's and problems that we should be worrying about, between things you think we can usefully understand and those things that only God can understand?

THATCHER. My remark was in response to a question about life after death; that is an area which seems to me to be very much beyond my comprehension. But I stand in a Christian tradition which affirms that there is a 'life after death'. I do not attempt to establish that by rational argument, but as part of the Christian faith, as part of the whole integrated way of seeing the world. This, I think, is firmer ground.

TRIGG. Is it only this question of life beyond death that is up to God?

THATCHER. No. For instance, I cannot say infallibly what the essence of God is.

TRIGG. I agree that how life after death will happen is obviously beyond our comprehension. But the question of whether or not there is a life after death is not a neutral one that can be put on one side. Either we are here 'by chance', and this life is all that there is; or what we do is of eternal significance, and each of us is of eternal significance, so that God will not let us die. That changes our attitude to people very crucially; so I think that this whole issue of life after death is of tremendous moral significance.

SWINBURNE. Traditional Christian orthodoxy has maintained that some things are provable by natural reason, and other things are only derivable from revelation. We know them through Christ himself, or through his Church. Life after death is not something you can prove by natural reason; rather, one proves first that there is a God, becoming incarnate in Christ, who is reliable. Then if he said that there is life after death, there is. That is the line to take. Proofs from the nature of the soul to its natural immortality do not work; but that does not mean that the belief in life after death is not justified. Given that, you then have to have a view of the person which makes it possible for God to give persons life after death. Even if they do not have a natural immortality, they have to be so constituted that God, if he chooses, may intervene and give them life after death. However, if the person's whole nature is his body, and his body is destroyed at death and the constituent elements dissipate into energy, then not even an omnipotent being can reconstitute it, because there is nothing to reconstitute. Whereas if there are in fact two parts to the person and the body is destroyed, then God can, if he chooses, re-form a new body around that remaining essential element. So Christian theology does require dualism, but it doesn't need dualism in which there is a *natural* immortality of the soul.

MICHAEL LOCKWOOD. One should not make the mistake of thinking that the only options here are Cartesian dualism and reductionist physicalism, such as is espoused by Peter Atkins. There are, it seems to me, powerful philosophical arguments for opposing Atkins's brand of reductionism, which have no particular connection with any elements of the Christian faith. What we know of our minds, of brains, 'from the inside', through introspection, shows, I believe, that a description couched purely in the language of physics is inadequate to the task of accommodating all that there is in the world.

My second point relates to a move made in the talk that I rather deplore – the bringing-in of quantum mechanics. The thought seems to be: matter and consciousness appear to be at odds with one another so long as our image of matter is of tiny billiard balls bouncing off each other in accordance with deterministic laws. But in contemporary physics this Newtonian picture has been largely abandoned in favour of something more shadowy and mysterious. So perhaps consciousness can more easily be accommodated within this new conception. But in fact there seems to me to be nothing whatsoever in the formalism of quantum mechanics that sheds any light at all on the phenomenon of awareness, or gives any hint as to why there should be such a thing. Moreover, it is wholly unclear, and hotly disputed, just what sort of reality we should think of as underlying the formalism of quantum mechanics anyway; and one can hardly resolve one mystery by pointing to another.

PEACOCKE. I think Thatcher meant that the realization that matter has the potentiality of self-organization into forms which display consciousness leads to a *de facto* recognition of the 'mental' porperties of matter in certain forms. This, I agree, is nothing to do with quantum theory.

ATTFIELD. We do not know what we mean by 'survival' unless we know that we mean 'survival as myself'. But I do not think this means that we are part body and part soul. If God exists with the powers attributed to him, it is not inconceivable that resurrection should take place with God bringing about the existence of an embodied person who in important respects resembles a former one, without there having to be a sort of identification tag 'soul', which is a constant link.

THATCHER. My point in discussing the resurrection and ascension of Christ was to draw attention to the corporealist assumptions underlying these early convictions of the Church and to say that they make sense. They involve a holistic view of the person which is what I think the Jewish view was at that time. We are now discussing this as a thesis about life after death, which was not my intention.

COLLINS. It seems to me deplorable to suggest that *either* we are here by chance *or else* God keeps us eternally significant. There are many actual and possible alternatives to such a simple dichotomy. In Buddhist thought, for instance, the view that there is a continuing and independent self is regarded as a fundamental religious mistake. Rather, there is a connected series of processes which at any given time we call a 'human being' or 'person'. In a process of conditioning which goes back over (beginningless) time, this connected series of processes, in one psychophysical unit in one life, is called one 'person'. The continuity involved here is seen as one of the patterns of consciousness and patterns of character, labelled karma. This means that *I*, insofar as I refer to myself in the ordinary sense, will not survive death, whereas the processes of which I am part will. The connections and continuities between lives are seen as comparable to those between, say, myself now and myself at the age of 75, or at the age of 7½ months. Thus, as Buddhism has it, the 'person' reborn after 'me' is neither the same nor different: just a further stage in the process of conditioned continuity. This view is just one example among many possible alternatives to thinking that we have a choice only between thinking that we are here by chance and are just a collection of atoms or else believing that it is God who invests us with eternal significance and an immortal soul.

13

The Unity of the Human Person According to the Greek Fathers

KALLISTOS WARE

PERSON AS MYSTERY

'The greatest secret is man himself,' said Novalis.[1] As David Jenkins, now Bishop of Durham, insisted in the first of his Bampton Lectures delivered at Oxford in 1966, personhood cannot be defined. We can do no more than 'point to what is meant and indicated', providing 'an ostensive definition'. From our living experience we have a sense of what it means to be a person, but this knowledge is far from exhaustive:

> There is a sense in which we do not know what is involved in being a person. Thus, we do not know how far being a person goes. That is to say we do not know what, if anything, could properly be described as the fulfilment of being a person, what are the possibilities as yet latent in human personalness, and what are all the demands which would have to be made on, and met by, men and women as persons, if men and women are to be truly and fully persons.

Personhood, he concluded, is something irreducible: 'the mystery of the fact of being a person' cannot be 'reduced to the facts of the appropriate sciences'.[2]

Novalis and Jenkins are saying something here that is of the utmost importance. The reality of our personhood is far more than any explanation that we choose to give of it. It is an intrinsic feature of personalness to be open, always to point beyond. The human person is that in which new beginnings are continually being made. To be human is to be unpredictable, creative, self-transcending.

With all this the Greek Fathers would agree. 'The greatest of all lessons is to know yourself,' says St Clement of Alexandria (*c*.150–*c*.215).[3] But he would have been the first to admit that to know oneself is not an easy task. What is my true self? What am I? Who am I? The answer, early Christian writers recognized, is far from obvious. For them, as for the Bishop of Durham, the bounds of each person are exceedingly wide – overlapping with those of other persons, interpenetrating, ranging over space and time, reaching out of space into infinity, out of time into eternity. There is, as they saw it, a specific reason for this mysterious, indefinable character of the person. It is to be found in the fact that the human being is made in God's image and likeness (Gen. 1: 26–7). The human person is a created icon of the uncreated God; since God is incomprehensible, so also is the human person. 'Has anyone ever understood his own intellect (*nous*)?' asks St Gregory of Nyssa (*c*.330–*c*.395). '...An image is only truly such in so far as it expresses the attributes of its archetype. One of the characteristics of Godhead is to be in its essence beyond our understanding; and so the image should also express this.'[4] In our talk about humans, as well as our talk about God, there needs to be an apophatic dimension; our negative theology demands as counterpart a 'negative anthropology'.

Thus far it is not difficult for a contemporary Christian to feel in sympathy with the approach of the Greek Fathers. But, if we read further in the patristic writings, almost at once we find ourselves confronted with a view of the person that strikes most of us as unhelpful, not to say dangerous. The majority of early Christian authors think in broadly Platonist terms, making a more or less sharp distinction between soul and body, and identifying the true person with the soul, which is seen as the unique, indestructible, and eternal element in each individual. Without rejecting the body as evil, and while continuing to affirm the New Testament faith in bodily resurrection, they seem to envisage our personalness in separatist terms as 'the ghost in the machine', in Gilbert Ryle's phrase. We miss the holistic standpoint affirmed by William Blake: 'Man has no Body distinct from his Soul; for that call'd Body is a portion of Soul discern'd by the five Senses.'[5] Instead of treating the body as the total person's 'mode' of existence, the manifestation to the outside world – as well as to ourselves – of the energies of our human nature as a whole, most Patristic writers appear to treat the body as no more than a part of the person, a separable and inferior component.

As soon as we look deeper, however, we discover indications of a more integrated, holistic conception. Take the well-known passage from the sermon on Christ's Nativity by St Gregory of Nazianzus (329–89),[6] for example, and compare it with another celebrated text, the forty-first of the *Ambigua*, or 'Disputed Questions', treated by St Maximus the Confessor (*c.*580–662).[7] I choose these two passages because they are typical, representative expressions of the patristic view of the person; although it should be emphasized that there is in the Greek Fathers no single, systematic theory of personhood, or even an agreed terminology, but only a series of overlapping approaches. We should not speak of *the* patristic doctrine of the person, as if there were only one such doctrine. Another reason for selecting Gregory of Nazianzus and Maximus is that they are both in the broad sense 'Christian Platonists', thinkers who contrast soul and body in what seems at first glance to be a characteristically Platonic manner. Yet, if we follow out the inner logic of their argument, we are brought to an understanding of the person that rises above any such dichotomy.

Gregory of Nazianzus begins by distinguishing between the two levels of creation: the invisible, or spiritual, and the material, or physical. Angels belong to the first level, animals to the second. Alone among living creatures, humans exist on both levels at once:

> Wishing to form a single creature from the two levels, from both invisible and visible nature, the Creator Logos fashioned man. Taking a body from the matter that he had previously created, and placing in it the breath of life that comes from himself, which Scripture terms the intelligent soul and the image of God [cf. Gen 1: 27; 2: 7], he formed man as a second cosmos, a great universe within a little one.

Gregory goes on to draw out the implications of this 'mixed' nature (as he styles it), both material and spiritual, with which we humans are endowed. Each of us is 'earthly yet heavenly, temporal yet immortal, visible yet intelligible, midway between majesty and lowliness; one self-same being, but both spirit and flesh'. It is our human mission to hold in harmony these two aspects of our dual nature. But our vocation extends beyond this. We are also to transcend ourselves: 'guided by God's providence', the human creature is capable of participating in the life and glory of God, of being 'deified', or 'divinized'. This experience of *theosis*, or 'deification', Gregory calls 'the supreme culmination of the mystery'. He concludes by speaking of bodily death, and by looking beyond this to the final resurrection: 'So God has bound together [soul and body]; and, though he separates them, he will hereafter bind them together once more in a yet more glorious way.'

Three words sum up this synoptic account of the human person: 'microcosm', 'mediator', *'microtheos'*.

MICROCOSM

In the first place, our human personhood, 'earthly yet heavenly', existing on both the spiritual and the material levels, is by virtue of its mixed, or dual, nature a microcosm, a 'second cosmos', reflecting and embracing the two different aspects of the created universe. Each of us is *imago mundi*, an icon of the world. Here Gregory of Nazianzus is making use of a *motif* which is found frequently in Greek classical and Christian authors, one that Jung has taken up and reinterpreted in our own day. The point is made with particular vividness by Origen (*c.* 185–*c.*254): 'Understand that you have within yourself, upon a small scale, a second universe: within you there is a sun, there is a moon, and there are also stars.'[8] 'You are a universe within the universe,' states St Nilus of Ancyra (early fifth century); 'look within yourself, and see there the whole creation.'[9] Maximus the Confessor speaks of the human person in similar terms as 'a laboratory (*ergasterion*) that contains everything in a most comprehensive fashion'.[10]

As we have seen, Gregory begins his account of the person by contrasting angels and humans: angels are spirit alone, whereas humans have a dual nature. In consequence of this mixed character, human nature is normally seen as occupying a level lower than the angelic in the hierarchy of being. There are some dissenting voices,[11] but this is the standard view. Human nature, however, if not at the summit of the created order, is certainly at the centre. An angel does not reflect and hold together in his person the entire creation, and so cannot serve a microcosm. This is a role fulfilled only by a human. Our human nature, precisely because it is mixed, is more complete than the angelic, and by virtue of its greater complexity, it also possesses richer potentialities.

MEDIATOR

What are these potentialities? This brings us to the second of our three terms: 'mediator'. Here a sympathetic modern inquirer, willing perhaps to use the notion of the human person as microcosm, is likely to feel less at home; for the patristic view of mediation presupposes a 'tiered', hierarchical vision of reality that is alien to most contemporary thinking. Let us attempt none the the less to understand what is being affirmed by this language of mediation. 'Earthly yet heavenly', it is our human vocation to reconcile and harmonize the differing levels of reality in which we participate, and so to draw them all into unity. This is a theme developed at length by Maximus the Confessor in *Ambigua* 41. He begins by distinguishing five divisions within reality:

between the uncreated and the created;
within creation, between the intelligible, or 'noetic', and the sensible;
within sensible or visible nature, between heaven and earth;
within earth, between paradise and the world;
within man (*anthropos*, i. e. human nature), between male and female.

Man, he continues, being in this way

a laboratory that contains everything in a most comprehensive fashion,
by virtue of his nature mediates through himself between all the extreme
points at all the various levels of division.... He has by nature full power
to unite all these divisions, because in the different aspects of his own
self he is himself related to all the extreme points and mediates between
them all.... It is thus his appointed task to make manifest in himself the
great mystery of the divine intention – to show how the divided extremes
in created things may be reconciled in harmony, the near with the far,
the lower with the higher, so that through gradual ascent all are eventually brought into union with God. That is why man was introduced last
into the creation as a natural bond of unity, mediating between the
extremes because related to them all through the different aspects of his
own self... drawing them all to unity within himself, and so uniting
them all to God their cause.[12]

We humans embark on our mediatorial task by first transcending the division
between male and female; and so with God's help we work upwards through
the other divisions, finally uniting created nature with the uncreated. This we
do by means of *agapē*, 'love,[13] a key concept throughout Maximus's theology.

Such is the way in which the human person constitutes what Maximus terms
the *physikos syndesmos* or 'natural bond' of the creation. We humans are, in
the phrase of St John Chrysostom (*c*.347–407), the 'bridge',[14] or, as the
Persian Sufis express it, the 'marriage song of the world'.[15] As a unity of
spirit and body, the human person has power to render the earthly heavenly,
to spiritualize the material order without thereby dematerializing it. We can
each act as priest and king of the creation, offering the world back to God
in joy and thanksgiving. Of God's creation, we alone can do this, for we alone
participate in the two realms at once, the material and the spiritual. We stand
at the crossroads, at the point of meeting. The ecological implications of this
are very plain: as mediators, we can transfigure the environment through our
acts of moral choice – or we can do the exact opposite, rendering it polluted
and poisonous.

This mediating function is a favourite theme among the Jewish Hasidim, as well as the Greek Fathers. In the words of Rabbi Shelomo of Karlin, man 'must go from rung to rung until, through him, everything is united'. According to Rabbi Hanokh of Alexander, man's task is to make of the earth 'something heavenly'. Rabbi Abraham Yaakov of Sadagora taught: 'All creatures and plants and animals bring and offer themselves to man, but through man they are all brought and offered to God. When man purifies and sanctifies himself in all his members as an offering to God, he purifies and sanctifies all the creatures.'[16]

So far the mediatorial function has been spelt out simply in terms of our basic humanity. But it is essential at this point to take a further step, and to express the idea of mediation in a specifically Christological way. In God's original plan, humanity was intended to act as mediator and priest, to unify the creation and offer it back to God. But instead of doing this, we humans have produced disharmony, not unity, within our own selves and between the world and God. Christ, the Son of God, has therefore come as true man to fulfil the task of mediation that we have left undone. Jesus Christ, the God-man, the *Theanthropos*, is *the* mediator. In his person all created things are 'summed up' and 'recapitulated' (Eph. 1: 10); he draws them all together, holds them all in unity (Col. 1: 17), and offers them all back to the Father. This work of cosmic mediation, inaugurated by Jesus Christ as 'head' (Col. 1: 18), is continued and extended by each member of Christ's Body the Church. Christ is in this way *the* man, the model of what it means to be human, the mirror in which I see reflected my own true face, and the incarnation – his human birth – is at the same time the 'birthday of the human race'.[17] For the Greek Fathers, anthropology is an aspect of Christology.

Those who enjoy exploring the roots of words will find this mediating vocation implicit in the Latin and Greek words for a human being. The Latin *homo* and *humanus* are linked etymologically with the word for the earth, *humus*; compare also the Greek *chamai*, meaning 'on the ground'.[18] The Greek word *anthropos*, on the other hand, is linked by classical authors with *anathrein*, meaning 'to look up'. Lactantius (*c.*240–*c.*320), for example, says that man is called *anthropos* 'because he looks upward'; and he quotes Ovid's *Metamorphoses*: 'All other animals look down upon the earth, but to man God gave a face that looks on high, and commanded him to turn his eyes towards the heaven and his upright gaze towards the stars.'[19] Such is our condition and opportunity as human beings: we have our feet planted on the ground, but our vision embraces the sky, and it is thus our unique human privilege to draw the spiritual and the material into unity, to express them as inseparable and complementary aspects of a single and undivided whole.

MICROTHEOS

Our role as mediators, however, is not limited to reconciling earth and heaven, the physical and the invisible, within the created world. We also have a higher task: to transcend the first of the five divisions indicated by Maximus the Confessor, to unify the created with the uncreated. Such, as he sees it, is the supreme and ultimate aim of every human person: '. . .mediating between the extremes. . .drawing them all to unity within himself, and so *uniting them all to God*' (emphasis added). In our work of mediation we pass beyond the limits of our own created nature and, as Gregory of Nazianzus expresses it, we become 'deified': our human personhood is taken up into the eternal life of God and, without ceasing to be human, it is rendered godlike. This ultimate stage in our mediatorial ministry is possible because the human person is not only microcosm, the universe in miniature, but also *microtheos*, god in miniature. Each of us is not simply *imago mundi*, image of the world, but also *imago Dei*, image of God. Each is a created reflection of the uncreated Deity, a finite expression of God's infinite self-expression.

That is why Gregory of Nazianzus states, in the passage that we have been quoting, that man is 'a second cosmos, a great universe within a little one'. The unwary reader might easily assume that there has been a mistake here; surely Gregory must have written 'a little universe within a great one' (and that is indeed the way in which the phrase is sometimes translated).[20] But no, there has been no mistake: what Gregory said, and meant to say, was 'a great universe within a little one'. The human person is 'megalocosmos', rather than 'microcosmos'. As Nazianzus's namesake and friend Gregory of Nyssa observes, our chief glory as humans is not to be microcosms:

> Those who magnify human nature by comparing it to this world, saying that man is a microcosm, a little world, composed of the same elements as the universe. . .fail to realize that they are dignifying man with the attributes of the gnat and the mouse; for they too are composed of these four elements. . .What great thing is it, then, for man to be accounted a representation and likeness of the world – of the heaven that passes away, of the earth that is subject to change?

The true greatness of our human personhood, concludes Gregory of Nyssa, consists 'not in our likeness to the created world, but in our being made according to the image of the nature of the Creator',[21] in the fact that we reach out beyond the created order into the realm of the uncreated.

It is not the physical world with its countless galaxies that is the 'great universe'. Incomparably greater is the universe that exists within each human person. Vaster than the distances of outer space measured in myriads of light-years is the inner space of the human heart.

It is our vocation, then, not only to unify ourselves and the world around us, not only to hold together the material and the spiritual and to express them as an undivided whole; reaching out beyond created limits, we are also to unite ourselves and the world with God, and so to divinize the creation. This means that we are to discover the hidden spark within ourselves, the secret shrine that Scripture terms the 'image of God' and Orthodox writers often call the 'deep heart'. We are to find within us the place of encounter between the human and the divine, the centre of the self where our created personhood opens out upon the uncreated personhood of God – what Thomas Merton styles *le point vierge*, the 'little point of nothingness and of *absolute poverty*' that is 'the pure glory of God in us'.[22] Having found this centre, or 'little point', we then become mediators in the truest and fullest sense, through the power and after the example of Christ, the unique Mediator. Ourselves 'deified', we unite all things to God, revealing the divine presence in our own persons, in one another, in every tree, rock, and stream, in the whole creation. As *microtheos*, each person has the possibility of making the creation articulate in praise of God, transparent, at once 'diaphanic' and 'theophanic'. In the words of St Leontius of Cyprus (seventh century): 'Creation does not venerate the Maker through itself directly, but it is through me that the heavens declare the glory of God, through me the moon worships God, through me the stars glorify him, through me the waters and showers of rain, the dew and all creation, venerate God and give him glory.'[23] 'Through me': the human person is the indispensable link in the great chain of being.

UNDIVIDED UNITY

From everything stated so far, there follows a vital corollary. We humans cannot fulfil our vocation as unifiers, as bridge-builders, unless we each see our own self as a single, undivided whole. The concepts of microcosm, mediator, and *microtheos* acquire their true value only within the context of a holistic view of the person. If we repudiate our bodies as alien, instead of regarding them as as essential expression of our total selves, then by severing our links with our material environment, we cease to be microcosm and are no longer able to mediate. If we wish to be microcosm and mediator, we must not think of our person as 'the ghost in the machine', 'an angel in a slot machine',[24] a soul temporarily imprisoned in a body, striving to escape. Avoiding the dichotomies of soul and body, or of mind and body, affirming the material and the spiritual as complementary, we are to think of the person as a psychosomatic unity, an integrated totality of the physical, the psychic, and the spiritual. For only if we acknowledge our humanity in these terms, as an undivided whole, can we draw the creation together and unite the cosmos with God, as Maximus the Confessor would have us do.

It cannot be denied that Gregory of Nazianzus and Maximus, along with other Greek Fathers, tend to employ the separatist language of Platonism, subdividing the person into parts and contrasting soul and body. Yet the inner logic of their anthropology, with its key notions of microcosm and mediator, cannot but imply a vision of the person that transcends all such divisiveness. It is no coincidence that Gregory should end his account of the person by looking beyond the sundering of the soul and the body at physical death to their future reintegration by God at the final resurrection: 'He will hereafter bind them together once more in a yet more glorious way.' A Christian view of the person commits us to affirming, not just the immortality of the soul, but also – and much more fundamentally – the resurrection of the body. In the words of Mircea Eliade:

> What a paradox: The [pagan] Greeks, who . . . loved life, existence in the flesh, the perfect form, had, as an ideal of survival, the survival of the pure intellect (mind, *nous*). Christians, who are apparently ascetics and scorn the body, insist on the necessity of the resurrection of the body, and cannot conceive of paradisiac blessedness without the union of the soul and the body.[25]

'The soul is man,' said Plato.[26] To this the Christian tradition responds, in words attributed to the second-century Greek apologist Justin Martyr: 'Is the soul by itself the person? No, it is simply the person's soul. Do we call the body the person? No, we call it the person's body. So the person is neither of these things on its own, but it is the single whole formed together from them both.'[27]

RELATIONAL UNITY

There is one further point to be made, implicit in much of what has been said already, but now to be made explicit. When we talk of the human person as *microtheos*, formed in the image of God, the *Theos*, or God, of whom we are speaking is God the Trinity. In affirming a holistic view of the person, is there not sometimes a danger of lapsing into individualism, of seeing our personhood as a self-contained monad? Belief in God as Trinity – not only as one but as one-in-three – helps to keep us from any such distortion. The doctrine of the Trinity is a way of saying that God is not merely personal but interpersonal. The divine unity is fulfilled in community; the divine simplicity is a complex simplicity. As love, God is not self-love but mutual love. The being of God is a relational being; there is within God an 'I-and-thou' relationship between Father, Son, and Holy Spirit. God is exchange, self-giving, reciprocity.

Having affirmed all this of God as Trinity, we then go on to affirm it equally of the human person formed in God's image. The divine image given to each one of us is specifically a trinitarian image. And this means that human personhood, like the personhood of God, is exchange, self-giving, reciprocity. As a person, I am what I am only in relation to other persons. My human being is a relational being. My personal unity is fulfilled in community. I am only truly human, truly personal, if I relate to others after the likeness of the Trinity; if I express myself, as God does, in a relationship of 'I-and-thou'. In the words of John Macmurray, 'Since mutuality is constitutive for the personal, "I" need "you" in order to be myself.'[28]

Because I am made in the image of the Trinity, I cannot be a mediator, a bridge-builder, unless I relate to my fellow humans. My vocation to divinize the world is essentially a vocation realized in common with others. There can be *one* person only when there is the possibility of *every* person, when there is a shared world. The concept of the human person as microcosm, mediator, and *microtheos*, then, acquires its true value only within the context of a holistic view that is at the same time trinitarian and interpersonal.

Notes

PREFACE

1 See, e.g., his contributions to *Biology and Personality*, ed. I. T. Ramsey (Blackwell, Oxford, 1965), pp. 1–8, 174–96; and to *Personality and Science*, ed. I. T. Ramsey and R. Porter, a Ciba Foundation Blueprint (Churchill Livingstone, Edinburgh and London, 1971), pp. 1–4, 125–32.

CHAPTER I INTRODUCTION

1 Clarendon Press, Oxford, 1984.
2 *The Category of the Person*, ed. M. Carrithers, S. Collins, and S. Lukes (Cambridge University Press, Cambridge, 1985).

CHAPTER 2 PURPOSELESS PEOPLE

1 P. W. Atkins, *The Creation* (W. H. Freeman, Oxford, 1981).
2 P. W. Atkins, *The Second Law* (W. H. Freeman, New York, 1984).
3 Ibid.
4 R. Dawkins, *The Selfish Gene* (Oxford University Press, Oxford, 1976).
5 See Thomas Nagel, 'What is it like to be a Bat?', in *Mortal Questions* (Cambridge University Press, Cambridge, 1979), pp. 165–80.

CHAPTER 3 THE STRUCTURE OF THE SOUL

1 Descartes, *Meditations*, 6.
2 To avoid possible criticism that this 'simple' argument contains some modal fallacy, I set it out more formally and rigorously in an Appendix to this chapter.
3 See, e.g., my *The Evolution of the Soul* pp. 158 ff.

4   See his 'Personal Identity', *Philosophical Review*, 80 (1971), pp. 3–27, and his
     more fully developed views in his *Reasons and Persons* (Clarendon Press, Oxford,
     1984), pt. 3.

5   For the initial statement of this view, which he developed more fully in later
     writings, see W. V. O. Quine, *From a Logical Point of View*, 1953 (Harper and
     Row, New York, 1963) pp. 42–6.

6   S. Kripke, *Naming and Necessity* (Blackwell, Oxford, 1980), pp. 144–55.

CHAPTER 4   THE PERSON AS OBJECT OF SCIENCE,
AS SUBJECT OF EXPERIENCE, AND AS LOCUS OF VALUE

1   For the logical difficulties of this idea, see my *Identity and Spatio-Temporal
     Continuity* (Blackwell, Oxford, 1968), pt. 1; *Sameness*, ch. 1.

2   Here I am much indebted to John McDowell, 'On the Sense and Reference of
     a Proper Name', *Mind* (1977). For further Fregean testimony, see also Gareth
     Evans, *The Varieties of Reference* (Oxford, 1984), ch. 1, and my 'Frege's
     Problem of the Morning Star and the Evening Star' in *Studies on Frege II:
     Logic and Philosophy of Language*, ed. M. Schirn (Bad Canstatt, Stuttgart,
     1976).

3   For an elaboration of this suggestion, which involves a repair to Frege's view of
     the predicative character of concepts, and for some further remarks about Frege's
     diagram, see my 'On the Sense and Reference of Predicates', *Philosophical
     Quarterly* (July 1984), and *Sameness*, p. 79 n. In the article just cited I propose
     that in philosophical usage, concepts should be distinguished from properties and
     that quantification over properties should be supplanted in philosophy by quan-
     tification over concepts. But I have judged that the present paper is not the place
     to follow that recommendation through. 'Property' and 'concept' are inter-
     changeable here. Maintaining Frege's distinction between concept and what falls
     under it (or as I shall sometimes say the extension) does not commit one to close
     the question Frege began by regarding as open, namely the criterion of identity
     for concepts. (There seems to be more to identity of concepts than the coincidence
     of their extensions.)

4   See *Sameness*, ch. 3, citing and modifying Hilary Putnam, 'How is Semantics
     Possible?', *Metaphilosophy* 3 (1970). I take a stereotype for the reference of 'f'
     to be a standardized or idealized set of *de re* beliefs about fs. For 'extension-
     involving', see *Samness*, pp. 10–11, 79–86, 210–11.

5   On this and the subsequent claim, see Hidé Ishiguro, 'On the Primitiveness of
     the Concept of Person', in *Philosophical Subjects*, ed. van Straaten (Oxford, 1980).

6   See Aristotle, *Nicomachean Ethics* I. 6, with (e.g.) the comment on this in my
     'Truth, Invention, and the Meaning of Life', *Proceedings of the British Academy*
     (1976) p. 375, n. 2, and at n. 53 in the reprinted version of this paper in my *Needs,
     Values, Truth* (Aristotelian Society and Blackwell, Oxford, 1986).

7   Methuen, London, 1959.

8   On elucidation, see *Sameness*, p. 4, with L. Wittgenstein, *Tractatus Logico-*

Philosophicus 3. 263, 4. 026, 4. 112; Mark Helme, 'An Elucidation of *Tractatus* 3. 262', *Southern Journal of Philosophy*, 17 (1979), pp. 323–34.

9   In the logicians' sense. See, e.g., Patrick Suppes, *Introduction to Logic* (Van Nostrand, Princeton, 1957), p. 154. For a cognate but potentially divergent criticism, see Bernard Williams, 'Strawson on Individuals', in *Problems of the Self* (Cambridge, 1973).

10 The argument following leans heavily upon M. Deutcher and C. Martin's 'Remembering', *Philosophical Review* (1966); and it recapitulates *Sameness*, Longer Note 6.14. For the ancestor of all these speculations, see H. P. Grice, 'The Causal Theory of Perception', *Proceedings of the Aristotelian Society*, 35 (1962).

11 The memory trace may be conceived under the specification 'the normal neurophysiological connection whatever it is, between rememberings and the incidents of which they are rememberings'. This is not a circular procedure: but even if it were circular, this would not matter for present purposes, which relate to the *necessary* conditions of remembering. Deutcher and Martin carefully explore a multiplicity of alternatives to the explicit memory-trace account of the causal connection between incident and experiential memory of incident. They show that none of these accounts can simultaneously allow for the possibility of prompting and define the particular sort of *operativeness* we are looking for between incident and representation.

12 The more one tries to conceive of such a thing, the less it can satisfy him; and it scarcely improves things to think of the memory trace as an immaterial imprint on immaterial stuff. This can only help to the extent that immaterial mind is made intelligible by being *modelled* on the material, and distinguished from it only by the apparently vacuous contention that it is immaterial.

13 For the materials for a similar argument about pain, see Richard Wollheim, 'Expression and Expressionism', *Revue Internationale de Philosophie*, no. 68–9 (1964). More generally, see my discussion in 'Identity, Necessity, and Physicalism', in *Philosophy of Logic*, ed. Korner, (Blackwell, Oxford, 1976), pp. 120–1.

14 See *Sameness*, p. 169, and my 'Identity', n. 12; also Joseph Woodger, *Biology and Language* (Cambridge, 1952), p. 267 n., p. 272, *et passim*.

15 See *Sameness*, p. 164.

16 See Woodger, *Biology and Language*, p. 278; 'Neither can the method which uses the physical language exclusively deal with persons except by means of the *abstract* notion of body.'

17 See *Sameness*, p. 173. On relativity in this sense, with acknowledgements to an idea of Williams's, see my 'A Sensible Subjectivism?' in *Needs, Values, Truth*, especially §11 and Longer Note 24.

18 On interpretation, see, e.g., Donald Davidson 'Radical Interpretation', *Dialectica* (1973); Richard Grandy, 'Reference, Meaning, and Belief', *Journal of Philosophy* (1973); Gareth Evans's and John McDowell's Editorial Introduction to *Truth and Meaning: Essays in Semantics* (Oxford, 1976); and §1 of McDowell's article in that volume, 'Truth Conditions, Bivalence, and Verificationism'; *Sameness*, at Longer Note 6.36.

19   On (a) and (b), see especially John McDowell, 'Truth Conditions'.
20   Shortly after I had published *Sameness and Substance*, my then colleague at London University, Peter Winch, presented a critique of chapter 6 of the book in his presidential address to the Aristotelian Society, October 1980. See 'Eine Einstellung zur Seele', *Proceedings of the Aristotelian Society* (1980–1). His critique was invaluable to me in making me see how far I had fallen short of making myself clear at various points, and in making me appreciate how much there was that Winch and I were jointly opposed to, albeit in very different ways. It is to reading Winch's critique that I also owe the idea of completing the second of the two suggestions offered in this paper by quotation from a book of Simone Weil, namely *The Iliad, or the Poem of Force*, tr. M. McCarthy (Stonewall Press, Iowa City, 1973). p. 6. For the first quotation, see L. Wittgenstein, *Philosophical Investigations*, p. 223.
21   By the claim of the irrationality of giving up these feelings I mean that, wherever these are our actual feelings and we have no specific reason to give them up, it is simply gratuitous to suggest that it is irrational for us not to try to wipe the slate clean in order to deliberate from a standing start of pure self-interest. But that is the suggestion implicit in the more rationalistic discussions of challenges to morality such as Glaukon and Adeimantus' tale of Gyges' ring in Plato, *Republic* II or the Prisoner's Dilemma 'paradox', discussions that often proceed as if the whole matter could be approached from a cool, fresh-starting-point reached without paying the cost mentioned in the text, and that often fail to acknowledge the intimate mutual involvements of the raw materials of morality – morality itself, not *ersatz* morality or self-love – with everything that is presupposed to interpretation.
22   See my 'A Sensible Subjectivism'.

CHAPTER 5   REASONING ABOUT PERSONS

1   D. Parfit, *Reasons and Persons* (Oxford University Press, Oxford, 1984).
2   T. Nagel, 'Brain Bisection and the Unity of Consciousness', in *Mortal Questions* (Cambridge University Press, Cambridge, 1979), p. 64.
3   Ibid, p. 164.
4   D. Parfit, 'Lewis, Perry and What Matters', in *The Identities of Persons*, ed. A. Rorty (University of California Press, London, 1976), p. 100.
5   Parfit, *Reasons and Persons*, p. 251.
6   R. Sperry, 'Brain Bisection and the Mechanisms of Consciousness', in *The Brain and Conscious Behaviour*, ed. J. C. Eccles (Springer, New York, 1965), p. 299.
7   Ibid.
8   A. R. Luria, *The Man with the Shattered World* (Basic Books, New York, 1972).
9   D. Davidson, 'Radical Interpretation', in *Inquiries into Truth and Interpretation* (Oxford University Press, Oxford, 1984).
10   Nagel, *Mortal Questions*, p. 164.
11   G. Seddon, 'Logical Possibility', *Mind*, 31 (1972), pp. 481–94.
12   D. Wiggins, *Sameness and Substance* (Blackwell, Oxford, 1980).
13   Parfit, *Reasons and Persons*, p. 298.

14 Ibid., p. 200.

15 Ibid., p. 199.

16 D. Hume, *Treatise of Human Nature* (1739), bk. 1, sect. 14.

17 I. Kant, *Critique of Pure Reason*, (1787) tr. N. Kemp-Smith, (Macmillan, London, 1929).

18 P. F. Strawson, *The Bounds of Sense* (Methuen, London, 1966).

19 L. Wittgenstein, *Philosophical Investigations*, tr. G. E. M. Anscombe (Blackwell, Oxford, 1953), vol. 1, p. 265.

20 Note that there is no need to appeal to a majority here.

21 Here I use the notion of criteria without reference to any particular theory, to indicate that certain ascriptions can, and certain others cannot, be justified by appealing to evidence.

22 One can imagine circumstances in which I might be in doubt about these ascriptions, but they would be most exceptional.

23 G. Evans, *The Varieties of Reference*, ed. J. McDowell (Oxford University Press, Oxford, 1982), p. 238.

24 Parfit, *Reasons and Persons*, p. 220.

25 Wittgenstein, *Philosophical Investigations*, vol. 1, p. 395.

26 D. Wiggins, 'Locke, Butler and the Stream of Consciousness; and Men as a Natural Kind', in *The Identities of Persons*, ed. A. Rorty, p. 168.

27 Parfit, *Reasons and Persons*, p. 251.

28 Cambridge University Press, Cambridge, 1982.

29 Here, and in what follows, 'reductionist' and 'reductionism' refer to the view outlined above.

30 *Philosophical Reviews*, 79, no. 2 (1970).

31 Oxford University Press, Oxford, 1976, pp. 199–203.

32 In *God and the Soul* (Routledge and Kegan Paul, London, 1969), pp. 2 ff.

CHAPTER 6   PERSONS AND SELVES

1 E. Husserl, *Cartesian Meditations* (Martinus Nijhoff, The Hague, 1973).

2 D. Hume, *A Treatise of Human Nature*, 1739; ed. D. G. C. McNabb (Collins, London, 1962).

3 I. Kant, *Critique of Pure Reason* (Riga, 1787).

4 G. H. Mead, *Mind, Self and Society* (Chicago University Press, Chicago, 1934).

5 L. S. Vygotsky, *Thought and Language* (MIT Press, Cambridge, Mass., 1962).

6 C. Darwin, *The Origin of Species* (London, 1859).

7 J.L. Austin, *How To Do Things with Words* (Oxford University Press, New York, 1965).

8 L. Wittgenstein, *Philosophical Investigations* (Blackwell, Oxford, 1953).

9 H. Morsbach and W. J. Tyler, 'Some Japanese-Western Linguistic Differences Concerning Dependency Needs: The Case of *Amae*', in *Life Sentences*, ed. R. Harré (J. Wylie, Chichester, 1976).

10 R. Benedict, *The Chrysanthemum and the Sword* (Routledge and Kegan Paul, London, 1967).

11 I. Morris, *The Nobility of Failure* (Secker and Warburg, London, 1975).

CHAPTER 7   THE PERSON IN LAW

1 *The Institutes of Gaius*, I. 8.
2 *Digest*, 4. 5. 11.
3 Early Roman legislation; see, for example, H. F. Jolowicz and Barry Nicholas, *Historical Introduction to the Study of Roman Law*, 3rd edn. (Cambridge Universtiy Press, 1972), p. 13 and ch. 7.
4 D. M. Walker, *The Oxford Companion to Law* (Oxford University Press, 1985), p. 951.
5 These examples are given in H. Kelsen, *General Theory of Law and State* (Russell and Russell, New York, 1945), pp. 3–4.
6 These examples are given in G. W. Paton, *A Textbook of Jurisprudence* (Clarendon Press, Oxford, 1946), p. 251.
7 J. A. C. Thomas, *Textbook of Roman Law* (North Holland, Amsterdam, 1976), p. 349.
8 M. Frankfort *et al.*, *Before Philosophy* (Penguin, Baltimore, 1949), p. 24.
9 *Pramatha Nath Mullick v. Pradyumna Kumar Mullick* (1925) LR 52 Ind. App. 245.
10 1909 SC (HL) 10; see also A. Sachs and J. Wilson, *Sexism and the Law* (Martin Robertson, Oxford, 1978), ch. 1.
11 Butterworths, London, 1984.
12 C. S. Kenny, *Outlines of Criminal Law*, 19th edn. (Cambridge University Press, Cambridge, 1966), p. 80.
13 [1952] 2 All ER 645.
14 *Smith* (1845) 1 Cox CCC 260 per Erle J.
15 18 NY (2d) 481 (1966).
16 [1982] QB 1166.
17 *Thake* v. *Maurice* [1986] 1 All ER 497; see also *Eyre* v. *Measday* [1986] 1 All ER 488.
18 See R. H. S. Tur, 'The Leaves on the Trees', *Juridical Review*, 139 (1976), pp. 139–55.
19 [1979] QB 276.
20 *Daily Mail*, 21 May 1985.
21 [1984] 1 All ER 365 (Woolf J.); [1985] 1 All ER 533 (Court of Appeal); [1985] 3 All ER 402 (House of Lords); see also All ER Rev., 1985, pp. 171–5.
22 [1981] 1 WLR 1421.
23 [1983] 2 WLR 539.
24 [1969] 1 QB 439.

CHAPTER 8   IS MEDICINE A BRANCH OF ETHICS?

1 T. S. Szasz, 'The Myth of Mental Illness', *American Psychologist*, 15 (1960), pp. 113–18.
2 R. E. Kendell, 'The Concept of Disease and its Implications for Psychiatry', *British Journal of Psychiatry*, 127 (1975), pp. 305–15.

3 C. Boorse, 'On the Distinction between Illness and Disease', *Philosophy and Public Affairs*, 5 (1975), pp. 49–68.
4 B. A. Farrell, 'Mental Illness: A Conceptual Analysis', *Psychological Medicine*, 9 (1979), pp. 21–35.
5 R. M. Hare, *The Language of Morals* (Oxford University Press, Oxford, 1952), ch. 7.
6 J. L. Austin, 'A Plea for Excuses', *Proceedings of the Aristotelian Society*, 57 (1956–7), pp. 1–30.
7 C. M. Culver and B. Gert, *Philosophy in Medicine* (Oxford University Press, New York, 1982), ch. 4.

CHAPTER 9 JUNG'S CONCEPT OF PERSONALITY

1 C. G. Jung, 'Mental Disease and the Psyche', in *Collected Works*, vol. 3 (Routledge and Kegan Paul, London, 1960), § 498.
2 Jung, 'The Tavistock Lectures', Lecture 2, in *Collected Works*, vol. 18 (1977), § 105.
3 Jung, 'A Review of the Complex Theory', in *Collected Works*, vol 8. (1960), § 201.
4 Ibid., § 202.
5 Jung, 'On the Nature of the Psyche', in *Collected Works*, vol. 8 (1960), § 435.
6 Jung, 'The Structure of the Psyche', in *Collected Works*, vol. 8 (1960), §§ 317–18.
7 Jung, 'Psychoanalysis and Neurosis', in *Collected Works*, vol. 4 (1961), §§ 563–4.
8 Ibid., § 570.
9 Jung, *Memories, Dreams, Reflections* (Collins and Routledge and Kegan Paul, London, 1963), p. 170.
10 Ibid., p. 191.
11 Jung, *The Psychology of the Unconscious*, ch. 4; *Collected Works*, vol. 7 (1953), § 57.
12 Anthony Storr, *Jung* (Collins, Fontana, London, 1973), p. 67.
13 Sigmund Freud, *The Interpretation of Dreams*, Standard Edition, vol. 4 (Hogarth Press and the Institute of Psycho-Analysis, London, 1958), p. xxxii.
14 Jung, 'The Practical Use of Dream Analysis', in *Collected Works*, vol. 16 (1954), §§ 317, 330.
15 Jung, 'The Aims of Psychotherapy', in *Collected Works*, vol. 16 (1954), §§ 83–4.
16 Jung, 'The Relations between the Ego and the Unconscious', in *Collected Works*, vol. 7 (1953), §§ 236, 240.
17 Jung, 'The Development of Personality', in *Collected Works*, vol. 17 (1954), § 289.
18 Jung, 'Commentary on "The Secret of the Golden Flower"', in *Collected Works*, vol. 13 (1967), § 68.
19 Jung, *Psychology and Religion*; *Collected Works*, vol. 13 (1958), § 138.
20 Jung, 'Commentary on "The Secret of the Golden Flower"', § 67.
21 Jung, *The Undiscovered Self*; *Collected Works*, vol. 10 (1964), § 588.
22 *The Freud/Jung Letters*, tr. Ralph Mannheim and R. F. C. Hull, ed. William McGuire. (London, 1974), p. 294.

23 Storr, 'Individuation and the Creative Process', *Journal of Analytical Psychology*, 28 (1983), pp. 329–43.
24 Jung, *Memories, Dreams, Reflections*, p. 76.
25 Ibid., p. 17.
26 Jung, 'On the Nature of the Psyche', in *Collected Works*, vol. 8 (1960), § 437.
27 W. Pauli, 'The Influence of Archetypal Ideas on the Scientific Theories of Kepler', in C. G. Jung and W. Pauli, *The Interpretation of Nature and the Psyche* (Routledge and Kegan Paul, London, 1955), p. 152.
28 Jung, *Mysterium Coniunctionis* ch. 6; *Collected Works*, vol. 14 (1963), § 768.

CHAPTER 10   PERSONALITY AND POETRY

1 Plato, *Phaedo*, 97E–99A.
2 C. S. Lewis, *A Grief Observed* (Faber and Faber, London, 1961).
3 N. Chomsky, review of *Verbal Behaviour*, by B. F. Skinner, in *Language*, 35 (1959), pp. 26–58.
4 D. Hume, *A Treatise of Human Nature*, ed. L. A. Selby-Bigge, repr. of 11th edn. (Clarendon Press, Oxford, 1966), 1.iv. 6.
5 Ibid., 1. iii. 10.
6 A. D. Nuttall, *A New Mimesis* (Methuen, London, 1983), p. 181.

CHAPTER 11   A THEOLOGY OF PERSONAL BEING

1 Reinhold Niebuhr, *Man's Nature and his Communities* (Geoffrey Bles, London, 1966), p. 42.

CHAPTER 12   CHRISTIAN THEISM AND THE CONCEPT OF A PERSON

1 St Augustine, *De Trinitate*, 7. 4. 7.
2 Locke, *An Essay Concerning Human Understanding*, 1690 (Collins, London, 1964), 2. 27. 8–9.
3 Descartes, *Meditations*, 1642, in e.g., *Discourse on Method and Other Writings* (Penguin, Harmondsworth, 1968), p. 105.
4 Kant, *The Metaphysic of Morality*, 1785, p. 276.
5 Sartre, *Existentialism and Humanism*, 1946 (Methuen, London, 1978), p. 28.
6 John Macmurray, *Persons in Relation* (Faber, London, 1961), p. 24.
7 Richard Swinburne, *The Coherence of Theism* (Clarendon Press, Oxford, 1977), p. 99.
8 J. L. Mackie, *The Miracle of Theism* (Clarendon Press, Oxford, 1982), pp. 1–4, 12.
9 Adrian Thatcher, 'The Personal God and a God Who Is a Person', *Religious Studies*, 21 (1985), pp. 67–70.
10 Sydney Shoemaker and Richard Swinburne, *Personal Identity* (Blackwell, Oxford, 1984), p. 31.
11 Derek Parfit, *Reasons and Persons* (Clarendon Press, Oxford, 1984), p. 275.

12   See Arthur Peacocke, *Creation and the World of Science* (Oxford University Press, Oxford, 1979), p. 189; Lynn de Silva, *The Problem of the Self in Buddhism and Christianity* (Macmillan, London, 1979), ch. 8; Grace Jantzen, *God's World, God's Body* (Darton, Longman and Todd, London, 1984), p. 5.

13   de Silva, *Problem of Self*, p. 75.

14   Biblical quotations are from the New English Bible, unless otherwise stated.

15   de Silva, *Problem of Self*, p. 85.

16   Other works that are illuminating in this regard are Harold Schilling, *The New Consciousness in Science and Religion* (SCM Press, London, 1973); Theodosius Dobzhansky, *The Biology of Ultimate Concern* (Collins, London, 1971); Ian Barbour, *Issues in Science and Religion* (SCM Press, London, 1966).

17   Peacocke, *Creation*, p. 66.

18   Ibid., p. 120.

19   John Macquarrie, *Principles of Christian Theology*, rev. edn (SCM Press, London, 1977); idem, *In Search of Deity* (SCM Press, London, 1984); idem, *Thinking about God* (SCM Press, London, 1975); Keith Ward, *The Concept of God* (Blackwell, Oxford, 1974); idem, *Rational Theology and the Creativity of God* (Blackwell, Oxford, 1982).

20   St Anselm, *Proslogion* (1078); in, e.g., J. Hick and A. McGill, *The Many-Faced Argument* (Macmillan, London, 1968), p. 6.

21   Ward, *Rational Theology*, p. 231.

22   I owe the use of the term 'homeostatic' to John Bowker, *The Sense of God* (Oxford University Press, Oxford, 1973), p. 51.

23   Macquarrie, *Principles*, p. 213.

24   P. F. Strawson, *Individuals* (Methuen, London, 1959), ch. 3.

25   Ward, *Rational Theology*, p. 141.

26   See, e.g., J. C. A. Gaskin, *The Quest for Eternity* (Penguin, Harmondsworth, 1984), ch. 1.

CHAPTER 13   THE UNITY OF THE HUMAN PERSON
ACCORDING TO THE GREEK FATHERS

1   Novalis (Friedrich von Hardenberg), *The Disciples at Saïs and Other Fragments* (Methuen, London, 1903), p. 75.

2   *The Glory of Man* (SCM, London, 1967), pp. 5, 10.

3   *The Pedagogue*, III. 1.

4   *On the Creation of Man*, 11 (*Patrologia Graeca* XLIV. 153D, 156B).

5   *Poetry and Prose of William Blake*, ed. Geoffrey Keynes (Nonesuch Press, London, 1948), p. 182.

6   *Orations*, 38, §11 (*PG*, XXXVI. 321C–324B). See Anna-Stina Ellverson, *The Dual Nature of Man: A Study in the Theological Anthropology of Gregory of Nazianzus* (Almqvist & Wiksell, Uppsala/Stockholm, 1981).

7   *PG*, XCI. 1304D–1308C. See Lars Thunberg, *Microcosm and Mediator: The Theological Anthropology of Maximus the Confessor* (C. W. K. Gleerup, Lund,

1965); *Man and the Cosmos: The Vision of St Maximus the Confessor* (St Valdimir's Seminary Press, Crestwood, 1985).

8   *Homilies on Leviticus*, V. 2 (*Griechischen Christlichen Schriftsteller*, ed. W. A. Baehrens, p. 336, ll. 22–24). Compare R. C. Zaehner, *Mysticism Sacred and Profane* (Clarendon Press, Oxford, 1957), p. 103.

9   *Letters*, II. 119 (*PG*, LXXIX. 252B).

10   *Ambigua*, 41 (*PG*, XCI. 1305A).

11   For Greek writers who affirm man's superiority to the angels, see, for example, Macarius, *Homilies*, XV. 22, 43; Anastasius of Sinai, *Questions*, 78 (*PG*, LXXXIX. 708A–B); Gregory Palamas, *Natural, Theological, Moral and Practical Chapters*, 63 (*PG*, CL. 1165C–D), cited in Georgios I. Mantzaridis, *The Deification of Man: St Gregory Palamas and the Orthodox Tradition* (St Vladimir's Seminary Press, Crestwood, 1984), p. 19; but cf. *Chapters*, 27 (*PG*, CL. 1140A), which asserts the superiority of angels. According to Thomas Aquinas, humans are by nature lower than the angels, but by grace higher (*Summa theologiae*, I, Q. 108, art. 8, 3; Q. 117, art. 2, 3; *Scriptum super libros sententiarum*, II, dist. ix, Q. 1, art. 8).

12   *PG*, XCI. 1305A–C.

13   *PG*, XCI. 1308B.

14   In his homily 'On the text "My grace is sufficient for you"', 1 (*PG*, LIX. 509). This is probably not an authentic work of Chrysostom; the author, whoever he is, also calls man the bond, or *syndesmos*, of creation. The term *syndesmos* is applied to man in another work, which is certainly by Chrysostom, *On the obscurities of the Old Testament*, II. 5 (*PG*, LVI. 182).

15   A phrase used by Pico della Mirandola in his *Oration on the Dignity of Man*; cited in Erich Fromm and Ramón Xirau, *The Nature of Man* (paperback edn, Macmillan, New York, 1968), p. 103.

16   Martin Buber, *Tales of the Hasidim: The Early Masters* (Schocken Books, New York, 1968), p. 275; *The Later Masters* (Schocken Books, New York, 1966), pp. 317, 70.

17   A phrase used in a sermon attributed to St Basil of Caesarea, 'On the Holy Nativity of Christ' (*PG*, XXXI. 1473A).

18   Cf. C. T. Lewis and C. Short, *A Latin Dictionary* (Clarendon Press, Oxford, 1951), p. 860.

19   Lactantius, *Divine Institutes*, II. i. 15–16; Ovid, *Metamorphoses*, I. 84–6. The idea is found in Christian sources as early as the second century, in the *Epistle to Diognetus*, X. 2. For pagan parallels in Cicero and elsewhere, see E. H. Blakeney, *The Epistle to Diognetus* (SPCK, London, 1943), pp. 77–8; Henry G. Meecham, *The Epistle to Diognetus* (Manchester University Press, Manchester, 1949), pp. 132–3.

20   Compare George Every, Richard Harries, and Kallistos Ware (eds.), *Seasons of the Spirit: Readings through the Christian Year* (SPCK, London, 1984), p. 26, where the phrase is incorrectly rendered. I take this opportunity to correct the mistake, for which I am responsible.

21   *On the Creation of Man*, 16 (*PG*, XLIV. 177D–180A).

22 *Conjectures of a Guilty Bystander* (Image Books, Doubleday, New York, 1968), p. 158; emphasis original.

23 *PG*, XCIII. 1604B.

24 J. A. T. Robinson, *The Body. A Study in Pauline Theology* (SCM, London, 1952), p. 14.

25 *No Souvenirs* (Routledge, London, 1978), p. 95.

26 *Alcibiades*, I. 130C.

27 *Fragments on the Resurrection*, 8 (ed. K. Holl, *Texte und Untersuchungen*, XX. ii. 45–6; *PG*, VI. 1585B).

28 *Persons in Relation* (Faber & Faber, London, 1961), p. 69. See also Kallistos Ware, 'The Human Person as an Icon of the Trinity', in *Sobornost incorporating Eastern Churches Review* (The Journal of the Fellowship of St Alban and St Sergius), vol. 8, no. 2 (1986), pp. 6–23.

List of Contributors

AUTHORS

DR P. W. ATKINS, Fellow and Tutor in Physical Chemistry, Lincoln College, Oxford, and University Lecturer in Physical Chemistry, University of Oxford.

DR K. W. M. FULFORD, Research Psychiatrist, Warneford Hospital, Oxford.

DR G. R. GILLETT, Fellow of Magdalen College, Oxford, and Research Associate of the Ian Ramsey Centre, Oxford.

MR H. R. HARRÉ, Fellow of Linacre College, Oxford, and University Lecturer in the Philosophy of Science, University of Oxford.

THE REVD PROF. J. MACQUARRIE, FBA, former Lady Margaret Professor of Divinity, Christ Church, Oxford.

MR A. D. NUTTALL, Fellow and Tutor in English, New College, Oxford.

MR D. A. PARFIT, Fellow of All Souls College, Oxford.

THE REVD DR A. R. PEACOCKE, Director, Ian Ramsey Centre, St Cross College, Oxford.

DR C. A. STORR, Emeritus Fellow of Green College, Oxford.

PROF. R. G. SWINBURNE, Nolloth Professor of the Philosophy of the Christian Religion, University of Oxford.

DR A. THATCHER, Principal Lecturer and Head of Religion and Philosophy, College of St Mark and St John, Plymouth.

MR R. H. S. TUR, Benn Law Fellow and Tutor in Law, Oriel College, Oxford.

THE RT REVD K. T. WARE, Fellow of Pembroke College, Oxford, and Spalding Lecturer in Eastern Orthodox Studies, University of Oxford.

MR DAVID WIGGINS, FBA, Fellow and Praelector in Philosophy, University College, Oxford.

OTHER DISCUSSANTS

Dr R. Attfield
Dr S. Collins
Dr R. Dawkins
Dr J. Durant
Dr M. J. Lockwood
Prof. B. G. Mitchell
Dr J. Robson
Prof. M. Ruse
Dr G. Scott
Dr J. M. Soskice
Prof. Sir Peter Strawson
Dr R. H. Trigg
The Revd Dr K. B. Wilson

Index of Names

Index by Joyce Kerr